American Political Thought

In Memory of
Isaac Kramnick

American Political Thought

An Invitation

KEN I. KERSCH

polity

First published in 2021 by Polity Press

Polity Press
65 Bridge Street
Cambridge CB2 1UR, UK

Polity Press
101 Station Landing
Suite 300
Medford, MA 02155, USA

ISBN-13: 978-1-5095-3032-8
ISBN-13: 978-1-5095-3033-5 (pb)

A catalogue record for this book is available from the British Library.

Library of Congress Cataloging-in-Publication Data
Names: Kersch, Kenneth Ira, 1964- author.
Title: American political thought : an invitation / Ken I. Kersch.
Description: Cambridge, UK ; Medford, MA : Polity Press, 2021. | Includes
   bibliographical references and index. | Summary: "The best
one-volume
   introduction to American Political Thought available"– Provided by
   publisher.
Identifiers: LCCN 2020027944 (print) | LCCN 2020027945 (ebook) | ISBN
   9781509530328 (hardback) | ISBN 9781509530335 (paperback) | ISBN
   9781509530359 (epub)
Subjects: LCSH: United States–Politics and government–Philosophy.
Classification: LCC JK31 .K469 2021 (print) | LCC JK31 (ebook) | DDC
   320.0973–dc23
LC record available at https://lccn.loc.gov/2020027944
LC ebook record available at https://lccn.loc.gov/2020027945

Typeset in 10/13pt Swift Light by
Servis Filmsetting Ltd, Stockport, Cheshire
Printed and bound in Great Britain by TJ Books Limited

For further information on Polity, visit our website: politybooks.com

Contents

Acknowledgments

In thinking about and writing this book, I am grateful for the assistance of my Boston College students, both the many with whom I have explored this subject in my classes, and the few who provided more extensive critiques, suggestions, and research assistance. Of the latter, I am especially grateful to Steven LeGere, Aaron Pezzullo, and, thankfully, once again, Ryan Towey. Kaylie Ramirez and Caleb Tansey from BC provided more targeted advice, as did Chris Bartlett, Richard Bensel, and Ted Holsten. My conversations with Clem Fatovic on this topic have been so numerous that it is hard for me to know where his understandings of key points and issues end and my own begin.

Anyone who has studied this subject with Isaac Kramnick at Cornell, as Clem and I did together, will know, as casual readers might not, that Isaac's influence on this book is pervasive. It is also hard for me to imagine having learned whatever I have about this subject without thinking of my initial conversations at Cornell with Ted Lowi, Richard Bensel, Jeremy Rabkin, and Elizabeth Sanders. I have learned an immense amount about this subject since, of course, especially from Keith Whittington, Mark Graber, and Carol Nackenoff, but from many others as well. Boston College provided generous financial assistance.

I am immensely grateful to George Owers at Polity, both for soliciting me to write a book on this topic – which I had long been pondering – and for being such a knowledgeable, engaged, and inspiring editor. The anonymous outside reviewers George assembled first for the book proposal and then for the completed manuscript provided extraordinarily penetrating critiques, sage advice, and essential corrections that significantly improved the book. I also would like to thank Julia Davies at Polity, whose expertise and attentiveness have been indispensable to whatever successes this book may have.

It was with great sadness that I learned of Isaac Kramnick's death as I was completing this manuscript. But it is with a resolute happiness that I dedicate it to his memory.

Timeline

Chapter 2 Settlement, the Road to Revolution, the Founding, and the Early Republic

1565: First permanent European settlement established by Spain at St. Augustine, Florida

1607: First permanent English settlement established at Jamestown, Virginia

1619: First African laborers imported to British North America

1620: English Puritans settle at Plymouth, Massachusetts

1624: First Dutch Settlement at New Amsterdam (seized by the British in 1664, when its name was changed to New York)

1630–1637: Massachusetts Bay colony established

1675–1678: King Philip's War

1688–1689: Glorious Revolution (England)

1689: Publication of John Locke's *Second Treatise on Civil Government*

1689: English Bill of Rights

1730–1755 (circa): First Great Awakening

1769: Spanish Catholic Franciscan missionaries establish twenty-one permanent missions along the California coast

1775: Pennsylvania Abolition Society founded

1775–1783: American Revolution

1776 (July 4): US Declaration of Independence

1781: Articles of Confederation ratified

1785: New York Society for the Promotion of the Manumission of Slaves founded

1787–1789: Constitutional ratification debates

1789 (September 17): US Constitution adopted

1789–1799: French Revolution

Chapter 3 Antebellum Political Thought

1790–1840 (circa): Second Great Awakening

1791: US Bill of Rights adopted

1791–1804: Saint-Domingue Slave Rebellion/Haitian Revolution

1793: Fugitive Slave Act of 1793

1800: First peaceful transition of power between national political parties

1803: Louisiana Purchase

1804–1806: Lewis and Clark expedition

1808: Atlantic slave trade ended

1812: War of 1812

1814–1815: Hartford Convention

1819–1821: Missouri Crises

1821: Mexican independence from Spain shifts large parts of what later will become the American West from Spanish to Mexican control

1822: Denmark Vesey Rebellion (aborted)

1823: Monroe Doctrine

1830: Indian Removal Act/Trail of Tears

1831: *The Liberator* founded

1831: Nat Turner Rebellion

1833: American Anti-Slavery Society founded

1845 (July 4): Henry David Thoreau begins residence at Walden Pond

1845: US annexation of Texas

1846–1848: Mexican–American War

1848: California Gold Rush

1848: Seneca Falls Convention

Chapter 4 Secession/Civil War/Reconstruction

1850: Fugitive Slave Act of 1850

1852: Publication of *Uncle Tom's Cabin*

1854: Republican Party founded

1857: *Dred Scott v. Sandford*

1858 (August–October): Lincoln–Douglas Debates

1859: Radical abolitionist John Brown's raid on US arsenal at Harper's Ferry, Virginia

1860 (December): South Carolina secedes

1861 (April 12): South Carolina fires upon Fort Sumter; hostilities begin

1861–1865: Abraham Lincoln presidency

1861–1865: US Civil War

1862: Homestead Act

1863: Emancipation Proclamation

1863: Gettysburg Address

1864: Sand Creek massacre

1865 (April 9): Robert E. Lee surrenders to Ulysses S. Grant at Appomattox Courthouse

1865 (April 15): Abraham Lincoln assassinated

1865 (June 19): First African-American Juneteenth celebration commemorating the Emancipation Proclamation

1865: First Ku Klux Klan founded
1865–1870: Civil War Amendments adopted
1865–1877: Reconstruction
1866: Civil Rights Act of 1866

Chapter 5 Industrial Capitalism, Reformism, and the New American State

1869: Transcontinental Railroad completed
1869–1874: Granger Laws passed
1871: Indian Appropriations Act
1872: First National Park established at Yellowstone
1875: Civil Rights Act of 1875 (voided by *Civil Rights Cases*, 1883)
1876: Alexander Graham Bell invents telephone
1876: Battle of Little Big Horn
1877–1880: Thomas Edison invents the phonograph, the electric light bulb, and electric power generation
1882: Chinese Exclusion Act
1886 (May 4): Haymarket Affair, Chicago
1887: Interstate Commerce Commission (ICC) established
1887: Dawes Act (Native American land allotments)
1890: Sherman Anti-trust Act
1890: Wounded Knee massacre
1890: American Frontier closed
1890: "Jim Crow" white supremacy re-established in South
1890s (circa): Populist movement
1890–1920: Progressive era
1892: Homestead Strike, Pittsburgh
1896: *Plessy v. Ferguson*
1898: Spanish–American War
1901–1909: Theodore Roosevelt presidency
1903: Wright Brothers invent airplane and fly at Kitty Hawk, North Carolina
1908: Introduction of the Model T automobile by the Ford Motor Company
1909: National Association for the Advancement of Colored People (NAACP) founded
1912: Theodore Roosevelt's third-party "Bull Moose" presidential campaign
1913: Federal Reserve established
1913–1921: Woodrow Wilson presidency
1914–1918: World War I
1917 (April)–1918 (November): US joins World War I
1918–1920: Spanish flu pandemic
1920: Nineteenth Amendment ratified
1920–1933: Prohibition

1921: Tulsa Race massacre
1921: Equal Rights Amendment proposed
1924: Immigration Act
1924: Indian Citizenship Act

Chapter 6 The New Deal Liberal Order: Collapse, Culmination, or "Great Exception"?

1929–1939: The Great Depression
1932: Great Plains dust storms
1933–1934: First New Deal
1933–1945: Franklin Delano Roosevelt presidency
1935: National Labor Relations Act
1935: Social Security Act
1935–1936: Second New Deal
1938: Fair Labor Standards Act
1939–1962: Civil rights movement sit-ins
1941 (December 7): Japanese attack on Pearl Harbor, Hawaii; US enters World War II
1941–1945: World War II
1944: Normandy Invasion
1945: US drops atomic bombs on Japanese cities of Hiroshima and Nagasaki
1945: Yalta Conference
1947–1991: Cold War
1947: Jackie Robinson breaks baseball color barrier
1948: Alger Hiss–Whittaker Chambers hearings
1948–1952: Chinese Communist Revolution
1949–1951 (circa): US television networks established
1950: Mattachine Society founded
1950–1953: Korean War
1950–1954: "McCarthy era" anticommunist crusade
1953: Soviets test hydrogen bomb

Chapter 7 Radical Stirrings, Civil Rights, the Contentious 1960s, and the Rise of Modern Conservatism

1954: *Brown v. Board of Education*
1955: Lynching of Emmitt Till
1955: Daughters of Bilitis founded
1955: *National Review* founded by William F. Buckley Jr.
1955–1956: Montgomery Bus Boycott
1955–1975: Vietnam War
1957: Russian Sputnik 1 satellite launched

1959: Nixon–Khrushchev "Kitchen Debate"
1960: Students for a Democratic Society founded
1960: Civil rights movement sit-ins begin at Greensboro, North Carolina
1960: Young Americans for Freedom founded
1960: Christian Broadcasting Network founded
1961: Bay of Pigs invasion (failed)
1961: Freedom Rides
1962: Cuban Missile Crisis
1963: March on Washington for Jobs and Freedom
1963: Birmingham 16th Street Baptist Church bombing
1963 (November 22): John F. Kennedy assassinated, Dallas
1963–1969: Lyndon Baines Johnson presidency
1964 (June): Murder of civil rights workers James Chaney, Andrew Goodman, and Michael Schwerner, Neshoba County, Mississippi
1964 (June–August): Mississippi Freedom Summer
1964: Civil Rights Act of 1964
1964: Barry Goldwater nomination
1964: UC Berkeley Free Speech movement
1964–1965: Great Society social welfare programs, including Medicare and Medicaid, launched
1965: Selma to Montgomery Voting Rights marches
1965: Voting Rights Act of 1965
1965: Delano Grape Boycott (Cesar Chavez)
1965: Malcolm X assassinated, New York City
1966: National Organization for Women founded
1966: Black Panther Party founded.
1967: Summer of Love, Haight-Asbury, San Francisco
1968 (April 4): Martin Luther King Jr. assassinated, Memphis
1968 (April–May): Urban riots
1968 (June 6): Robert F. Kennedy assassinated, Los Angeles
1968: Democratic National Convention riots, Chicago
1969: Stonewall uprising
1969 (July 20): Apollo 11 moon landing
1969 (August): Woodstock Music Festival
1969–1974: Richard M. Nixon presidency
1970: First Earth Day
1972: Eagle Forum established by Phyllis Schlafly

Chapter 8 The Identity and Post-Materialist Left, the New Right, and Third Way Liberalism

1972–1974: Watergate scandal; Nixon resigns
1973: *Roe v. Wade*

1973–1974: OPEC Oil Crisis
1979: Moral Majority founded
1981–1989: Ronald Reagan presidency
1982: Gay Men's Health Crisis founded
1985: Democratic Leadership Council founded
1986: Operation Rescue founded
1987: ACT-UP founded
1990–1991: Persian Gulf War
1992: Los Angeles Riots
1992: North American Free Trade Agreement (NAFTA)
1993: First World Trade Center bombing
1995: Oklahoma City federal building bombing
1998: Bill Clinton–Monica Lewinsky scandal
2001 (September 11): Al-Qaeda terrorist attacks on New York and Washington, DC
2001: US invasion of Afghanistan
2001– : "War on Terror"
2002: Department of Homeland Security founded
2003–2011: Second Iraq War
2005: Hurricane Katrina

Chapter 9 Conclusion

2008 (September): Financial Crisis/Great Recession
2008: Election of Barack Obama
2010: *Citizens United v. Federal Election Commission*
2010: Affordable [Health] Care Act
2011: Occupy Wall Street movement
2013: Boston Marathon bombings
2013: Black Lives Matter founded
2014: Ferguson, Missouri, uprising
2015: *Obergefell v. Hodges*
2016: Donald Trump elected; "American Carnage" Inaugural
2019: Green New Deal Resolution introduced
2019–2020: Donald Trump impeachment and acquittal
2020 (March)– : Coronavirus/Covid-19 pandemic
2020: George Floyd uprising against racist police violence and white supremacy

1

Themes and Frameworks in American Political Thought

Who gets to tell you what to do? Asking that question about a group of people comprising a political community – a *polis*, or polity – is the foundational question of the study of politics.

The question can be considered in two senses: the *positive* and the *normative*. The first takes up the question of who gets to tell you what to do as a matter of real-world fact. As a real-world fact, it can be studied empirically by asking: "Who, in fact, has demonstrated the *power* to direct, or coerce, you into doing A rather than B?" *Positive* approaches to the exercise of political power bracket judgments about authorized or unauthorized, justified or unjustified, good and bad, right and wrong. They aspire only to accuracy: the facts of the world, as it actually works, and is. The second – the normative – sense of the question, by contrast, takes up the question of who gets to tell you what to do by asking if the person, official, or institution claiming that power has been authorized to do so, is justified in doing so, does so for good or for ill, rightly or wrongly. *Normative* approaches to the exercise of political power – arising out of what the sociologist Max Weber called the "fact–value" distinction in the social sciences – invite and require moral judgment either of the particular commandment issued by a political actor, or of the underlying foundations of the authorization of power to that superintending actor. Normative approaches to the exercise of political power ask questions about authority, legitimacy, legality, and justice.

In studying political thought, we ask fundamental *positive* and *normative* questions about how power (positive) and authority (normative) has been wielded, exercised, and justified within politics generally – the more abstract study of "political theory" or "political philosophy" – and within particular political communities, that is, within a given *polis* or polity. The study of *American political thought* is the study of how political power and authority have been both wielded and justified within the United States over the length and breadth of its history. Undertaking such study invites both more general and abstract "universal" questions of political theory and thought, and more "particularistic" questions about the political power and authority within a single, delimited political community, in a world comprised of many, and diverse, political communities, with both overlapping and disparate approaches to the same foundational political questions.

While quotidian contention over who gets to tell whom what to do is as old as human society itself, the public raising of hard and sustained questions about the legitimacy of the social and political order was once rare. To do so (if it even occurred to people) was considered not only presumptuous and hubristic, but also potentially destabilizing, if not subversive: it was dangerous. In almost all human societies, longstanding, deeply rooted, and entrenched assumptions about who gets to tell you what to do pervaded the community. The question was rarely raised in part because, within the community, that answer – whatever it was – was taken to be obvious: what always had been, and what forever will be. Among the most common of these answers were God or the Gods; those chosen by the Gods as their earthly agents (clerics and an ecclesiastical hierarchy; monarchs chosen by divine right); tribal elders; parents; or your lord, master, or owner. The matter of who gets to tell you what to do was decided by presumptively eternal, natural, or divinely ordained hierarchies. In the western political tradition, the animating assumption of these hierarchies setting the relationship between rulers and ruled was that the higher and better rightfully commanded the lower and lesser. To subject these hierarchies to questioning, and to imagine a menu of alternative possibilities, was the beginning of political philosophy. One of the first men to devote his life to political philosophy and to teaching it to the young, the ancient Athenian Socrates, it is worth recalling, was put to death. The charge was the corruption of the city's youth and the (dangerous and destabilizing) challenging of its Gods.

Do nations like the United States have shared and pervading political philosophies? My own view, as reflected in this book, is that – in complicated ways, to be sure – they do. But there is a pre-history, and context, even to that. Modern nation-states like the US are just one type of polity, and a relatively new one at that. Families, tribes, cities, city-states, and even churches set the rules of group life within a community long before modern "sovereign" nations were imagined. The modern nation first emerged as a distinctive type of polity in seventeenth-century Europe. By that time, under the pressures of economic transformation and a Renaissance humanism fueled in significant part by the rediscovery of ancient Greek and Roman political thought, the political authority structure of medieval Europe had decayed and declined. In medieval Europe, worldly political and religious ecclesiastical authority were extensively intertwined. While disputes sometimes arose, political authority, it was nevertheless said, ran from God to his Church – and, as such, to his appointed agent on earth, the Pope, who sat at the pinnacle of the Christian (Roman Catholic) Church's clerical hierarchy. As God's divinely chosen agent, the Pope's authority extended downward both within and without the Church. In the latter realm, it extended downward to monarchs – Kings and Queens – held to rule by "divine right." Under the feudal system, that hierarchical line of authority extended downward from the monarch to his or her

Lords and Nobles, to their vassals and serfs. Under a feudal political order, the lines of authority concerning who got to tell whom what to do were clearly defined, running vertically from top to bottom. These lines of authority were understood to be not only the reality, but rightful.

The dawn of modernity, which was characterized by a new focus on men as unique, worldly, self-determining agents, was reflected in, and driven by, a series of revolutionary new departures: the invention of the printing press (c. 1440); the (Protestant) Reformation (c. 1517–1648) and, relatedly, the first translations of the Bible into vernacular languages, the Protestant elevation of the laity above the clergy, and the democratization of church structures. The new humanism, an incipient capitalism, and Protestantism generated a cascade of disputes that repeatedly raised more persistent questions about who gets to tell whom what to do, challenging in a more substantial and systematic way society's long-settled hierarchies. Europe's monarchs began to push back against the commands and dictates of the Pope. Feudal lords and nobles pushed back in a more pervasive way against the political power and authority of the monarchs. Vassals, serfs, and peasants began pushing back more vehemently and insistently against the authority of their Lords and masters.

As the feudal order unraveled at the dawn of modernity, a sense of crisis descended concerning the legitimacy of the full array of claims to authority. New, "modern" or "liberal" theories of the origins of political authority – of who gets to tell you what to do – emerged out of this crisis. These theories were forged with the aim of reconstructing some sense of legitimate, rightful authority that would underwrite a workable political order in a context of spiraling chaos, occasioning a succession of wars, rebellions, and acts of insolent disobedience. In time, "modern" political theorists like Thomas Hobbes, John Locke, and Jean-Jacques Rousseau alighted upon a new – and revolutionary – social contract theory of political authority, which emerged in conjunction with new understandings of sovereignty and nationhood. Who got to tell you what to do? The authorized ruler of your (geographically bounded and delimited) nation. Who was the foundational and authorized ruler of your nation? The sovereign (which, for some radical theorists, was constituted by the people as a whole).

With moderns chafing at hierarchies underwritten by the understanding that the stronger, the better, or the powers-that-be from time immemorial got to tell them what to do, a new group of political theories began with what, under conditions of dissension and disagreement concerning first principles, they assumed would be the least controversial starting point promising the broadest common ground. They proposed that each individual person (answering to his own understanding of God's commands) *got to tell himself* what to do (the "his" here is deliberate: gender played a major role in structuring the public realm). Modern political theorists asked next, "Under what conditions would this person delegate the authority to tell himself what to do to someone other than himself?" The answer was: "Under conditions in which that person could help them get something that they needed or wanted but could not otherwise get if sovereignty were held only to reside in their lowly selves – all equals in the state of nature – and no higher." In *Leviathan* (1651), the English political theorist Thomas Hobbes described the state of nature as a condition in which

> there is no place for industry, because the fruit thereof is uncertain, and consequently no culture of the earth, no navigation nor use of the commodities that may be imported by sea, no commodious building, no instruments of moving and removing such things as require much force, no knowledge of the face of the earth; no account of time, no arts, no letters, no society, and, which is worst of all, continual fear and danger of violent death, and the life of man solitary, poor, nasty, brutish, and short.

Hobbes posited the state of nature, bereft of common political authority, as a hellscape. His countryman John Locke's subsequent understanding of the state of nature (*Second Treatise on Civil Government*, 1689) was somewhat more benign, but still undesirable. It was a condition in which the protection of highly valued natural rights to "life, liberty, and property" vouchsafed to all by nature was perpetually uncertain. Under such conditions, these modern political theorists proposed, men would agree to a "social contract" by which they would cede either all power, save that of self-defense (Hobbes), or all powers which did not transgress upon their core natural rights (Locke), to a sovereign who would stand, by their own hypothesized grant of political authority, above them. The sovereign would then have the good and rightful authority to tell them what to do, since the sovereign's power was a power they themselves, acting in the posited state of nature as sovereign individuals of their own free will, would have logically conferred upon – delegated to – the sovereign to advance their own best individual and common interests. These modern ideas of the origins of political authority underwrote the rise of a distinctive species of modern nation-state. And they were enlisted by the American Revolutionaries as the basis for their Declaration of Independence (1776), and, under the theory of "popular sovereignty" – "We the People" – for the Constitution of the United States (1787/1789).

As such, many have argued that, from its inception in the "Age of Revolutions" (English, 1689; French, 1789), American political thought represents an apotheosis of the new genus of "modern" political thinking. In part by dint of its fictional and imaginatively willed origins in the settlement of an (ostensibly) unpopulated blank-slate wilderness, with none of the on-the-ground monarchical and ecclesiastical baggage of palimpsest England and France, the United States was heralded by many – not least the proud Americans themselves – as the first "new" nation, founded upon modern principles on the origins of legitimate political authority, free from the encrusted hierarchies and traditions of Old World assumptions and understandings. Indeed, John Locke himself was looking across the ocean to this altogether new departure: "In the beginning," he wrote of the hypothesized state of nature in his *Second Treatise*, "all the world was America."

While there is certainly something to this, the reality is considerably more complicated. For one thing, of course, the settlers who came to North America were hardly stripped clean of their prior understandings of political and other forms of authority – of their faiths, folkways, traditions, and hierarchical assumptions. All – including a belief in the rightfulness of monarchy – were imported, to greater and lesser degrees, into the North American settlement. To complicate matters further, the polity – or polities, since British North America was initially organized as a contiguous arrangement of separate self-governing colonies – was far from static or impermeable. From the beginning, new immigrants and new ideas were introduced into the polity, either from the outside, or as cultivated from within. These layered over and interacted with the peoples and the political thought already there. As such, "New World" or not, the US polity was its own palimpsest. The result was a lively political culture, and distinctive tradition of American political thought, grounded, dynamic, and perpetually becoming.

The Traditional Framing: Lockean Liberalism, Civic Republicanism, and the Liberal–Republican Debate

---

Frameworks of American Political Thought

1. (Lockean) liberalism ("The Hartz Thesis")
   – Other liberalisms:
     J. David Greenstone's liberal bipolarity
     Judith Shklar's liberalism of fear
     Rawlsian liberalism
2. (Civic) republicanism
3. Ascriptive Americanism

Lockean Liberalism

Some of the first phrases to fall from the lips of contemporary scholars seeking a core essence of American political thought (if they are so inclined) – whether to praise, condemn, or simply describe it – are "Lockean liberalism," "liberal individualism," "individual liberty," and "individual freedom." The belief in "American exceptionalism" – the idea that the United States as a polity is unique, and *sui generis* – has been closely (if not solely) associated with an understanding that the United States is quintessentially, and to a peerless degree, a Lockean liberal nation. By this, these scholars mean that the American people have defined themselves as a nation defined not, as other nations have been, by race or ethnicity, its people (*volk*), spirit (*geist*), or its primordial traditions, but rather by a pervading commitment to a set of political-philosophical ideas and ideals associated with Lockean liberalism or liberal individualism – by its foundational commitment to the political liberty of free and equal individuals.

The most prominent contemporary articulation of this view is known as the "Hartz thesis," advanced by the Harvard political scientist Louis Hartz in *The Liberal Tradition in America* (1955). The Hartz thesis holds that the key to understanding how Americans think about political authority is that, as modern liberals, they collectively subscribe to the belief that all claims to political authority ultimately derive from the will of sovereign individuals. Acting of their own free will, in their own self-interest, these individuals chose to unite with others, via a social contract, to create a government to protect their foundational natural rights to "life, liberty, and property."[1] Hartz argued – critically, rather than in celebration – that, for the length of its history, American politics, and, indeed, the political imagination of Americans, has been fundamentally shaped and bounded by a consensus commitment to Lockean liberal premises and principles.

Liberal political thought as a genus is defined by a set of themes and touchstones. First, liberalism takes the individual as the foundational unit of analysis. It considers political questions initially from the standpoint of the individual, as opposed to, say, communal bodies or groups, like a tribe, family, or *demos* (the people, considered as a self-governing unity, and whole) – although, to be sure, each of these can be reimagined in accord with liberal premises. Second, liberalism posits that the chief purpose of government is to protect the *rights* of individuals. In line with liberalism's *a priori* individualism, those rights are considered pre-political: they exist in nature, prior to the establishment of political society, by virtue of simply being human. Third, liberalism promises individual freedom, guaranteed equally to all individuals, under a legitimately authorized government limited by constitutional constraints and the rule of law (an understanding that political philosophers call "negative freedom").[2] Fourth, by necessary implication from its commitment to limited government under the rule of law, liberalism enacts a separation between the public and private spheres, and distinguishes the proper realms of state and civil society. While as a practical matter the boundaries can be disputed, liberalism tends to push, if not confine, matters of economic production, religion, and family to the private sphere, removing them from the purview of public concern and government policy. Liberalism, moreover, typically valorizes the private over the public sphere, the latter of which it tends to regard as a necessary evil. Finally, liberalism's touchstone thinker John Locke placed special value within his framework on the duty to work, and the productive value of labor ("God gave the world . . . to the industrious and rational") – the "producer ethic" – from which Locke derives the right to private property, the third of his posited troika of foundational natural rights (life, liberty, and property). Locke highly valued religious liberty, which he considered an essential sphere in which (most) individuals would be free to follow their inner lights and consciences in the private sphere, without interference from worldly governments. Locke's *Letter Concerning Toleration* (1689) is a seminal argument for that fledgling commitment. Locke's call for religious liberty and toleration reflected the incipient tendencies of liberal political thought to valorize secular government and the separation of Church and State.

While liberal individualism is a fairly abstract political theory, it has considerable real-world implications for how Americans think about politics. (Hartz considered Lockean liberalism to be a hegemonic political ideology that had lamentably circumscribed the collective aspirations and political possibilities of the American people.) While Locke's social contract theory was designed to justify and legitimize government power (in Locke's case, England's Glorious Revolution, 1688–1689) – to put it on firm foundations derived from the free will of sovereign, independent individuals – it also has the perhaps ironic effect of simultaneously subverting that power by implication. It is potentially subversive of the power it legitimates by underlining that, if government does not serve the ends for which it has been created, the social contract has been violated, and, as such, is rendered null and void. A contract, in other words, can be broken. And, if it is, the parties are released from their obligations, and all bets are off. Pursuant to what Locke deemed the (natural) right of revolution, the people perpetually retain the sovereign right "to alter and abolish" the government for a failure to achieve, or for betraying, its contracted aims.

The Lockean liberal understanding of the origins of free governments holds that government powers are delegated by the sovereign people for specific ends – and those ends only. Any powers exercised by the government not directed toward those ends, or in violation of the rights for which government was created to protect, are, under the paradigm, considered illegitimate exercises of governmental power. As such, many attribute familiar features of American political thinking – the deep (and sometimes conspiratorial) suspicion that the government is exceeding its rightful powers (anti-statism); the persistent demands for the recognition of individual rights by proponents of civil liberties and civil rights; and hot-headed threats of rebellion and revolution in the name of freedom (think the recent militia or Tea Party movements on the Right) – to the Lockean liberal paradigm that has ostensibly held the country in its grip from its inception. Many have commented on what seems like the country's congenital suspicion of authority, *per se* – the prickly affinity of Americans for the idea that nobody gets to tell someone what to do unless he or she has (expressly?) delegated that authority to that person. They have fingered that suspicion as the root cause of the much remarked upon sense of atomization and isolation in American life, arising out of the orienting liberal assumption that it is, in the end, everyone for him- or herself.

Surveys of public attitudes suggest that, in contrast to Western Europeans, most Americans believe that we are all free to rise by our own efforts. The sometimes unstated implication is that if someone fails it must have been for a lack of such efforts, a personal failing. By these lights, in a free country individuals are authors of both their own successes and their own failures. Society's "losers" are not entitled to any assistance from the government, whose chief, and perhaps sole, purpose is to set the rules of the game for the free play of the ordered liberty of free individuals. This thoroughgoing individualism, Louis Hartz complained, made Americans especially resistant to any recognition of class consciousness, perhaps pre-eminently among the working class. The Lockean liberal framework may also be responsible for the generalized sense of anxiety, workaholism, and competitiveness, for the special attraction Americans seem to have for naming winners and losers, and even the culture's running undertone of violence. A saying displayed in the entryway of a prominent American business school in Texas nicely captures the general mood, and anxiety: "There is no status quo in American life: you are either on your way up, or on your way down."

Liberal Foundations, Themes, and Political Preoccupations

1. Individualism
2. Individual rights/rights consciousness, with special value placed on rights to labor, property, and religious toleration and liberty
3. Limited government, held to have originated by consent, pursuant to a social contract
4. Rule of law
5. [Liberal] constitutionalism
6. Separation of the public and private spheres
7. Right of revolution for violation of the terms of the original agreement upon which government was founded

---

(Civic) Republicanism

In the 1960s, the historians J.G.A. Pocock, Bernard Bailyn, and Gordon Wood launched the first scholarly salvo against the Hartz thesis. These historians of the founding era argued that in that seminal period at least – and, hence, perhaps in others going forward – a quite different political thought tradition, republicanism (sometimes styled "civic republican" or "classical republicanism"), had been ubitquitous for anyone who troubled to look. This challenge to the Hartz thesis launched "the liberal–republican" (or, in a slightly different guise, the "liberal–communitarian") debate among scholars of American political thought. For a time, scholars lined up as partisans arguing for the ideological predominance of one framework or the other, either at the founding, in other periods or moments of American history, or across it, or within identifiable spaces and subcultures within the American political order.

While liberalism is a product of political modernity, republicanism's lineage dates back to ancient Greece and Rome. "Classical" republican thought was rediscovered and revived during the Renaissance (including by the Italian political philosopher Niccolò Machiavelli in his *Discourses on Livy*, 1531; interestingly, Machiavelli was also the author of the proto-modern political theory masterpiece *The Prince*, 1532). That current of classical and Renaissance thought was then – most proximately as concerns American political thought, as revised and, in some sense, reimagined for a modern context – drafted into service in the extended seventeenth- and eighteenth-century political struggles between the English Crown and Parliament. As Englishmen, the American colonists were steeped in this politics of their mother country. That politics was the prism through which the American colonists came to understand their crescendo of grievances with the English Crown in the aftermath of the French and Indian War (1754–1763). This framing informed the political thought that fomented the American Revolution.

Instead of starting with a posited sovereign individual in a state of nature, republicans, following Aristotle, began by stipulating the social and political – the inherently communal nature – of man. (Aristotle, *Politics*: "Man is a political animal.") The republican writers of ancient Greece and Rome – Aristotle, Polybius, Cicero, and others – were widely read by the North American colonial, revolutionary, and early republic elites as part of their classical educations, which often included instruction in the original ancient Greek and Latin languages of such works. Seventeenth- and eighteenth-century English "country" political thought had enlisted classical republicanism to challenge the authority of the English "Court" and Crown. When, not long afterward, the colonists found themselves with their own growing list of grievances against the Court and Crown (George III), they were primed by both these ancient and English predecessors to read their grievances through republican lenses.

Classical republican thought struck themes that were different from – and, in some cases, the antithesis of – individualistic liberalism. Perhaps foremost was the foundational, *a priori* commitment to the common good (the word "republic" itself derives from the Latin *res publica* – "public things"). Republicanism glorified the "free state" – the independent polity, understood as one body, indivisible, directing its own collective life and destiny, free from foreign subjugation or constraint. Liberty is of surpassing value to republicans.

But the emphasis within republican thought was on the understanding that no individual within the polity was truly free unless the community of which he was a part was itself, as a body, free. Republican thought, moreover, placed surpassing value on the virtue – the "civic virtue" – of republican citizens, with virtue itself defined as involving the pursuit of the common good. Republicanism holds that the preservation of individual and collective freedom depends on the virtue of ordinary citizens, their selfless and patriotic devotion to the principles of a free republic, and the common political project. This entailed, and was evidenced by, a willingness of citizens to sacrifice their own personal or private interests for the greater good. As such, whereas liberalism valorizes individual rights, republicanism entails a strenuous, and even austere, devotion to duty. Virtuous republican "citizens" (a republican concept) are expected to directly and actively participate in public life, not to advance their private or partial interests, but to work together with their fellow citizens to advance the common good. (The reliance on elected "representatives" in deliberative bodies, or mercenaries in war, was considered by republicans to be a corruption – evidence of a want of responsibility, citizenship, and duty.) Put otherwise, citizens were understood to be directly responsible for the exercise and preservation of their own freedoms. (As such, republicans traditionally spurned standing armies in favor of citizen militias.) In this regard, many speak of liberalism being anchored in "negative" conceptions of liberty (where liberty is preserved by the limitations imposed on the powers of government) and republicanism in conceptions of "positive" liberty (where liberty is manifested as a free people's active exercise of their power to make their own laws, to set their own collective path, and realize their own common political project).[3] It is characteristic of republicans to be perpetually apprehending the freedom of their polity to be under threat, whether from internal corruption or external subversion or predation.

Republican thought holds that corruption – the worst fate that can be befall a republic – can come from diverse sources: it can be brought on by a falling away from the state's founding principles, and from a decline in virtuousness in the citizenry, including – in a refusal of the abstemious self-denial required of republicans – when citizens' personal or private interests come to prevail over the commitment to virtuous life and the common good. This may be evidenced by a succumbing to the spirit of party, or to the spirit of commerce, the latter of which is doubly suspect as both being based in the pursuit of private interests and for its tendency to distract citizens from their strenuous responsibilities to actively participate in public life. Subversion is enabled by weakness and selfishness, treachery, disloyalty, and treason.

Unlike liberalism, which posits that the end of the state is the preservation of individual rights, republicanism posits a moral purpose or end for the state. As such, following Aristotle, republicanism places surpassing value on establishing the conditions for the cultivation of personal or civic virtue conducive to human flourishing. In this regard, republicans value laws directed to the improvement of men's morals, at making men good. Consequently, as per the Swiss/French political thinker Jean-Jacques Rousseau, republican states will often hew to a "civil religion."[4] Many republicans understood theistic religions as instrumentally valuable in advancing the social and political order sustained by virtuous citizens in a free state – but only to the extent that they were consistent with, or lent support to, the society's civic religion, which they privileged.

Despite their many differences, there are some commonalities among liberal and republican political outlooks. These include a commitment to limited government and the rule of law (albeit each according to its own distinctive concerns, aspirations, and idioms). Because it begins with mostly self-interested individuals, liberalism valorizes the establishment of institutional mechanisms of countervailing powers to enforce limitations on government power, to steer the exercise of the powers of government, to the extent possible, toward the best approximation of the public good. (Liberals vary in the degree to which they are sanguine about the possibility of doing so.) In its own more hopeful visions for the realization of the common good, republicanism, by contrast, places a higher value, and greater hopes, on inculcation through education and other formative practices (like patriotic exercises and military service), and on the strict adherence by a virtuous citizenry to rules and legal and institutional forms.

While it has its uses, the stark opposition often posited between the conceptual universes of liberal and republican thought – sometimes by contemporary scholars who joined one team or the other in the "Liberal–Republican" Debate – can distort the way that these different currents of thought have actually informed the American experience. Ancient, Renaissance, and modern republicanism, for one thing, were not identical. While their core preoccupations and commitments mark them as a continuation of the same family of ideas, modern republicans were more inclined to regard participation in the public sphere as an instrumental means to the achievement of private ends, as opposed to an independent means to human flourishing to be valued for its own sake. In this regard, while they valued direct civic engagement in public life more than liberals, their expectations and standards for that participation were much less strenuous than those of ancient Greece or Rome. They were certainly more amenable to commerce, and, although they lauded it when it appeared – in the courage and sacrifices of George Washington, for example, as a citizen and soldier – they lowered their expectation of the manifestation of heroic virtues by ordinary citizens in mundane times. Modern republicans certainly placed a much greater emphasis on individual liberty than did classical republicans. For these reasons, many of those moderns whose writings are considered core texts of American political thought, like Montesquieu, Thomas Jefferson, and Alexis de Tocqueville, are classed by some, sometimes, as republicans and by others, at other times, as liberals. The truth is that they drew from the well of both political thought traditions, which, moreover, cross-pollinated, and were far from static. The same was true for less well-known thinkers, and, indeed, of ordinary Americans as they have thought about and participated in public life over the course of American history.

Republican Foundations, Themes, and Political Preoccupations

1. Devotion to the common good
2. Pursuit of moral and civic virtue
3. Idea of a morally aspiring free state
4. Patriotism and sacrifice for the community
5. Valorization of public duties over private rights
6. Civic commitments/civic religion given priority over theistic private faith
7. Concern with decline, decay, or defeat through internal corruption or foreign subversion
8. Call for renewal through return to founding principles

Complications and Refinements: Other Liberalisms, Other Republicanisms, and Other Thought Traditions

It is hard to deny the remarkable ability of the Lockean liberal and republican frameworks to illuminate longstanding patterns in the way that Americans from the country's inception have tended to think about, and practice, politics. In addition to arguing about the respective influence of one framework versus the other, generally, among different groups and actors, and across time, some scholars who broadly subscribe to the Hartz thesis positing Lockean liberal hegemony have suggested that it might be either more accurate or more helpful to look at American political thought through the prism of other American liberalisms that, in a positive sense, *have* served as foundations for American political thought, and/or, normatively, *should* serve as the basis for that thought.

In *A Theory of Justice* (1971), the Harvard analytic philosopher John Rawls (1921–2002), for instance, following liberal philosophers before him, including John Locke, but also David Hume, Immanuel Kant, and John Stuart Mill, explicated a new social contract considered and agreed upon, as he imagined it, by individuals in an "original position" under a "veil of ignorance" about how well they would fare in the new society, economically and in social status. The liberal Rawls posited that these hypothetically contracting individuals would place surpassing value on liberty and equality, via limited constitutional government by consent committed to the appropriate guarantees for individual rights. Rawls argued, broadly speaking, moreover, that in addition to securing these foundational guarantees, individuals operating behind a veil of ignorance would insist that the new political order be just, with what is just defined as what is fair ("justice as fairness"). This, Rawls argued, entailed not simply a commitment to maximizing individual liberty (so long as that liberty did not infringe upon the equal liberty of others – Mill's "harm principle"). It further entailed a certain level of distributive justice – a floor, guaranteed by the liberal state, that set limits to the level of economic and social status inequality. Rawls enlisted the "minimax" principle (minimizing the maximum possible loss) in specifying how his theory of justice would ensure the realization of basic individual freedoms and equal opportunity of access to offices and positions. In this way, his liberalism sought to model a just political order that offered the fullest possible commitment to liberty and equality (equal rights to basic liberties), under conditions of universal access to power consistent with the full civic membership of free and equal citizens. This liberalism, unlike Locke's, provided a clear justification for the modern redistributive (liberal) social welfare state.

For her part, Judith Shklar (1928–1992), a Harvard political scientist, argued, at least implicitly, that Rawls's grand theoretical bid for an intricately constructed systematic liberalism in *A Theory of Justice* (and his other books offering refinements of his initial model) was perhaps a bit illiberal in its totalizing ambitions. Informed by her direct encounters with the totalitarian horrors of the twentieth century, including Nazism and Stalinism, Shklar, a Latvian-Jewish refugee, eschewed efforts to forge grand systems. Ever alert to the menace of overwrought utopian ambitions – even in pursuit of ostensibly noble ends – Shklar's liberalism spent less time positing first principles, and then constructing an elaborate theory of government on those foundations, than focusing our attention on attending to the greatest danger and problem in collective life: human cruelty. Putting "cruelty first" entailed what Shklar called a "liberalism of fear." Such a liberalism was decidedly non-perfectionist – it held to a (seemingly) modest, but firm, commitment to the project of staving off, to the maximum extent possible in an imperfect world, the greatest ravages and evils of human societies.

While retaining the schematic ambitions of Hartz, and retaining his emphasis on the importance of liberalism, two frameworks of American political thought with ties to the University of Chicago posited the thought tradition of the United States as essentially plural, and contested. The University of Chicago political scientist J. David Greenstone (1937–1990) accepted Hartz's thesis about the predominance of liberalism in the United States. Greenstone, however, rejected Hartz's view that this had entailed an American "consensus" – to a one-dimensional hegemonically liberal political culture. Where Hartz had posited widespread and reflexive agreement among Americans, Greenstone found a history of political conflict. Taking Abraham Lincoln's thought as his point of entry, Greenstone proposed that, if one looked at the nation's actual politics over the long term, one could discern two different and distinguishable ("bipolar") liberalisms that were offered in opposition to each other in contests for political power. One emphasized "negative liberty," or freedom from coercion by government. The other promised "positive liberty," or the purposive and affirmative direction of public power to expand the scope of individual freedom, in a practical, real-world sense, in everyday life. This concrete contestation over the meaning of liberty, with divergent views over the legitimacy of the enlistment of government power to achieve it, Greenstone argued, was a defining feature of American politics.

Although he wrote almost nothing about American political thought, the German-Jewish émigré University of Chicago political philosopher Leo Strauss (1899–1973) sired a line of scholars who came to write extensively about American political thought from a "Straussian" perspective. Contemporary Straussians – a mostly conservative cohort – have their own distinctive take on, idioms concerning, and disputes over the nature of the American political "regime." In *Natural Right and History* (1953), Strauss drew a fundamental distinction between the "ancients" and the "moderns" in political thought. The former, he argued, were devoted to understandings of political communities as committed to knowing and, in turn, pursuing the highest substantive philosophical ideals of truth, virtue, and justice. The latter, Strauss argued, as exemplified by Niccolò Machiavelli, Thomas Hobbes, and John Locke, in formulating their theories of political life, set these normatively desirable philosophical ideals to the side, and focused their attention instead on the "low but solid" goal of establishing social peace among members of a polity, who, in the nature of things, disagreed about the content of those ideas, and, indeed, had a tendency to go to war over them. While the ancients, one might say, believed that politics was about truth, virtue, and justice, the moderns believed it was about self-preservation and self-interest.

Liberalism is an instantiation, *par excellence*, of the modern view. Its theory of the social contract posits a Hobbesian (or, somewhat more benignly, a Lockean) unsafe – if not dog-eat-dog – state of nature. It then theorizes a contractual agreement that brackets any questions concerning hotly disputed substantive ideals. On these the parties to the contract agree to disagree, and move forward. They create a government that preserves the individual's right to follow his or her own understandings of what he or she believes those ideas entail and require ("liberal neutrality").

Strauss mourned the transition of western societies from the ancient understandings to the modern ones as a falling off. It involved, in important ways, a civilizational decline, entailing the abandonment of the pursuit of the highest human ideals in favor of the more grubby and delimited. At the same time, however, Strauss seemed to suggest at various points that this movement toward modernity may have been inevitable. It may even have had some distinct advantages, though this was far from clear. One virtue liberal modernity did have, however, was that it was far from pristine. There were cracks in the pavement through which flowers could bloom. A commitment to the pursuit of the highest ideals in the modern world was retained, for instance, in classic education in the liberal arts (chiefly the "Great Books" of western thought). It was also retained in the teachings of what Straussians have called "revealed religion." To the extent that we in the modern world were willing to study and construct our institutions to invite, to the extent possible, the salubrious influence of Athens (standing for reason) and Jerusalem (standing for revelation), we might be able to construct a morally and philosophically admirable and decent polity.

Most Straussians writing about American political thought adopted a self-consciously (and, some would say, unduly self-aggrandizing) patriotic stance toward the American polity, although they do not all think about it in the same way. Some, in implicit agreement with Louis Hartz, consider the United States an essentially modern, liberal (and, perhaps, bourgeois and commercial) polity. And they do not hesitate to pass judgment on the political regime. Straussians do not believe that one can separate positive from normative political analysis, in the way that most contemporary social scientists do. They either believe that it is good that the United States is liberal and modern, or they believe that, felicitously, in conjunction with its continuing commitment to normatively desirable non-liberal institutions inside the overarching liberal order (e.g. belief in God; loyalty to family and country; and commitment to traditional [natural] hierarchies), the US regime is worthy of full assent, and possibly even celebration, as the best possible political regime under modern conditions. These Straussians, however, are ever alert to the threats posed to these institutions by the country's secular liberals, who, as they see it, have waged war against them. For their part, other Straussians either challenge the foundational liberalism of the American political regime, such as by emphasizing republican themes (though they rarely declare themselves as simply proponents of republicanism as against liberalism), or by promoting the religious commitments of the American people and the religious (often Christian) grounding of the American political experiment. Alternatively, some Straussians reimagine liberalism, in the United States, at least, along lines that reject the concepts of liberal neutrality and individual autonomy and posit in their place a commitment within liberalism to a set of substantive moral and philosophical ends. These Straussians will define the content of individual rights in the American liberal order by the lights of a substantive *telos* informed by a robust understanding of what is just, right, and good. If what is said to be a "right" does not square with that substantive requirement, the claim is held to be mistaken – it is, after due consideration, no right at all.

Straussians pursue their scholarly agendas in American political thought in a family of ways. Many undertake studies of key figures – often of those they hail as "great men," like the nation's founders, Abraham Lincoln, and Frederick Douglass – who, as ostensible exemplars of virtue and statesmanship, nobly arrived, in diverse ways in different times, at understandings of the rightful admixture of the ancient and the modern in striving to steer the American polity. In contrast, they will also – at times ominously – set their sights on the ways in which other figures in American politics – often the early twentieth-century Progressives, and their (ostensibly) secular liberal successors – have abandoned the unique blend of the ancient and modern that, from the Straussian perspective, constitutes the glory and nobility of the American polity. Following Strauss, these scholars will spy in these purportedly faithless Americans the moral and philosophical heresies of positivism, historicism, secularism, and relativism. Besides focusing on individual great men (and sometimes women), Straussians have studied a broad array of the country's political institutions and creedal documents with an eye to the ways in which those, rightly read, square with their broader understandings of the distinctive nature of the American polity. Although they sometimes critique these documents or institutions, and detail the ways that they fall short, Straussians' general predisposition – in part arising out of their sense of duty as teachers of the (it is hoped, virtuous) citizenry – is toward (informed) patriotism and celebration, to the inculcation, through an appropriate liberal arts education, of a philosophical grounding, historical knowledge, and national pride.

Theories Positing the Inadequacy of the Traditional Frameworks and Proposing Alternatives

There have long been scholars who, while still harboring conceptual ambitions, nevertheless rejected claims that Lockean-liberal political thought has been hegemonic in the United States or, alternatively, that it is subsumable under the aegis of the liberal–republican tension. As they saw it, there had always been multiple frameworks and perspectives that had vied for prominence and pre-eminence in the country's aggressively contested public sphere.

> Whoever is an avowed enemy to God, I scruple not to call him an enemy of his country.
> John Witherspoon (1776)

> Mingling religion with politics [must] be disavowed and reprobated by every inhabitant of America.
> Thomas Paine (1776)

Many have long believed – and still do – that the United States is inherently a Christian nation: that it was founded upon Christian principles by Christian founders who both assumed and stipulated that the country's political institutions "presuppose" a Christian epistemology, theology, and faith. As such, one does not venture far into American political thought without encountering Christian – and, more specifically, Protestant – assumptions, imagery, eschatology, and theology.

While Protestant theology has been a constant force in American life, political and otherwise, from the first settlements to the present, the degree to which the country's core political institutions were founded on Christian principles is far from clear. Excepting its closing flourish announcing that the document had been done "in the Year of our Lord" 1787, the US Constitution neither claimed the authority or blessing of, nor referenced, God: it was designed as an entirely secular plan for government.[5] Just a few years earlier, Thomas Jefferson, the principal author of the Declaration of Independence (1776) which declared that "all men ... are endowed by their Creator with certain unalienable Rights" – had stated firmly that "The legitimate powers of government extend to such acts only as are injurious to others." An unorthodox Christian who denied the divinity of Christ, Jefferson explained his position by noting that "it does me no injury for my neighbour to say there are twenty gods, or no god. It neither picks my pocket nor breaks my leg." While a number of state governments at the time of the founding had established churches, the trendline concerning establishments in the early republic was resolutely downward: Massachusetts rang down the curtain on the country's last religious establishment in 1833.

In the founding era and subsequently, secular Enlightenment rationalism committed to the progress of human reason, as exemplified most prominently by the likes of Jefferson and Benjamin Franklin, developed parallel to, and, in some cases, in alternation in influence with, commitments to, and waves of, Protestant Christian religious fervor and enthusiasm. These have significantly shaped American public life from the first Puritan settlement to the First and Second Great Awakenings (c. 1730–1755 and 1790–1840, respectively) to the present.

While there was some initial religious diversity (Maryland was settled largely by Roman Catholics, and Virginia by adherents of the established – albeit Protestant – Church of England), the most pervasive influence was of England's dissenting Protestant religious sects. The core elements of their reformation theology, set in motion by Germany's Martin Luther (1517), who helped start a process that sheared much of Christendom off from the Roman Catholic Church, held, first, that Scripture – the text of the Holy Bible – was the only source of Christian doctrine, and, second, that belief and faith in Jesus was the only path to salvation. The former provided the law for human conduct, and the later the gospel that promised forgiveness from sin, and eternal life, by dint of God's grace. To be a Christian was to know God, and live by His commandments and His plan.

The Reformation splintered Christendom from a mostly unified body under the auspices of the Church of Rome into a multiplicity of sects holding diverse convictions regarding humanity's sinfulness, God's plan for its salvation, and the meaning of Jesus's resurrection for human redemption. John Calvin's *Institutes of the Christian Religion* (1536), a major Protestant text (directing, for example, the practice of Lutherans, Presbyterians, and Congregationalists), in turn, placed a heavy (Augustinian) emphasis on original sin and man's total depravity, as well as the sovereignty of God in all things – including His (inscrutable/unknowable) predetermination (predestination) of who would ultimately be saved (the elect), and who would be eternally damned. Salvation, for "Calvinists," would not be by good works or earthly deeds, but by God's grace alone. Other sects, by contrast, promised salvation through diverse means, typically involving not simply the adherence to God's law in pre-mortal life (righteousness), but also inner faith.

As we shall see in the chapters that follow, Christian theology played a direct role in shaping how Americans thought about core political issues, whether it be the relation of the individual to the community, the origins and limits on government, the role of morals and conscience in public life, the nature of liberty, equality, and justice, the imperative of social reform, or the duty to obey or defy the law. From the Puritans, to antebellum reform (including temperance, prison reform, abolitionism, and women's rights), to the progressive social gospel, the emergence of fundamentalism, the civil rights movement, the anti-Vietnam War movement, the Cold War, and the rise of the Religious Right, an increasingly pluralistic cohort of Protestants, joined more and more over time by politically active Roman Catholics, Jews, Muslims, Buddhists, and others, did politics in ways that were deeply informed by their religious outlooks and convictions.

At the time of the nation's founding, moreover, American political thought was clearly inflected by strains of statist nationalism – "statist" not in the sense that there were understood to be no constitutional or natural limits on the powers of government, but in the sense that, born as the country was into the Westphalian world order premised on geographically demarcated, interacting, and competitive national states pursuing their own interests, many Americans were concerned with the would-be power, fame, wealth, and glory of the United States as a nation-state, akin to – and in competition with – Great Britain, France, and Spain. Isaac Kramnick, an important proponent of the argument that the American founders drew upon and debated a range of antagonistic thought traditions, argued that a number of the founders, most prominently Alexander Hamilton, understood themselves to be statebuilders, aimed at creating a new commercial nation-state that could hold its own – protect and advance its "national interest" – in a global arena. To do so, the country would need a powerful and energetic centralized government with wide-ranging powers to tax, spend, promote economic development, aggressively protect its interests in the international arena through trade regulations, and, indeed, once possessed of a mighty military, fight. In this, localism was a potentially sapping centrifugal force. A relatively passive government chiefly concerned with administering justice and protecting private rights, moreover, would be wholly inadequate to the task.[6]

The political scientist Benedict Anderson has argued that, in the modern world, nationalism, which he famously defined as the sense of the nation as "an imagined community," was born of the colonial encounter between the "Old" and "New" worlds, and, arising out of empire and expansion, came into its own in the modern world as a distinctive species of political thought. Across history, American nationalism has come in different forms, from patriotic-militaristic statism, to cultural-chauvinistic, to religious. All, of course, have in some sense blended together in a mixture that has come to characterize the United States as a distinctive (and perhaps "exceptional") imagined community.

Religious – or, more precisely, white Protestant – nationalism has been a remarkably consistent strain of American political thought. Many Americans have long conceived of their country as a faith community, founded on Protestant (or, much later, in response to the rise of twentieth-century totalitarianism, "Judeo-Christian") principles, which, they believe, have both constituted its populace as moral beings, actors, and citizens, and provided the theoretical foundations for its political institutions. As such, there is a long tradition of white Protestant nationalist political thought that spans all of American history, and has informed and underwritten the country's politics.

One common form of this religious nationalism has been *Christian providentialism*: the idea that the nation's founding was divinely ordained. Christian nationalists believe that the nation's very purpose was to provide a sanctuary for persecuted Christians, a place where they would be free not only to live in accord with the precepts of their faith, but also to live together collectively as a Christian polity – as a Christian commonwealth. While the country that eventually became the United States of America was initially settled for many reasons, not least commercial, it is nevertheless true that certain of the early settlements, particularly in Puritan New England, clearly imagined themselves as founding a "New Israel" – a place where, persecuted in their home countries, the godly and righteous could freely worship God, and realize their common faith. Indeed, many colonists often spoke of the new land in messianic terms – as providentially given to them by God for the advancement of His Truth and Word (also, in a different way, an "exceptionalist" vision). These settlers were concerned less with the "civic virtue" prescribed by republicans than with Christian virtue.

Other scholars have observed that ostensibly ascriptive, prepolitical ethnic and racial identities have long been constitutive of the self-understandings of Americans as an imagined community. Forms of ethno-nationalism or racial nationalism have long held that membership in the US political community is premised upon ascriptive racial or ethnic characteristics, such as whiteness (racial), or Anglo-Saxon (ethnic), or white Anglo-Saxon (racial-ethnic)

> The American Negro has the great advantage of having never believed that collection of myths to which white Americans cling: that their ancestors were all freedom-loving heroes, that they were born in the greatest country the world has ever seen, or that Americans are invincible in battle and wise in peace. . . . Negroes know far more about white Americans than that.
>
> James Baldwin (1963)

identity. These ascriptive nationalisms have been founded on different under-standings, ranging from genetic to cultural. In practice, they have commonly intersected across American history with religious nationalism (e.g. the United States as an inherently white, Anglo-Saxon, Protestant nation). All of these forms of nationalism have underwritten understandings of civic membership, belonging, and exclusion. To the extent that they are founded on ascriptive categories positing a fixed "identity," they are presumptively unbridgeable and permanent.

The University of Pennsylvania political scientist Rogers M. Smith has argued that the standard inventory of American political thought paradigms – first, the Hartz thesis positing a hegemonic Lockean liberalism, and then the republican thesis – not only failed to recognize what he called "ascriptive Americanism" as a major current of American political thought, but also in critical ways contradicted those prevailing paradigms' ostensibly orient-ing commitments to civic solidarity and free and equal liberty under law – the country's purported "Idea" or "Creed."[7] More broadly, Smith argued that Americans have long ascribed certain traits and characteristics to mem-bers of certain groups and groupings, whether identified by race, ethnicity, sex, or gender – that is, they have long made ascriptions based on identity. Those holding political, economic, social, and cultural power, in part via the privileging of their own (favored) ascriptive characteristics, have denied full (or even *any*) recognition to the members of those groups as civic equals on the basis of those ascribed characteristics. Until the mid-nineteenth cen-tury, most African-Americans were enslaved – treated as species of property. Native Americans were considered savages, to be, variously, Christianized and assimilated, removed, or exterminated. Women were, in many ways (via, for example, coverture laws) considered to have legally merged with their husbands, and could not vote. These exclusions were not only practiced and legally enforced but spoken of and justified openly and extensively in the public and private spheres. As such, Smith argued, it makes little sense to describe the American political thought tradition as exclusively liberal and republican, as if the principles which those frameworks purported to cherish were applied and invokable by all.

Both before and after Smith, however, some have pushed back against this understanding, insisting that "the American idea" or "creed" is real, and that these aberrational blots on the nation – even when they involved an over-whelming majority of the populace – are better conceived of not as evidence of the falseness of American claims to being a "creedal nation" but as a failure, slowly remedied across time, to live up to the noble and catechistic ideals on which the country had (genuinely) been founded.

Creedal nationalism defines Americanism not ascriptively but as a will-ingness to subscribe to a set of normatively desirable and foundational principles – in most iterations, liberty, equality, and democracy. "True" or

"Real" Americanism – full civic membership – is defined by a willingness to fully commit oneself to – and perhaps even give one's life to defend – such principles. In contradistinction to ascriptive Americanism, creedal nationalism promises an open and inviting form of civic membership – on display, for instance, each year when thousands of immigrants of diverse races, ethnicities, nationalities, and religions take a solemn oath of American citizenship. Upon swearing the oath – professing fidelity not only to the country's laws, but also to its catechistic creed – they are presumed as American as anyone else, even those whose ancestors have been living in the United States for generations: they join the American national community as full civic equals.

It may seem that, when compared with ethno-racial ascriptive or religious nationalism, creedal nationalism is inviting, inclusive, and egalitarian. But creedal nationalism has its own cast of outsiders: those who do not subscribe – or who are held by others to not subscribe – to the creed's constitutive beliefs. Their beliefs – and, by extension, their persons – are classed as "anti-American," or "un-American." While these epithets would clearly be applied to those who expressly repudiate the polity's creedal political principles, they have also been wielded against those – for example, socialists – whose political views, despite their protestations, are held by their opponents to have repudiated those principles. If their views are in the minority, their insistence that their views are consistent with the American creed, or even provide the best opportunity for its fullest realization, are likely to fall on deaf ears. As such, its apparent universalism notwithstanding, creedal nationalism can unleash its own forms of civic exclusion, and conduce to intellectual orthodoxy, conformism, and a reluctance to express political disagreement or dissent for fear of being labeled a traitor.

Two of the most emblematic statements of American creedalism were made by outside observers of US political culture, the French aristocrat and sociologist Alexis de Tocqueville (1805–1859) and the Swedish sociologist Gunnar Myrdal (1898–1987). Both are at once celebrations and critiques.

De Tocqueville's *Democracy in America* (1835) has been widely adopted by Americans as a seminal text of American creedalism. Tocqueville was part of a flotilla of European visitors who came to the Jacksonian United States to observe and reflect upon the extraordinary spectacle of a country in which the constituent people, the *demos*, were their own rulers. *Democracy in America* is an engaging mixture of dispassionate observation, sociological description and reportage, analytical-philosophical reflection, and normative evaluation and assessment – much of which was speculative, provisional, and prognosticative. An early social scientist in the modern sense, Tocqueville observed that Americans professed certain principles of political thought and, moreover, that, in some ways, they lived, or sought to live, by the lights of those principles. Tocqueville then went out and observed what Americans actually did and said, and identified patterns. He additionally observed the ways that key institutions of American life functioned. Tocqueville then stepped back to consider both the present and future implications of their dynamics. Where he saw problems, he considered the possibility that other dynamics and institutions might offer potential remedies, or at least mitigations.

Tocqueville's observations – about the role of women and religion, about lawyers, about New England township government, and innumerable other aspects of American life as he observed it – and his often prescient analysis of their implications, are too extensive to canvass here. But one preoccupation of his is worth setting out: his extended consideration of the implications of what he took to be the pervasive American belief in (democratic) equality – for which, it is worth underlining, his point of comparison, his yardstick, was not an abstract ideal (or, for that matter, twenty-first-century standards) but contemporaneous Western Europe. Tocqueville was attracted by the trend toward equality he saw in America. He thought it boded well for the future of liberal freedom in the world. At the same time, however, he tempered his celebration with reservations and concerns. The faith of Americans in democracy and equality threatened traditional understandings of hierarchy and authority, many of which had long undergirded much of the peace, good order, manners, and mores of western societies, and their core institutions like families and churches. Throughout history, most people had taken their basic opinions and understandings from hierarchical authority and traditions. What might happen, Tocqueville wondered, as the commitment to democracy and equality, with the critiques they entail of hierarchy, tradition, and authority, unspooled to reach new and previously unimagined destinations?

Tocqueville pondered, and speculated. He expressed concern about the emergence of a "tyranny of the majority." In the absence of the traditional sources of authority and hierarchies in a democracy, the people, he predicted, would increasingly take their opinions from what those around them were thinking. As such, he posited that democratic America's ironic fate might be that its thorough-going individualism might end, paradoxically, in a stultifying conformism: while everyone would ostensibly be free to think and do as they pleased, most would end up thinking and doing what everyone else was. The country's loudly professed commitment to freedom of speech and freedom of thought would end up, Tocqueville ventured, with very little freedom of opinion.

Gunnar Myrdal's *An American Dilemma: The Negro Problem and American Democracy* (1944) was a landmark study commissioned by the New York-based Carnegie Corporation that influenced the American civil rights movement and public thinking about civil rights more generally. In that two-volume report, Myrdal posited an "American Creed" that largely reflected liberal values of liberty, equality, and justice for all – which he took to be widespread among Americans, and sincerely held. That said, Myrdal argued that, in key respects, chiefly with regard to race, the country had as yet failed to live up to its creedal ideals, (Similar views had long been expressed, in diverse ways, by the abolitionist Frederick Douglass, the feminist framers of the Seneca Falls Declaration on Women's Rights, and other "aspirationalists" – and, for that matter, by "declinists," who focused on corruptions and fallings away.)

Critical race theorists and Rogers Smith have taken exception to Myrdal's framing. The commitment to ascribed identities, they have argued, had always been constitutive of the nation's laws, practices, and self-understandings. Put otherwise, it was not the exception but the rule. As such, according to Smith's "multiple traditions thesis," American political thought needed to afford "ascriptive Americanism" full and equal status as a constitutive paradigm of American political thought.

Many others of note both before and after Myrdal, ranging from Hector St. John de Croevecoer, to Hartz's *The Liberal Tradition in America*, to Ernest Tuveson (*Redeemer Nation: The Idea of America's Millennial Role*, 1968), to Samuel Huntington (*American Politics: The Promise of Disharmony*, 1981), have articulated creedal understandings and visions of American political thought. A closely associated genre are works that have posited an "American character" or an "American mind," such as Frederick Jackson Turner ("The Significance of the Frontier in American History," 1893), David Potter (*People of Plenty: Economic Abundance and the American Character*, 1954), or David Hackett Fischer (*Albion's Seed: Four British Folkways in America*, 1989). Both the creedalist and "American character" genres posit a set of quintessentially American beliefs and inclinations. They advance a diverse set of arguments about their ostensible roots, ranging from the country's distinctive geographic and material conditions to the national/ethnic/racial characteristics – the demographics – of the people who populated it. Notably, it was only a short step from this approach, in the minds of some of these scholars, to the positing of the underlying values and principles to which "we," as Americans, are ostensibly committed, and the mind and character "we" ostensibly share. Such homogenizing and essentializing theses, while they remain attractive to many, are also, these days, quite controversial. This is because they not only tend to posit a broad consensus among a diverse and disparate collection of people, but additionally suggest that that consensus has been largely fixed across time, across which the United States experienced many changes, not least in the composition, and political agency, of its populace.

While these understandings, and American creedalism, are typically taught as philosophies or coherent wholes, a variety of observers have seen their importance in American life not as rooted in a deliberate philosophical choice among Americans but in the conditions of their settlement and demographics, and their economic status and class. They have also been embodied in and informed by narratives and stories.

Stories About America

Among political theorists especially, liberalism and republicanism are typically understood, and taught, as political philosophies. They start from core premises and build outward to construct logically coherent and cohesive theories of government, which can then be critiqued, criticized, revised, refined, or rejected. While the political thought of Americans has certainly been informed by underlying political philosophies, however, it has also been informed by narratives and stories, which have their own dynamics different from those involved in arguing a point of political philosophy.

In later work, Rogers Smith wrote about American political thought as (also) being informed, if not foundationally structured, by a set of "people-making," "ethically constitutive stories." These stories look to and interpret the nation's past, offering shared readings of the country's mores in light of stories about where their tellers imagine the country has been and is going. These might be stories of spiritual aspiration, or prodigal wandering, of anointment or chosenness, or foresakenness, of belonging, privilege, or exclusion, of restoration or redemption, of treachery or betrayal, of decline or triumph. One way to think about such stories is that they are bids at meaning-making, whether by an individual, a group, or the political community as a whole. To be effective, such stories (or narratives) will appeal not just to the intellect but also to the emotions, inspiring feelings of loyalty, resentment, pride, anger, hope, and even love. Such stories are a staple of everything from political speeches and campaigns to national anthems and pop songs, and of the design of flags, government buildings, and public monuments like the Lincoln or the Vietnam memorials. The relationship between the stories Americans have told themselves over the course of their history interact with political philosophies in diverse and complicated ways. Sometimes the stories are enlisted to illustrate and reinforce a particular political framework or philosophy. At other times, they evince their own distinctive, and orthogonal, dynamics.

Conclusion

Many Americans are inclined to treat the study of American political thought as a catechism. In this catechism, the country is held to adhere to a set of abstract, and celebrated, creedal commitments – liberty, equality, democracy, justice – which its institutions were designed to honor and implement. Individuals and the nation may not always live up to these American ideals, and its institutions may from time to time fail to realize them, but, if that is the case, a course correction is always on order, to set the nation – "man's last best hope on earth" (Lincoln) – back on the right path to the realization of its noblest ideas.

Others, however, approach the subject entirely differently. Many of these other approaches emphasize pluralism, contention, and an open-endedness, provisionality, and perpetual incompleteness that does not lend itself to catechism. In one important study, for instance, *Contested Truths: Keywords in American Politics since Independence* (1987), the Princeton historian Daniel Rodgers posited a cynosure set of words (utility, natural rights, the people, government, interests, the state, and freedom) around which the conceptual debates of American political life have dilated over the course of American history. Given who they are and what they do, great poets – Robert Frost in "The Black Cottage" (1914), for instance, or Tracy K. Smith in "Declaration" (2018) – have also emphasized the open-endedness of core American events and ideas, while still gesturing toward the idea of a discernable American political tradition. Argument, contestation, and irresolution may, by some lights, be as constitutive of a political culture and tradition as unity and finality. Power might matter. But power might be challenged, and shift. In this regard, in her poem, Smith acts not only as legatee subject, but also as self-determining agent of American political thought.

For native-born Americans, the tradition of American political thought is presumably a birthright and inheritance. For naturalized Americans, it is often a chosen history and family. For non-Americans, given the global reach and influence of US power, politics, institutions, and ideas in the twenty-first century, whether undertaken willfully or not, it is commonly an encounter. Knowing the history, habits, perils, and promise of American political thinking is an illuminating part of any rounded political education.

Questions

1. Is there a substantive content to "American" political thought as a distinctive subject of study (as opposed, for instance, to the study of political theory, intellectual history, or even the study of American politics more generally)? If so, in what sense?
2. Is it possible to construct a canon of American political thought? If so, what are the standards enlisted to determine selection for inclusion in, or exclusion from, the canon?
3. In studying American political thought, how accurate or helpful is it to talk about core, shared understandings of concepts like "liberty," "equality," "democracy," or "justice"?
4. How might we think about the political thought of particular individuals across the temporal span of their lives and experiences? Does it make sense to speak of the political thought of, for instance, James Madison, Abraham Lincoln, Martin Luther King Jr., Malcolm X, or Ronald Reagan as if they had a stable philosophy that extended across the entirety of their lives?

5. How useful, or dangerous, is it to posit an "American exceptionalism"?
6. What is gained or lost in positing either a hegemony or a (delimited) pluralism of overarching ideologies or frameworks to understand American political thought? Relatedly, does it ever make sense to enlist the category of "we" in our discussions of American political thought?
7. Do you think political philosophies or ethically constitutive stories have been more influential in shaping the contours of American political thought? How and in what ways?
8. How much of the American political thought tradition has been determined by broad, impersonal social forces (geography, demography, economics, ideology), and how much by individual agency?
9. In studying American political thought, how useful, or dangerous, is it to avail ourselves of apparently hermetic categories – often in the form of binaries – to get an analytic grip on the politics of a moment (e.g. founders v. loyalists; liberal v. republican; Federalists v. Antifederalists; the people v. the interests (or elites); progressives/liberals v. conservatives)?
10. What role does time (chronology/development) play in American political thought? Is there a consistency to ideational frameworks across time? Or do things change over time in critical ways? Relatedly, how might we think about the forces driving chronological patterns? How is the influence of ideas, ideologies, and frameworks temperally reproduced or institutionalized or, for that matter, interrupted and de-institutionalized?
11. How much of the study of American political thought should be about what *is* (in a positivist sense), and how much should be about what *ought to be* (in a normative sense)?
12. Are progressives/liberals and conservatives likely to study American political thought in different ways? Americans and non-Americans? Members of historically powerful and historically marginalized groups?
13. Is the American political thought tradition one of which Americans should be proud, ashamed, or something in between? Why?

2

Settlement, the Road to Revolution, the Founding, and the Early Republic

The Theological Dimensions of Colonial American Thought

In the early seventeenth century, European colonists began to settle the original strip of land that became the United States on North America's Atlantic coast, previously populated exclusively by native aboriginal tribes. Commerce provided much of the impetus for the European migration, including the early Dutch settlement of New Amsterdam (later, New York). Over time, fueled as well by the forces of imperial ambition and competition, the thirteen North American colonies matured into an estimable outpost of the globe-spanning British Empire.

Other European settlers, however, were drawn to the colonial settlements for religious reasons. While, as noted, the Southern colonies were initially settled by Anglicans, and Maryland by Catholics, the New England colonies were disproportionately settled by members of England's "dissenting" Protestant religious sects. A religious minority in the mother country (7%), members of these sects were subject to discrimination, and even persecution. They were Calvinists of different sorts (Congregationalists, Presbyterians, Baptists), but also Quakers. Given their predicament as dissenters from the prevailing political order, undergirded by the officially established Church, ministers and theologians in the colonies spent time reflecting upon questions of the sources of legitimate worldly political authority, the relationship between that and otherworldly, divine authority, the respective claims of the individual and the community, and the appropriate relation between Church and State. As such, theological investigations by Christian ministers (and other Christians) in the American colonies addressed some of the most significant political questions. These investigations and discussions were transatlantic.

The English Enlightenment political philosopher John Locke had contemporaneously argued for "the reasonableness of Christianity" (1695) – that reason could be used to test the soundness of religious beliefs, and measure and confirm the authenticity of revelation. Locke's views were widely disseminated by Puritan preachers in the American colonies. While the epithet "Puritanism" came to be associated with religious, and often sexual, oppressiveness, the most significant calling card of the Puritans was the role its theology afforded to reason, particularly as that reason was practiced outside of – and even against – the strictures of a government-sponsored, officially established Church. As such, Puritan thought in the Anglo-American tradition was allied, albeit imperfectly, with developments that led to modern conceptions of both religious and political liberty. It was the English Puritan writer and poet John Milton, for instance, who, in *Areopagitica* (1644), penned what is still one of the seminal arguments against censorship, and in defense of the freedom of speech. The Cambridge-educated Puritan minister Roger Williams (1603–1683), whose radical views concerning the liberty of conscience and the separation of Church and State led to his expulsion from the Massachusetts Bay colony, was a peerless champion of religious freedom. Puritan theologians authored pioneering challenges to the claim of the divine right (authority) of Kings.

As their name suggests, Puritans were additionally preoccupied with what they took to be the worldly corruption of the Church of England. They responded by founding new "purified" churches, where they could live and worship in the true light of God. It is this critical, moralizing impulse, and passion for purifying the corrupted and debased, that provides the basis for the epithet "puritanical" commonly directed not only toward Puritans (or their latter-day epigones), but also toward American culture more generally, which Puritan thought, in this regard, is held to have foundationally influenced and pervaded.

Protestantism, born in the call by Martin Luther, in his Ninety-Five Theses, for "Reformation," had itself originated from similar concerns about the worldly corruption of the Roman Catholic Church, as manifested by a rampant materialism and a decadent, venal, and power-hungry clergy (including, at the apex, the Pope), at the expense, it was said, of genuine spiritual concerns. England underwent its own Protestant Reformation when, after King Henry VIII sought an annulment which the Pope refused to grant, reformationists helped underwrite Henry's break from Rome and establish the Anglican Church, with the English monarch replacing the Pope as its head.

Some English Protestants expressed increasing disappointment and dissatisfaction with the course of the English Reformation. The Puritans thought that the Church of England had not gone far enough in cleansing itself of the vestiges of Catholicism. The growing body of dissenters complained that the monarchically decreed practices, rituals, and forms of worship prescribed by the Anglican Church, including the Church's purportedly un-scriptural ornate clerical vestments, smacked of popery (a pejorative that frequently recurs in colonial American thought). By not excluding the self-evidently wicked from their communion, the Church of England was courting the corruption of the spiritually pure, imperiling their immortal souls. If even its ministers were worldly sinners, it was said, what hope could the Anglican Church offer the humble parishioner?

The English Puritan John Field (1545–1588) had defined a church as "a company or congregation of the faithful called and gathered out of the world by the preaching of the Gospel, who following and embracing true religion, do in one unity of Spirit strengthen and comfort one another, daily growing and increasing in true faith, framing their lives, government, orders and ceremonies according to the word of God." Puritans like Field endeavored to form churches of "visible saints": voluntary associations of the holy, predestined for salvation. Such a spiritual community would admit only those of manifest probity; the faith community would be characterized by a rigorous discipline enforced by admonishment, censure, and excommunication.

A growing number of Puritans interpreted seventeenth-century England's economic and political troubles as a sign of divine displeasure. This led to further reflection on the appropriate origins and organization of churches. Some sought greater reform of the Church of England. A cohort of more radical Puritans called for separation. Among them was Robert Browne, who in 1581 went so far as to declare the Church of England to be a false church, organized with utter disregard for biblical principles. Brown called for assemblies of the godly to establish new churches on Biblical principles. The Puritans who made landfall in Massachusetts, first at Provincetown (in whose harbor they drafted the Mayflower Compact of 1620), before settling at Plymouth, established the first separatist Church in what they called "New England."

Many more – separatist and non-separatist alike – would follow, especially after the Anglican leadership moved to forbid Puritan liturgical practices and harass nonconforming ministers. Beginning in 1630, a "Great Migration" of seven hundred Puritans, including John Winthrop, aboard the *Arbella*, re-settled in North America and founded the Massachusetts Bay colony. In doing so, they imagined their migration to the New World as a biblical Exodus of world-historical significance: on those distant shores they would found a "New Israel" rooted in Christian governing morals and ideals.

Notwithstanding that many settlers of the American colonies came simply to make a livelihood, or even as punishment for crimes, the providentialist and exceptionalist idea of the United States as "the redeemer nation" (Ernest Tuveson) – a recycled idea many of them had formerly applied to England – started early, and here. Ever since Winthrop described the Puritan settlement of Massachusetts Bay "as a city upon a hill" with the eyes of the whole world watching, many Americans have understood the United States as God's chosen country, with a divinely ordained mission in the world. For good and for ill, Americans throughout their history have exhibited a marked tendency to imagine their nation's historical and political trajectory as a religious drama. And, not infrequently, especially in times of crisis – or perceived crisis – they have shown a tendency to script that drama in apocalyptic terms: as an epic, God-haunted battle of Good versus Evil, with Satan's snares perpetually tempting, and eternal damnation an impending threat.

The pietist strain of American political thought took strongest root in New England, where Church and State were most densely intertwined (church membership, for instance, was required to vote). The American Puritans set up distinctive governing structures anchored in their religious principles and codes. Although fleeing persecution based on their religious practices and beliefs, the American Puritans did not institute religious toleration. As they saw it, in migrating they had sought the freedom to establish their own self-governing communities where they could live according to their faith. As such, Puritans in America meted out severe discipline to those who spurned or transgressed against the community's theological convictions. America's early Puritans were aggressively moralistic. They expected community members to live up to the highest moral standards, and were quick to ferret out and punish immorality. Puritans like Winthrop spoke frequently of liberty. But they did so by the lights of the distinction they drew between a dangerous "natural liberty" (anarchic license) and a virtuous "civil liberty" harmonizing with just and legitimate authority. For a community and the individuals who comprised it to live according to just, legitimate, and true laws, both temporal and moral, as discerned and enforced by a legitimate governing authority, was to be truly free. Liberty, for Puritans, meant living by the commands of biblical (Christian) teaching under the authority of Our Lord Jesus Christ.

The Puritans practiced – indeed, helped pioneer – government by consent in the way they organized their churches. As explicated by Winthrop and John Wise, among others, Puritan churches – in contradistinction to both the Church of Rome and the Church of England – were voluntary associations of "visible saints," organized by mutual consent through covenants. As such, Puritan church governance reflected proto-democratic instincts about self-government that foreshadow important elements of later democratic thought. In a plea for forbearance for his human foibles and errors, as well as a reminder of his high authority, Winthrop reminded those who had entrusted him with governing power that "It is yourselves who have called us to this office, and being called by you, we have our authority from God." Given the organization of their churches, by the standards of their time – again, as compared with the organization of the Church of Rome and the Church of England – this allowed for considerable diversity. By the standards held by most in our own time, however, that diversity looks tightly circumscribed: it had sharp, and sometimes harshly (and even cruelly) enforced, limits.

These limits were perhaps most dramatically tested by the case of Roger Williams, a Puritan separatist critical of the decision of the Massachusetts Bay colony founders to retain their ties to the Church of England. Stubbornly hewing to his own inner light, Williams persistently antagonized his religious community, to the point where he was banished from the colony. Williams moved south, first founding the city of Providence (1636), and then securing a formal charter for the new colony of Rhode Island (Providence Plantations) (1644). Chafing at Massachusetts Bay's Congregationalist structures and strictures, Williams became a Baptist.

In the *Bloudy Tenent of Persecution* (1644), Williams penned one of the first arguments in English (following some Dutch predecessors) for both religious toleration and the total separation of Church and State. Williams's arguments for both were foundationally, if not exclusively, theological. Coerced or compelled faith, he argued, was not genuine faith. As such, it was contrary to Scripture. Persecution for alleged error made a travesty of the teachings of Jesus Christ (Williams called it "soul rape"). It was, moreover, a menace to civic peace. Williams additionally argued that the Bible itself had firmly distinguished the realms of Church and State. In uniting them, Massachusetts Bay had flouted the commands of Holy Scripture. The Bible, he elaborated, had commanded that worldly government should be secular. Being a good Christian and a good magistrate or citizen were separate matters. Any attempt to establish a purported "Christian Commonwealth" in this world would end by afflicting the faith, and the faithful: to the extent it got involved in worldly politics, the Church would find itself complicit in, and corrupted by, worldly politics. Williams championed the view, later enshrined in the US Constitution (Article VI, Cl. 3), that "no religious Test shall ever be required as a Qualification to any Office or public Trust under the United States."[1]

Williams's arguments for toleration and the complete separation of government and religion evinced a profound concern for the claims of individual conscience. Williams considered an individual's conscience man's most valuable, God-given possession – and, indeed, responsibility. Williams's arguments left a strong imprint on American political thought. Claims on behalf of the individual's self-discerned inner moral light of conscience found a sustained life in what some have called the nation's alternative "dissenting tradition," which held obedience to conscience to be both a requirement of the soul and a pillar of political liberty. It was palpably in evidence, for instance, in Henry David Thoreau's refusal to pay his taxes that supported an immoral war (the Mexican-American War, 1846–1848), and in Thoreau's, and others', refusal to lend any sustaining support for chattel slavery.

Many contemporary scholars have argued that Williams's theological arguments on behalf of Church–State separation, which became rooted, if uneasily for some, in the United States, at least at the national level, underwrote the US's exceptional religiosity. As compared with a secularizing Western Europe, where established churches ended up shouldering the blame for the decisions and behaviors of the worldly politicians with whom they had publicly and closely associated themselves, Church–State separation in the United States, such as it was, reinforced, it has been said, the purity of the Church. A separation, moreover, in which the state showed no favoritism toward any of the country's competing religious sects – gradually adopted by all of the

American states by the early nineteenth century – proved especially conducive to the liberty of conscience. Some have latterly argued, moreover, that
non-establishment and the wide scope given for a multitude of competing
religious sects spurred competition among churches to effectively meet the
needs of their current and potential congregants, strengthening the churches,
and promoting Christian evangelization.

New England's Puritan churches were notable, and precedent-setting,
exercises in self-government, offering clear models for secular political rule.
Each church was independent of every other church. As its own independent,
self-governing faith community, each church selected its own minister, who
served at the congregation's pleasure. (The congregational structure instituting self-government in ecclesiastical matters was codified in the Cambridge
Platform of 1648.) While there were strong elements of what Alexis de
Tocqueville later called "individualism" in these new departures, the colonial
Puritan congregations were nevertheless intensely communal: the emphasis
was on the collective spiritual, moral, and temporal needs of the group over
and above those of the individuals who comprised it – an emphasis explicated
in John Winthrop's speech "Modell of Christian Charity" (1630), delivered
shipboard during the *Arbella*'s Atlantic crossing. New England's Puritans
understood their communities as organic wholes: their individual members
were the organs and limbs of a single human body, inextricably joined and
sharing a common fate. Winthrop enjoined his flock on the *Arbella* that to
"love one another with a pure heart fervently we must bear one another's
burdens, we must not look only on our own things, but also on the things of
our brethren." He called for common devotion to mercy and charity. Notably,
Winthrop's injunction to communal duty and care was directed toward the
"private" institutions of "civil society" (here, churches), rather than toward
the "public sphere" institutions of (secular) government. Concern for the
needy was considered a matter of divine Christian obligation.

The Christian communions that formed churches made no claims to universal inclusion. The "people" with the authority to enter into the covenant
organizing a church was a highly circumscribed class, in accord with the
stringent purposes that had motivated the association in the first place. Full
membership was limited to saints. And claims to sainthood required proof –
visible evidence of having had a conversion experience, of being "Born Again."
A 1646 Massachusetts law mandated that all within a township attend its
church. But only full members of the church were afforded governing privileges. In time, however, this orthodoxy began to clash with the more casual
inclinations of others, who may not have been able to provide personal evidence of religious conversion.

As the Protestant theologians were often deeply learned men – educated,
for instance, at England's Cambridge University – their understandings of the
proper government of churches were not fashioned from Christian sources

alone. Puritan theologians in the colonies were also informed by ancient and modern texts of political philosophy, from Aristotle to (in time) John Locke. John Wise's reflections on church governance, for example, drew upon Aristotle's consideration of the virtues and debilities of rule by the one, the few, or the many (monarchy, aristocracy, democracy), and the possibility and potential of mixed political regimes. Wise was also persuaded by his near contemporary John Locke's theories of government by consent, arising out of the state of nature. These understandings were disseminated in the American colonies not only in books and pamphlets, but also from the pulpit. As such, in their concern with questions of natural equality, the relationship of the individual to the community, the claims of conscience, of self-government, and significance of the individual's voice in directing the affairs of the community – and, indeed, of political liberty – Puritan thought anticipated and informed colonial thinking concerning fundamental questions of (secular) American political thought.

Americans still debate the extent and nature of the Puritan legacy in US political thought. Religious traditionalists recur to the Puritans' strict moral standards, their enlistment of public authorities to aggressively police personal and public morals, and their privileging of claims of the community over those of the individual. Many also claim that the Puritanism of early New England set the template for the country's core political philosophy. Less remembered, perhaps, is the profoundly subversive strain of Puritanism's more radical and persecuted dissenters – like Anne Hutchinson, Roger Williams, and the Quakers, who, like Hutchinson and Williams, had been banished from Massachusetts Bay. The same was true for many who remained, like the liberal Congregationalist minister Jonathan Mayhew of Boston's Old West Church. In the role it afforded individual conscience, some of this thought was intensely individualistic. Mayhew's and Wise's voluntarist understandings of the nature of governing authority and non-submission and active resistance to illegitimate authority may have been initially developed as part of their reflections on the organization of churches. But their thought on these matters powerfully appealed to the American revolutionaries. Puritan theology figured into the theorizing about the rights of representation and, in time, of resistance and revolution. And, indeed, Mayhew took an early stand against illegitimate government power, adducing the divine right of Kings and British colonial rule as cases in point. Mayhew held biblical teaching to be consistent with Whig and Lockean premises holding the public good to be worldly government's only legitimate end. He argued that subjects had not only a right but a duty to resist and overthrow any government that failed to promote the public welfare and preserve fundamental rights, and to fight for liberty against tyranny.

This line of Puritan thought, to be sure, was in tension with more conservative strains holding that non-submission and disobedience would tend "to the total dissolution of civil government; and to introduce such scenes of wild anarchy and confusion, as are more fatal to society than the worst of tyranny." Romans 13 – whose conventional implications Mayhew had brilliantly inverted by emphasizing the failure of worldly leaders to faithfully adhere to their high responsibilities and duties, which lent legitimacy to their presumptive authority – had declared, after all, that "The powers that be are ordained of God." Hierarchy and deference to legitimate authority – of wives to husbands, children to parents, and servants to masters – it was also said, conduced to healthy, well-ordered families, households . . . and polities. Both strains of Puritanism were present from the country's earliest settlement.

Soon, however, major developments were afoot. Between the time of the first Puritan settlement in New England and the American Revolution, the transformation, and diversification, of American Christianity was well under way. The trans-denominational evangelical Christianity that has shaped American politics – including reformist campaigns like temperance/prohibition, abolitionism, the social gospel movement, and the contemporary Religious Right – was forged during the transatlantic First Great Awakening (c. 1730–1755). The English evangelist George Whitefield, who toured the colonies preaching at open-air revivals, set himself against the arid formalism and indifference amongst his Protestant brethren. Whitefield urged Christians to turn their gazes inward, examining their propensity to sin, to repent, and to commit themselves anew to a holy, Christian life. Whitefield, his countryman John Wesley, and other home-grown colonial evangelists like T.J. Frelinghuysen, Gilbert Tennent, James Davenport, and Jonathan Edwards, encouraged their flocks to feel deeply both their depravity and the pure joy they would experience when they made the momentous decision to re-commit themselves to Christ – to be "Born Again." In joining the community of "New Light" Christians in a flood of fervor and enthusiasm, the evangelists promised, they would be welcomed with a surpassing love of a kind they had never before experienced.

While this was happening, most of the "Old Light" churches in the colonies went about their business, and often set themselves against what they took to be the unhinged emotionalism and questionable theology of the camp meeting revivals. There were schisms between Old Light and New Light versions of the Methodism of Whitefield and Wesley, the Dutch Reformism of T.J. Frelinghuysen, the Presbyterianism of Tennent, and the Congregationalism of Davenport and Edwards. The New Light evangelists met Old Light attacks with their own accusations that the stolid Old Lighters were more concerned with their respectability and worldly status than with the Gospel of Jesus Christ.

The New Light evangelicals also diverged from each other, both in their theology and in their temperaments. The more cerebral evangelicals like Jonathan Edwards, influenced by the Enlightenment, closely examined the natural world, and explained how it intricately demonstrated the Creator's superintending plan and design. (This theological project would be taken up in the nineteenth century by academic natural philosophers like Williams College's Mark Hopkins, who, prior to the rise of the secular German-style research university toward the end of that century, played a central role in higher education at the nation's then mostly Christian colleges and universities.)[2] On the other hand, evangelicals like the fanatical James Davenport – who denounced other clergy as heretics, bragged about assessing at a glance whether an individual was destined for heaven or hell, and burned worldly luxuries, books, and, in one case, his own pants (which, in a fit of righteousness, he stripped off before an appalled crowd) – made it hard to know where the godliness ended and prurience, exhibitionism, and mental disturbance began.

The effects of the First Great Awakening on the later life of the nation are hard to exaggerate. Besides transforming its theology, the revival significantly augmented and diversified American Christianity. (The ranks of the Methodists and Baptists in particular swelled.) The First Great Awakening inspired a transformative introspection amongst colonial women. It, moreover, played an important role in the adoption of the Christian faith by the country's enslaved African peoples, fundamentally reshaping black American life and thought.

At the most general level, the understanding of many Americans of the world as superintended by God's plan, of life as beset by sin, but with a promise of redemption and salvation, and of this condition as constituting not only a great truth but also an emotion-drenched drama of world-historical significance with everything at stake, has plainly been informed by the United States' Protestant heritage. So, too, has one major strain of what has come to be called "American exceptionalism," which understands the United States as "New Canaan," or "New Israel": a promised land and people, chosen by God, with His great plan in mind, serving as a beacon – and perhaps even savior – to the world.

Race and Indigeneity during the Settlement and the Road to Revolution

When Spanish, Dutch, French, and English explorers and settlers first arrived in North America, they encountered a land inhabited by millions of indigenous peoples who had been living there for over 10,000 years. As such, the political thought of and concerning America's native peoples, like that involving its coercively imported Africans, has been a constant throughout US history. This indigenous political thought falls into two categories. First, there is the political thought of the native tribes themselves concerning their own collective lives, considered independently of their relationship to the European settler-colonizers. And, second, there is the political thought of the

tribes (and, for that matter, of the Europeans and their American descendants) underwriting, informed, and generated by the European conquest,
settlement, and rule. The former, given the structure of modern scholarly
disciplines, has historically – and, some would say, problematically – been
considered the proper subject less of political science than of anthropology.
It involves deep considerations of native concepts, cosmologies, epistemolo-
gies, philosophies, religions, and cultural practices of a far-flung landscape
of different indigenous tribes. This thought advanced diverse understandings concerning the origins and nature of the community, clan, and kin,
the relation of native peoples to the land and other living beings, and the
sources and locus of authority. The latter species of indigenous thought,
developed of necessity, frequently sparked political debates and contention among natives and white settler-colonialists alike. This second type of
thought formulated views concerning native sovereignty and the desirability
and terms of acculturation, assimilation, conversion, or accommodation
in the face of a relentless demographic onslaught. Tribal thinkers raised
questions concerning the normative or strategic desirability of adopting
the concepts and practices of European political thought, like sovereignty
(with its assumptions concerning the fixed territoriality of states, petitions,
treaties, and citizenship), property ownership, race, ethnicity, (minority and
liberal individual) rights, and the Christian faith.

As might be expected, some of the most prominent voices of Native
American political thought in British North America – and, in turn, the early
republic and antebellum United States – were evangelical Christian minister-
missionaries like Samson Occom and William Apess, fired, in some cases by
the First Great Awakening, to bring the gospel to the land's indigenous hea-
thens, while simultaneously arguing for their just and humane treatment.
Others, like the Seneca orator Red Jacket (Sagoyewatha) or the Sauk warrior
Black Hawk, either advocated on behalf of their tribes' traditional religions, or
simply continued to practice their native cosmologies and faiths.

While Africans in America were relative newcomers when considered in
relation to the continent's indigenous peoples, they arrived on its shores
at about the same time as North America's white European explorers and
settlers. Although there were sixteenth-century antecedents in short-lived
Spanish settlements dotting the littoral southeast, the forced labor of Africans
brought against their will to North America began in earnest in Virginia in
1619 – the year before the Puritan settlers landed at Plymouth. At the time,
forced labor was not a unique burden of coercively imported Africans: inden-
tured servitude of whites, to say nothing of women (who in many respects
were conceived of as living in service to their husbands), was a pillar of the
settler-colonial economic, social, and political order. In time, however, this
form of servitude faded, and slavery in the Americas, in contradistinction to
bondage in the ancient world, was racialized.

Opposition to the enslavement of human beings, albeit fledgling, traces back nearly as long. From as early as the 1680s, Quakers, concentrated in the Pennsylvania colony, distinguished themselves as outspoken opponents of slavery. As Enlightenment ideals of liberty, equality, democracy, and human progress began to take hold in the mid-eighteenth century,[3] and then set the framework for the colonial grievances with the mother country (and, eventually, for the American Revolution), whites and free blacks alike noted the contradiction between the colonists' ever more loudly professed moral and political ideas and both chattel slavery and racial inequality. In what has come to be called abolitionism's "First Wave," interracial coalitions sustained and inspired by Christian and secular humanitarian ideals alike began the process that resulted in gradual, state-by-state emancipation in the North. This ongoing process collided with the country's founding, raising serious political problems that would bedevil the Constitutional Convention that framed the nation's core political institutions.

The American Revolution and the Founding

In the mid-eighteenth century, Great Britain's North American colonies were increasingly implicated in that era's global imperial wars, struggles, and crises. The metropole's initial oversight was light, and its authority weak: while not forgotten, those colonies were an afterthought. To be sure, they were enmeshed in a web of (it was said, mutually beneficial) imperial regulations concerning imports and exports. But the colonies were taxed only lightly, and left largely to govern themselves. Each colony had an elected representative legislature that directed its own internal affairs. Their economies thrived, and the population grew.

Things began to change, however, with the French and Indian War (1756–1763), the North American front of the globe-spanning Seven Years War, which ultimately pitted a coalition led by Great Britain against a rival coalition led by France. Britain won the war, leading France to surrender nearly all of the territory it had previously claimed in North America east of the Mississippi River, including in what is today Canada. This drew Britain into an increased focus on its North American colonies and on the extensive – and expensive – responsibilities it now bore for defending them. Britain argued that it had shielded the free Protestant colonies – at the urging, for that matter, of New Englanders – from the threat of tyrannical popery (French Canada), marauding (French-allied) Indians, and foreign attacks and bids for conquest. The British believed that, under these new circumstances, it was only proper for the colonies to bear some of the massive costs of Great Britain's titanic war debts, and their own self-defense.

A succession of revenue acts followed across the 1760s and 1770s, sparking increasingly spirited colonial resistance. A cascade of pamphlets – the most popular form of political writing at the time – flowed, most prominently in resistance to the direct tax on printed material authorized by the Stamp Act (1765). The debate turned on the power of Parliament to tax the people of the North American colonies, when the colonists did not have power to vote for and elect members of Parliament. The colonists argued that they were being taxed without representation, and hence their property was being taken without their consent. If Parliament could strip them of their natural, pre-political rights to property (Locke), it was said, Parliament, by implication, had free rein to strip them of any and all of their God-given natural rights – to say nothing of their rights as British subjects.

The argument expanded over a series of thrusts and parries concerning subsequent revenue acts (and partial retreats, but with a British refusal to cede the authority to tax). These included not only boycotts and other incendiary protests (some led in Boston by Samuel Adams's Sons of Liberty), but also outsized explosions of rage and violence against what many were now complaining was a system of unjust and, finally, intolerable rule by a distant and tyrannical government. English "country" party and republican political thought (James Harrington, Algernon Sydney, and others) had descried the corruption of the distant urban elite governing class under the sway of and resident at the King's "Court." In seeking to understand their growing list of grievances and predicament, the American colonists drew from this thought, in the process forging penetrating new reflections on sovereignty, government by consent, representation, and rights, with frenzied outrage over ostensible depredations of rights that, in a less fraught context, might have seemed like lesser slights. (An inflamed "rights consciousness," many have observed, has continued to characterize the American temperament.) In time, as the British increasingly took extraordinary steps to suppress resistance – including closing Boston harbor; altering and then suspending Massachusetts's colonial charter to reinforce their control; landing waves of troops, some of whom were coercively quartered in colonial residences; disarming colonial militias; and expatriating rebellious colonists for trial in England – a critical mass of the most vocal colonists moved from complaining of transgressions of their traditional, common law and natural rights as Englishmen under the British Constitution to contemplating a permanent political break.

The First and Second Continental Congresses were convened (1774, 1775) to coordinate support for the resistance in Massachusetts, and, before long, a military battle broke out between British troops and the colonists at Lexington and Concord which is generally taken as the start of the American Revolution. At this point, however, debates were still ongoing in the colonies about whether to seek reconciliation (as initially advocated by John Dickinson, James Wilson, and Thomas Jefferson, among others, and a clear majority of the delegates to the Second Continental Congress) or separation (advocated by radicals like Samuel Adams and John Adams). Samuel Adams had already authored "The Rights of the Colonists" (1772), in which, in Lockean high dudgeon, he denounced the British for trenching on the rights of the American colonists to life, liberty, and property (with the rights to representation, toleration, and conscience thrown in for good measure, although Adams was careful to acknowledge a duty to pay taxes in support of a legitimate government). Where fundamental rights had been violated, Adams insisted, there was a clear right of revolution. By contrast, even two years later, while denouncing "parliamentary tyranny," in "A Summary View of the Rights of British America" (1774), Thomas Jefferson appealed to King George III to intervene to settle the ongoing grievances. In his appeal, Jefferson underlined the individualist roots of the colonial settlement, where the colonists had labored unceasingly and sacrificed much to build their own societies. But Jefferson too noted the right to revolution, cheekily citing England's own Glorious Revolution (1689) as a case in point.

The game-changer, however, was the anonymously published incendiary pamphlet *Common Sense* (1776), which turned public opinion sharply in favor of separation. Authored by the radical revolutionary Thomas Paine, *Common Sense* went through fifty-six editions in 1776 alone – selling 120,000 copies in its first three months, and ultimately reaching a total of half a million. "'Tis time to part," *Common Sense* unequivocally declared, in the first full-throated call for total independence. In contrast to many others, like Jefferson, far from praising the genius of the British Constitution and appealing to its principles and protections, Paine gave it the back of his hand: he disdained its murky historical roots, its obscure and arcane foundations in the common law, and its unwieldy and ambiguous assemblage of proclamations, statutes, judicial rulings, and traditional practices and precedents, devoid of any clear and readily discernible boundaries, forms, and rules. Paine condemned the elaborate balances the British Constitution had calibrated between the country's diverse social estates – including aristocracy and hereditary monarchy, no less – which violated fundamental principles of human equality. This was too complicated and opaque, Paine complained. To its great discredit, the British Constitution was not readily knowable by the common man. Its elaborate system of check and balances was, moreover, nonsensical: it was an invitation to illegitimacy and injustice.

In all this, Paine evinced a deep suspicion of government. He drew a sharp distinction between "society" and "government" – the former "a blessing," the latter, "even in its best state is but a necessary evil, in its worst state an intolerable one." Government was established by consent for sake of the security and liberty of the people. Besides proving tyrannical, government by Great Britain no longer made sense given the current interests of the North American colonies. An Old World power, Britain, a tiny far-away island, after all, was continually embroiling itself in wars. For all intents and purposes at

this point the colonies were a different polity, with their own distinct interests and preferences. They stood ready to stand apart – and up – and govern
themselves. The decision to do so, Paine entreated, in an exceptionalist vein,
would be a historical event, of great moment both for the American people
and the world: "'Tis not the concern of a day, a year, or an age; posterity are
virtually involved in the contest, and will be more or less affected even to the
end time by proceedings now." The country, Paine had announced, would be a
beacon to the oppressed of the world, to those who yearned to live free.

By May 1776, the Second Continental Congress called upon the colonies to
write new constitutions for themselves – to "adopt such government as shall,
in the opinion of the representatives of the people, best conduce to the happiness and safety of their constituents in particular and America in general."
Not long after, on July 4, the Declaration of Independence, drafted chiefly
by Thomas Jefferson (with assistance from John Adams, Benjamin Franklin,
Robert Livingston, and Roger Sherman), and drawing upon the by now widespread political theories that had been articulated in the American colonies
with increasing precision and vehemence, declared to the world that "a long
train of abuses" – including a refusal of "Representation in the Legislature" to
assent to laws "wholesome and necessary for the public good," to provide an
impartial judiciary, and to adequately protect both the colonies' domestic and
national security – had so transgressed their natural rights to "life, liberty,
and the pursuit of happiness" that they were impelled to claim their natural
rights to separate from Great Britain and establish by consent an independent
country that would better protect the rights vouchsafed them by "nature, and
nature's God." In so doing, the colonies took the grand leap from aggrieved
British subjects to Americans.

Discussion and debate concerning the best form of government for the
newly independent colonies began. The diverse and divergent views held
by the Americans on these matters were reflected in the varying institutional designs of the new country's state constitutions. Pennsylvania's, for
instance, was radically democratic: it not only manifested a deep suspicion
of executive power, but also kept its elected representatives on a short leash.
Massachusetts's John Adams, the principal drafter of that state's constitution, was much more skeptical of the governing capacities of ordinary
people. In the dense and learned *Thoughts on Government* (1776), which drew
broadly on the lessons of the English Constitution, the history of ancient
Greece and Rome, classical and modern political theory (Aristotle, Locke,
and English republicanism), and the new nation's state constitutions, Adams
reflected at length on fundamental questions concerning the legitimate ends
of governments and the institutions with the best prospects for achieving
them. Following Aristotle and republican thought more generally, he placed
particular emphasis on character and the need to cultivate a virtuous citizenry, and on institutions conducive to character formation, such as militias

(service and sacrifice), public education, and sumptuary laws restricting the consumption of luxuries and extravagances. Adams also argued for the importance of a balance of powers, rotation in office, an independent judiciary, and the rule of law.

The Creation of the Constitution

In many respects, things did not go well for the new United States, whose independent status, in a world of global imperial contention, was precarious. Domestic squabbling, disorder, and dysfunction were perhaps even greater problems. This troubling state of affairs led to another round of serious reflection and disputation over the nature and requirements of good government.

The initial governments established both in the states and at the national level, it was soon being argued, had over-corrected for the perceived debilities of British rule. If the colonists had been systematically deprived of popular input and representation in Parliament, the new governments would radically empower the population: they would be structured to be highly responsive to ordinary people (via, for example, short terms and frequent elections to emphasize accountability). It was in this context that many American founders, like John Adams, James Otis, and Gouverneur Morris, hurled the term "democracy" as an epithet – or at least complained of its excesses. The ignorant populace, inflamed by their passions and private interests, these founders charged, were making outlandish appeals to their all-too-responsive representatives. The people were demanding relief from their debts, and the redistribution of wealth. Along these lines, they were calling for the printing of paper money (most famously in "Rogue's Island") to inflate the currency, easing the repayment of their debts, in the process menacing the rights to contract and property that were so highly valued in liberal political and (in fledgling form, capitalist) economic thought. These unruly people, in the estimation of these founders, were a shockingly far cry from the virtuous, self-sacrificing, and public-spirited citizenry for which so many American revolutionaries, perhaps unrealistically, had so fervently hoped. As inflation and financial instability roiled the polity, the cerebral Virginia planter and politician James Madison grew alarmed by the "multiplicity," "mutability," and "injustice" of the laws. Madison's fellow Virginia planter – and Commander of the victorious revolutionary Continental Army – George Washington, his protégé, the New York lawyer and financial wizard Alexander Hamilton, and the erudite Pennsylvania legal scholar and politician James Wilson, joined Madison in newly concluding that republicanism as they knew it – the idea that ordinary citizens had enough virtue to govern themselves responsibly and protect liberty – was proving a failed experiment. Wouldn't the country be better off if there were a correction, putting what John Jay called "the better sort of people," whose rights and prosperity were increasingly menaced by this madness, in the drivers' seat? Democracy was threatening ordered liberty. Something needed to be done.

Efforts were undertaken to offer a more comprehensive diagnosis, and consider possible cures. When it came to the design of political institutions, the radical Thomas Paine had emphasized transparency, simplicity, and direct empowerment of the people, without the sort of checks featured in the British Constitution (and praised by the more conservative John Adams). The spirit of Paine had been more than a little present in the country's first national constitution, the Articles of Confederation (drafted by John Dickinson in 1776; approved by Congress in 1777; ratified in 1781). The Articles reflected a strong republican antipathy to distant power, especially, but indeed for government power, *tout court*. They reflected republican demands for devolved and highly accountable local control, and placed their hope for effective rule in sacrifice and service by the nation's ostensibly virtuous citizens. The Articles, James Madison later complained, were "in fact nothing more than a treaty of amity and of alliance between independent and sovereign states" (a status the Articles had expressly affirmed). Under the Articles of Confederation, almost all governing power was left to the states. There was only a nominal executive, and no federal judiciary. The powers afforded to the Confederation Congress were few, and sharply limited. (There was, for instance, no power to tax, and thus raise money directly to support the national government.) Representation was not by population, but by state: one vote for each, with both the size and manner of the state's delegation to the Confederation Congress to be determined by the state. Most decisions required a super-majority vote and, in some cases (including the case of constitutional amendment), unanimity.

The effects of these choices were soon apparent. Almost no money came in, hobbling the fledgling country's efforts to conduct foreign policy, and jeopardizing its national security – and, indeed, its continued independence. Discriminatory tariffs were instituted, and trade wars broke out, wrecking a fragile economy and portending armed conflict between the states, which some feared would be inclined to enlist the assistance of distant foreign powers. The few national initiatives that did pass could not be enforced. Alexander Hamilton warned ominously of "impending anarchy." An impressive cohort that included Hamilton came to believe that the need for reform was critical. But there was strong resistance from those who benefited from or otherwise supported the *status quo*. As the farmer/debtor uprising (Shay's Rebellion, 1786–1787) in western Massachusetts was unfurling, Hamilton and a select group of compatriots, including Madison, finally took action. They met first in Annapolis, Maryland, in September 1786 to consider revisions to the Articles of Confederation. The Annapolis group quickly concluded that reform would be insufficient, and that comprehensive change was needed. They decided that a more broadly representative body would gather in closed session in Philadelphia from May to September 1787, ostensibly to consider reform of the Articles, but in fact to debate and draft an entirely new national constitution. That gathering became the US Constitutional Convention.

Framing and Ratifying the Constitution: "The Great National Discussion"

As he would later emphasize in *The Federalist*, a series of newspaper articles advocating ratification of the Constitution that he co-authored with James Madison and John Jay under the pseudonym Publius, Alexander Hamilton understood the chief problem under the Articles to be inadequate "energy" in the national government. George Washington concurred in the view that effective governments are possessed of adequate power to sanction, coerce, and enforce to secure the common good, and that the proposed Constitution provided the framework for such a government.

Convinced that the country had entered a "critical period" in which its survival was at stake, fifty-five delegates from every state save Rhode Island met in closed-door session in Philadelphia from May to September 1787, with George Washington presiding – silent until the end – and James Madison, Gouverneur Morris, and James Wilson driving much of the discussion. The convention lost a few delegates along the way, a number of whom, fired by the republicanism that had informed the Articles of Confederation, smelled a rat.

The challenge was to devise a popular government that would remain true to its core principles while proving institutionally effective and sustaining popular support. James Madison and Edmund Randolph seized the initiative – illegally, given the limited mandate of the convention – to propose an entirely new framework of national government. They proposed the creation of a national executive (the President) and a federal judiciary, as well as a legislature, the Congress, directly elected by the people according to population, with real powers to levy taxes and establish an army. In addition, they expressly proposed that appropriately authorized national laws would take precedence over those of the states. A challenge to this "Virginia" (or "Large States") plan was mounted by the less populous states (the "New Jersey Plan," spearheaded by William Paterson), which called, among other things, for the retention of the unicameral legislature of the Articles of Confederation, with one vote per state. The proposed institutions of the new government were discussed and debated at great length at the Philadelphia Convention, some, to be sure, more extensively than others. (The deeply divisive subject of chattel slavery was barely discussed, though it was clearly understood that guarantees for its continuation in pro-slavery states had to be scrupulously provided.) In the end, a Great (or "Connecticut") Compromise, brokered by Roger Sherman and Oliver Ellsworth, divided the Congress into an upper and lower house, with the former comprised of two representatives from each state, elected by the legislatures of those states, and the latter directly elected by the people on the basis of population.

Departing from the design of the Articles, the proposed Constitution's Preamble announced that "We the people" (not "We the undersigned delegates of the states") were promulgating the country's fundamental law. Citizens were represented directly in the House of Representatives rather than through the intermediary of their state governments. They were taxed directly as well, giving the national government the wherewithal to act and spend without applying cap-in-hand for requisitions from the states. There was provision for a strong, independent executive, and a potentially powerful federal judiciary. Of those delegates who remained for the duration of the constitutional convention, the product of these sustained deliberations won overwhelming, though not unanimous, support.

The men who gathered at Philadelphia to frame the new Constitution were an elite and learned lot who had undertaken additional studies in both ancient and modern history and political theory to inform their momentous deliberations. They would draw on this political science extensively in explaining and justifying their handiwork to what, they knew, might be a skeptical and divided polity. Convincing arguments mattered. But those supporting ratification put their thumbs on the scale. While maintaining the "one state, one vote" principle of the Articles, they altered the unanimity requirement by providing for ratification by nine of the thirteen states. They circumvented entrenched interests in the state legislatures while taking care to avoid creating new rival power centers by allowing (temporary) state ratifying conventions. This, moreover, would lend the new Constitution "downstream legitimacy" by providing for ratification by the people themselves. They would be temporarily mobilized to directly exercise their sovereign authority in a moment of high importance that Alexander Hamilton, among others, suggested would do nothing less than decide the fate of all mankind, and then be immediately shuffled off the national stage.[4]

The lesson learned during the 1780s by those who supported the ratification of the new Constitution – the Federalists (a name advisedly chosen to avoid the scare-mongering labels "nationalists" or "consolidators") – was that the country needed a more powerful centralized government than the Articles of Confederation allowed, and a more competent, virtuous, and responsible leadership than the locals had chosen in the states. There was agreement on this – in theory at least – between, on the one hand, Federalist supporters of the 1787 Constitution like John Adams, James Madison, Alexander Hamilton, and George Washington and, on the other, Antifederalist opponents like Samuel Adams, Richard Henry Lee, George Mason, and Patrick Henry. They had radically different concerns, however, about the proffered solutions.

The Federalists argued that the new Constitution achieved the necessary vigor and competence at the national level while simul-

> We are now one nation of brethren. We must bury all local interests & distinctions. . . . No sooner were the State Governments formed than their jealousy and ambition began to display themselves. Each endeavored to cut a slice from the common loaf, to add to its own morsel, till at length the confederation became frittered down to the impotent condition in which it now stands. . . . To correct its vices is the business of this convention.
>
> James Wilson (1787)

taneously, and ingeniously, providing for popular rule and protecting the fundamental rights whose violation had occasioned the American Revolution. The Antifederalists, by contrast, were convinced that the new Constitution would lead to the ultimate evisceration of the rights the American revolutionaries had fought to preserve, through the (re)creation of a distant, overly centralized government, and a dangerously empowered elite, who would institute despotic, quasi-monarchial rule under new auspices. The battle was hard-fought: the future of liberty, and the survival of the nation, many believed, was at stake.

Alexander Hamilton and James Madison were the pre-eminent proponents of the new Constitution. Hamilton, a fiercely intelligent and peerlessly ambitious Caribbean immigrant of obscure origins, was the chief proponent of the creation of a strong, active national government both as a solution to the country's current problems and as a foundation for the nation's future glory as one of the world's most powerful, eminent, and prosperous states – the equal, if not the better, of Great Britain or France. The young Hamilton, a financial genius, had penned brilliant pamphlets in support of the Revolution, and quickly came to the attention of the head of the revolutionary army, George Washington, with whom he became an *aide-de-camp* and an unusually close confidant. Hamilton spearheaded, and was the most prolific author of, *The Federalist*, a series of eighty-five essays published in the *New York Independent Journal* which his future rival, Thomas Jefferson, called "the best commentary on the principles of government which ever were written." The *Federalist* essays struck "Hamiltonian" themes, such as a reiteration of the surpassing need for "energy" in government: that is, the idea that the national government should have power to act quickly, decisively, and effectively in carrying out its responsibilities. Hamilton insisted that, as the country's travails under the Articles had made all too clear, the revolutionary era opposition between liberty and authority had to be rethought. The order and stability that a well-framed, energetic government could provide were not inherently a threat to liberty and justice but, ultimately, their guarantor. An appropriately empowered and effective national government, Hamilton argued, was worthy of the respect and esteem of all true republicans.

Hamilton's argument for the ratification of the new Constitution centered on the relationship between (constitutionally) authorized means in the service of (legitimate) governmental ends, an approach he deployed most emblematically in the *Opinion on the Constitutionality of the [National] Bank* (1791), which he later prepared for President Washington while serving as the country's first Treasury Secretary. Given the ultimate requirement of national self-preservation, some governmental powers, particularly those related to existential threats to the nation's security, must be all but unlimited. On this, the ultimate test was success. But the national government also required all the powers essential to actively and energetically realize the full range of its constitutionally legitimate objectives. As such, the national government needed the power to tax. Federal law, moreover, where legitimate, had to be clearly supreme to any countervailing centrifugal assertions of control by the states. Weak government, Hamilton emphasized, is bad government. Borrowing from Hamilton, the Federalist Chief Justice John Marshall would soon insert this argument into one of his most celebrated – and excoriated – opinions: "Let the end be legitimate, let it be within the scope of the constitution, and all means which are appropriate, which are plainly adapted to that end, which are not prohibited, but consist with the letter and spirit of the constitution, are constitutional."[5]

Given these concerns, Hamilton was perhaps the leading proponent of broad understandings of executive power. The unity of the office of the President was not accidental. Presidents often had to act quickly, with a keen eye to ever-changing threats and important national objectives. Hamilton was also a fervent proponent of a powerful federal judiciary, possessed of all the power necessary to void laws in contravention of the Constitution – what we now call "judicial review."[6] He was especially concerned that the courts could guarantee the rights of property and contract essential to the development of a dynamic capitalist economy. The requirements of the Constitution are the nation's fundamental law, ratified by "we the people," acting, in a rare moment, in their sovereign capacity, he explained in Federalist #78. As such, its requirements are foundational, and superior to ordinary legislation, adopted as part of the day-to-day business of representative legislatures. It is in the nature of things that in the case of conflict, the fundamental trumped the ordinary: the solemn stipulation of the people themselves trumped the actions taken by their agents. It was the job of independent, life-tenured federal judges, exercising their apolitical, legal judgment, to impartially enforce these foundational constitutional requirements. This would conduce to a government that would exercise – to the fullest extent of its authority – only its constitutional powers, while guaranteeing fundamental constitutional rights.

> The latent causes of faction are . . . sown into the nature of man. . . . The regulation of these various and interfering interests forms the principal task of modern legislation.
>
> Federalist #10 (Publius [James Madison]) (1787)

Albeit to a different degree with somewhat different preoccupations and concerns, James Madison was similarly alarmed by the national government's fecklessness under the Articles of Confederation, and especially by the inflamed popular excesses of a state and local politics disturbingly heedless of rights.

Madison was adamant that the new Constitution provide the national government with an absolute veto power over state laws via a "council of revision" – and was chagrined when a measure proposing one failed to pass. Forced to take this defeat in his stride, Madison, in his contributions to *The Federalist*, explained the safeguards that the basic structures of the Constitution would provide for rights, given the document's creation of the significantly stronger national government that he supported. ("[Y]ou must first enable the government to control the governed; and in the next place oblige it to control itself," he wrote.) Madison reasoned his way through these countervailing concerns most succinctly in Federalists #10 and #51. There, he limned the core of the problem as one of "faction," which in Federalist #10 he defined as "a number of citizens, whether amounting to majority or minority of the whole, who are united and actuated by some common impulse or passion, or of interest, adverse to the rights of other citizens, or to the permanent and aggregate interests of the community."

Unlike some of his peers, Madison did not trust that a virtuous citizenry would cure the problem of faction and guarantee liberty. His proposed solution was instead to establish a geographically extended "republic." (Here he used his own, novel definition of the term, which departed from ancient understandings that were synonymous with direct citizen rule in small, unitary polities.) This would encompass a multiplicity of contending factions that would mitigate the effects of each through opposition, filter popular passions by instituting representative (as opposed to direct) democracy, and divide power with an eye to the encouraging clashes between contending governmental power centers. This design instituted a system of checks and balances through the mechanisms of federalism (the "compound republic"), the separation of powers (legislative, executive, and judicial), and the multiplication of civil society's opposing factions through the extension of the sphere made possible by a large country.

The Antifederalists, a diverse group socially, culturally, ideologically, economically, and politically, were united by their alarm at the new Constitution, and unconvinced by the arguments made in its defense. They set themselves in fervent opposition to its adoption. Their objections were many, and they gave it all they had. The proposed Constitution had been hatched by a secret cabal, making an illegal end-run around the Articles. It had done away with the sovereign states in favor of a consolidated, all-powerful central state. It had abandoned core principles of republican government, which political philosophers from Aristotle to Cicero to Montesquieu had taught was impossible over such a broad geographic expanse. There were too few representatives, rendering the system democratically deficient. This fatal deficiency was especially troublesome since Antifederalists held that the role of representatives in a republic was not to act freely as their trustees but to mirror and register the views of their constituents.[7] Given the Constitution's ambiguities, and a host of dangerous clauses, moreover, its grant of powers to government was, in effect, plenary. Astonishingly – especially given the country's English constitutional heritage – there was no national Bill of Rights, which left critical guarantees like the freedom of speech, rights of conscience and religious liberty, due process of law, and the right to keep and bear arms to the whims of a distant governing class. Alas, bemoaned the Antifederalists, this was as one would expect from a document that had sprung from the minds – and served the interests – of a scheming and remote aristocratic elite.

Some contemporary scholars have argued that, rather than simply being naysayers, those who objected to the Constitution – the likes of Edmund Randolph, George Mason, Elbridge Gerry, and Patrick Henry, and pseudonymous authors like Cato, Brutus, and the Federal Farmer – were informed by a coherent, republican political outlook and philosophy.[8] Evincing a pronounced affinity for the political ideas that sustained the ancient Greek and Roman republics, the Antifederalists, it has been observed, celebrated the political life of small, pastoral republics, comprised of a virtuous and engaged citizenry. They were ever alive to the threats to self-government posed by moral corruption and decline, fomented by distant elites, lacking in patriotism and lusting for power. Rule by these corrupt and distant elites was heedless, if not a self-conscious enemy, of the institutions of local civil society – family, church, school, and local government – which promoted and sustained character and civic and Christian virtue. All this portended either decline or tyranny. As such, the Antifederalists affirmatively advanced the republican values of active political participation aimed at the common good, sacrifice, localism, and the promotion, both institutionally and otherwise, of civic and personal character and virtue.

Against this resistance, which might well have succeeded, it helped that the Federalists counted some of the new nation's most illustrious figures – not least the revolutionary hero George Washington, who it was understood would serve as the nation's first President – among their number. Although published in New York with an eye to the ratification vote there, *The Federalist* essays were widely distributed. The Federalists quickly agreed to add a Bill of Rights immediately after the document's ratification. The politically savvy Alexander Hamilton fashioned a brilliant financial plan – soon to be implemented via the plan set out in his *Report on Credit* (1790) and *Report on Manufactures* (1791) – that made it in the interest of the country's business and financial classes and the highly indebted states to support ratification. In a sop to the commercial and financial periphery, the country's capital city was moved south from the northern financial centers of New York and Philadelphia to Virginia (today, Washington, DC).

Hamiltonian and Jeffersonian Visions

One of the more notable features of American political thought is the longevity of the original Federalist–Antifederalist debates, which in many ways have continued to define American political oppositions to the present day. Once the Constitution was adopted, the former opponents of the Constitution almost immediately – and, some have recently argued, strategically, and perhaps insincerely – sloughed off their resistance like an old skin, becoming as fervently loyal to the Constitution as the most ardent Federalists.[9] The new institutions of government were up and running. In that sense, things were settled. Vehement debates over the concrete assertions of powers by these institutions – about distant national power, consolidation, and threats to rights – were, however, carried forward, now transposed from debates about constitutional design into debates about constitutional interpretation.

These antagonisms moved into a new stage almost immediately during the First Congress. Within President Washington's administration – which understood itself as unaffiliated with anything so disreputably factional as a political party – Alexander Hamilton, now Secretary of the Treasury, worked to advance the Federalist program of a powerful central government, including a strong federal judiciary. Thomas Jefferson, now Secretary of State, while a supporter of the Constitution, took up many concerns and themes of the now ostensibly defunct Antifederalism: pushing for the decentralization of power and a weak federal judiciary. Each was convinced that the plans, policies, and plots of the other menaced fundamental rights and rendered precarious the nation's hopes to stand before the world as a beacon of liberty.

A proponent of a prosperous commercial republic that would compete on the world stage as an industrial powerhouse, Hamilton had linked the new government closely to powerful capitalist and financial interests, in the process confirming the worst fears of the country's erstwhile Antifederalists. In time, convinced that the President was fatally in sympathy with Hamilton, Jefferson left Washington's cabinet, recruiting his fellow Virginian James Madison to his cause. In this way, the country's two-party system – in its first iteration, the Federalists versus the Democratic-Republicans – was born. So, too, was a template for debate that pitted proponents of a strong central government against those championing decentralization and states' rights; proponents of the federal courts as guarantors of an individual liberty endangered by the tyranny of the majority against those who held federal judges to be unelected, life-tenured elitists less committed to the dispassionate application of laws than to imposing their own politicized understandings on the polity by fiat; and proponents of one political party as the friend of freedom against the opposition as its most implacable foe.

Because they considered a powerful strong and active central government a crucial tool in setting the nation's direction and meeting its problems, and because they believed a feeble government stinted on guaranteeing liberty and promoting justice, Hamiltonians were proponents of the broad construction of the federal government's constitutional powers. In this, they emphasized that government's inherent powers in service of its legitimate ends. They looked to the nation's vibrant urban centers as critical to the development of a vibrant commercial republic. As proponents of business and commerce, they also prized the rights of property, regularity, stability, and institutional and social order.

Because they hewed to a republican faith in a "constitutionally and conscientiously democratic" people, in whose wisdom and judgment Jefferson – unlike his compatriot Madison – had surpassing confidence and trust, Jeffersonians called for the devolution of government downward, from states, to counties, to small, locally governed "ward republics" of self-sustaining – independent – yeoman farmers. Like the ancient Athenian Aristotle, they believed that the people's virtues would be cultivated through their active participation in the responsibilities of governance. As Jefferson explained in *Notes on the State of Virginia* (1785), the self-sufficiency and independence of farmers – which, given slavery, of course, was anything but – was uniquely conducive to the development of the liberal, democratic, and egalitarian character that he placed at the core of the nation's promise. For these reasons, Jefferson championed universal public education that would similarly cultivate a republican spirit, character, and virtue. (He regarded his founding of the University of Virginia as one of his greatest achievements.) These views underwrote the Jeffersonians' vigorous advocacy for the reserved powers of the states, to the point of insisting on the right of states to resist unconstitutional federal laws, like the Alien and Sedition Acts (see *The Virginia and Kentucky Resolutions,* 1798). They also underwrote suspicion about the powers of judicial review claimed by the federal courts – which they understood as not only parts, but also agents of, the national government.

Unlike the consummate New Yorker Hamilton, the Sage of Monticello loathed cities, with their bustling web of often far-flung and anonymous interdependencies. Cities were seedbeds of vice and scourges of virtue. Jeffersonians celebrated rural, agricultural life; the property-holding, ostensibly independent yeoman farmer; the common man; deliberative, participatory majoritarian democracy (rule by popular will) – albeit with appropriate protections for minority rights; and even orneriness and resistance. (Jefferson's heart leapt with excitement – at least when he was not President – when the people resisted moves to trench upon their fundamental rights.) Although a profoundly compromised proprietor of what was, in effect, a slave labor camp at Monticello, Jefferson was nevertheless, as a political theorist at least, perhaps the founding era's most fervent proponent of equality, which he held a hallmark of republicanism. His condemnation of hierarchies, for example, especially hereditary ones, informed his campaign for placing sharp limits on the inter-generational inheritance of wealth.

While he criticized what he held to be artificial aristocracies, Jefferson celebrated natural aristocracies – the aristocracy of talents. He was a tireless proponent of what we today call the equality of opportunity. His support for public education and his founding of the University of Virginia evinced a commitment to the notion that, if a fair and equal start in life is given to all without distinction, those who cultivated their individual talents and virtues would – and should – rise. The belief in such opportunities, with the promise that merit would be rewarded, of course, is one of the surpassing appeals of the liberal world-view, and of an exceptionalist reading of American political culture as the world's pre-eminent land of opportunity.

In the broadest sense, like the pioneering Enlightenment scientists of America's founding, Benjamin Franklin and Benjamin Rush, Thomas Jefferson was a meliorist who was passionate about the all-but-limitless possibilities for individual, social, and human progress. He looked hopefully to the future, where, ultimately, truth would win out. One of his great hopes in this regard was that human reason might ultimately triumph over the scourge of religious fanaticism, which history had shown to have done such damage to individual minds, lives, and nations. History, alas, was replete with instances in which religious orthodoxies and superstitions had thwarted the progress of reason. (One of Jefferson's more notorious sallies was to take his scissors to his Bible, leaving the good stuff, but excising caked-on layers of fantasy, absurdity, and mumbo-jumbo.) Needless to say, Jefferson was the founding's most relentless proponent of building "a wall of separation between Church & State," and religious liberty and toleration. "The legitimate powers of government," he wrote in *Notes on the State of Virginia*, in a quintessential statement of the role of liberal government, "extend to such acts only as are injurious to others. ... [I]t does me no injury for my neighbour to say there are twenty gods, or no god. It neither picks my pocket nor breaks my leg." As such, Jefferson was a proponent of secular government, and of a polity that consigned religion to the private sphere, where all manner of belief – and unbelief – was to be strictly voluntary, a matter between the individual and his God – or not. (In addition to the authorship of the Declaration of Independence, and the founding of the University of Virginia, Jefferson counted his third and final great accomplishment to be the authorship in 1777 of the Virginia Statute for Religious Freedom.)

Most of the original American colonies and, subsequently, states – with the exception of Rhode Island, Pennsylvania, Delaware, and New Jersey – had either single or multiple Christian establishments. In these, individuals were required to support the state's official church, or a church of their choosing. In some cases, they were required by law to attend worship services. (There were also a host of other mandatory supports for established religions, and debilities for disapproved faiths.) Jefferson opposed these establishments, and their systems of privileges, supports, and penalties. The country was already moving in his direction at the time of independence, a trend reinforced by ideas concerning individual liberty that had driven the American Revolution. Joining Jefferson's campaign on this, and continuing the Puritan legacy of Roger Williams, was James Madison's *Memorial and Remonstrance on Religious Assessments* (1785), which marshaled a phalanx of religious and secular arguments in opposition to the religious establishment of Virginia, their home state. The country's last state religious establishment (in Massachusetts) was repealed in 1833.

As one might expect given all this, Jefferson was a fervent proponent of free inquiry and the freedom of speech, convictions the tetchy statesman failed to consistently support, against his own stated principles, when he ended up being its target. Jefferson's compatriot in opposing the Sedition Act (1798), James Madison, did better in this regard. Madison explicitly recognized, in his great statement in his *Report to the Virginia Assembly* (1800), that abuse of the exercise of a right was probably inevitably inseparable from its promise.

> The acceptance of, and continuance hitherto in, the office to which your suffrages have twice called me have been a uniform sacrifice of inclination to the opinion of duty.
>
> George Washington (1796)

As Hamiltonian and Jeffersonian political understandings came to set the poles of political contestation in the early republic, both sides resented and resisted the charge that their views were those of an interested party or faction. They, at least – though plainly *not* their scheming, obnoxious opponents – were thinking only of their country, and of its long-term national interest. Within the framework of republican thought, they apprehended themselves and theirs as self-abnegating, civic-spirited public servants, a mindset elegantly expressed in George Washington's *Farewell Address* (1796) – the very same President in whose cabinet these opposing poles began to be charged, each powerfully repelling the other.

Conclusion

The political thought of the colonial settlements that would eventually unite – minus the loyalists – to become the fledgling United States was a honeycomb of affinities, arguments, dissonances, and what today look like contradictions, many of which continue to shape, and vex, the country. The Puritans who emigrated to Massachusetts Bay seeking and celebrating religious freedom found it next to impossible to respect the religious liberties of those they took to be misguided, if not heretical. Those who dissented from their orthodoxy were harassed, jailed, and banished. Some Quakers were even executed. The voluntarist organization of the Puritan churches both pioneered proto-democratic and proto-liberal understandings of government by consent, and were premised – as was the participatory democracy of ancient Athens – on the community's powers of expulsion and exclusion.

The American Revolution, fueled by appeals to universal Enlightenment values like liberty and equality, popular sovereignty, and national self-determination, was clearly one of world history's most significant anticolonial uprisings. But vis-à-vis the land's indigenous peoples, the Americans who made that revolution were themselves an ascriptive, expansionist, and often brutal colonial power who rarely afforded those who stood in their way universal recognition as fellow human beings. The same was true for their treatment of the enslaved Africans, who were bought and sold as chattels. What Jefferson celebrated as an "empire of liberty" was an empire of dispossession and slavery. Many, including Jefferson himself, recognized these contradictions. Some, to be sure, challenged these injustices in the name of liberal Enlightenment values. Others, however, either saw no contradiction at all, or justified their beliefs and their practices. Liberty, as they would have it, was for those who had the capacity to rationally and intelligently exercise it. And equality was for equals.

The liberal and republican strains of colonial and early American political thought also vied for pre-eminence, with these different frameworks being enlisted in different times and different places by different people – and sometimes by the same person in a single sermon, speech, or pamphlet. In many cases, the opposition could seem a false one, especially when we take into account that classical and Renaissance republican thought was being retooled in the modern world for that new political animal, the "commercial republic" nation-state.

These tensions and dynamics played out in debates over the governing structures set out, first, in the country's state constitutions, then in the Articles of Confederation, the US Constitution, and, following the hard-fought ratification of the Constitution, in the question of how the powers and limits on them would be applied and interpreted. Far from resolving matters concerning the legitimate powers of government generally and more specifically (legislative, executive, judicial; the states versus the national government), the oppositions that structured the debates between the Federalists and the Antifederalists flowed into George Washington's administration, where the New Yorker Alexander Hamilton, a proponent of an energetic federal government taking an active role in building a finance-capitalism-fueled urban-industrial economy, with hopes for wealth, glory, and national dominance on a global scale, fought for Washington's ear with the Virginian Thomas Jefferson, a proponent of rural agrarianism and localism, who was deeply suspicious of both finance capital and powerful (especially centralized, distant) government.

These affinities, antagonisms, arguments, and dissonances lent the American founding a multivalent – and sometimes contrapuntal – character that left Americans with a powerful but complicated ideational and institutional legacy.

Questions

1. Were the Puritans a force for progress or reaction? Was Puritan thought "liberal" or "illiberal"?

2. Is the American Revolution best understood as conservative or radical? Was it really revolutionary at all? In what sense?
3. How much of a distinction is there, ultimately, between the categories of "constitutional design" and "constitutional interpretation"?
4. How do the oppositions between Federalists and Antifederalists, and Hamiltonians and Jeffersonians, map onto the politics of subsequent American history, including the present day?
5. Does it make sense to speak of the American founding as instituting a "democracy"?
6. Does it make sense to speak of any coherent group under the label of "the founders"?
7. Does the existence and acceptance of chattel slavery by the new nation vitiate any moral or political value that the American founding might otherwise have?

3

Antebellum Political Thought

The Federalist, which advanced views about how to implement popular government, both celebrated the new regime and made recommendations on how
to bridle democracy's debilities through institutional design. As the founding
generation left the stage, however, it became increasingly apparent that the
country was writing a new chapter in the progress of popular government,
with a roiling mass populace as its stars.

To be sure, mass mobilization of the common man was not an entirely new
departure for Americans: the revolutionary fervor itself had often assumed
this form. The post-revolutionary state constitutions, and the governing structures of the Articles of Confederation, had reflected it. The Antifederalists
had been outspokenly anti-hierarchical, anti-centralist, and mass democratic.
In violent debtor and tax resistance uprisings in western Massachusetts and
western Pennsylvania, the enraged and put-upon common man bared his
teeth. But the "republic" instituted by the 1789 Constitution was deliberately
fashioned to order, structure, discipline, and filter an unruly public sphere.

Many of a more conservative bent thought it their duty to continue this
project. The Supreme Court Justice Joseph Story of Massachusetts denounced
"King Mob." Story's fellow jurist James Kent opposed the expansion of suffrage
to non-property holders for state Senate races in his home state of New York.
On balance, though, the country was moving in a different direction.

Antebellum Americans rethought and reinvented democratic politics. The
founding generation's political thought was suspicious of party spirit, which
they thought encouraged vices over virtues, privileged passion over reason,
and promoted private interests over the public good. Tory Federalists like
John Adams, Gouverneur Morris, and Fisher Ames were more than ready to
issue moralizing harangues and exhortations. Realists like James Madison,
however, mistrusted the ultimate effectiveness of civic blandishments. More
useful, they thought, given human nature, would be designing institutions
of government that "suppl[ied], by opposite and rival interests, the defect
of better motives" (Federalist #51). Still, the old hope sprung eternal. As he
ended his two terms as the country's first President, George Washington, who
had thrilled to performances of Joseph Addison's tragedy *Cato* (1713), sternly
warned against party spirit, and called upon his countrymen to put their
nation first.

Washington had observed the developments close at hand in his cabinet, where Thomas Jefferson and Alexander Hamilton, whom he had hired as wise and selfless notables, soon found themselves not only butting heads personally, but also taking intransigently opposed positions on matters of principle and policy. Washington's Federalist successor John Adams understood the Jeffersonian Democratic-Republicans not as legitimate rivals but as traitors, culpable for fomenting a scurrilous and radical politics, hostile to rights, resistant to law, and devoted to stirring up unreasonable popular demands and civic unrest. The Federalists passed the Naturalization and Alien and Sedition Acts (1798) to keep the Democratic-Republicans from augmenting their ranks with immigrant radicals and to suppress challenges to what they considered (their) legitimate governing authority. The deportations and prosecutions began.

> [E]very difference of opinion is not a difference of principle. We have called by different names brethren of the same principle. We are all republicans: we are all federalists.
> Thomas Jefferson (1801)

The resistance to these measures assumed many guises, including formal declarations of constitutional resistance from the states drafted by Jefferson and Madison themselves (*The Virginia and Kentucky Resolutions*, 1798/1799). It soon took the form of a political campaign in the election of 1800 to wrest the national government from the Federalists, putting Thomas Jefferson in the White House, and his party in the majority in Congress. The opposition succeeded in a landslide. In his first Inaugural Address, President Jefferson sought to settle the fractious party spirit that had torn the nation apart by magnanimously pronouncing his opponents to be one with members of Jefferson's own party in their love of country, and their pursuit of the common good. While partisan contention continued, the election of 1800 was notable for its navigation of the first peaceful (if perilous) transfer of powers between rival parties in American history – a harbinger, in its own way, that mass democracy on a scale well beyond that of the ancient Greek city-states just might work.

Democratic-Republican dominance might have portended a sharp reversal of the Hamiltonian Federalist political vision and policies. One wing of the party, the "Old Republicans," led by the fiery Virginia Supreme Court Justice Spencer Roane, took a hard line in emphasizing a strict constitutional construction sharply limiting the powers of the national government, and listing heavily toward the states. In the disastrous aftermath of the War of 1812, weak leadership, barely able to steer an under-resourced and inept federal government, brought the country to the precipice of financial ruin, and enabled a string of humiliating military defeats. Against this backdrop, another wing of the Democratic-Republicans, the party's mainstream "National Republicans" – which included both Jefferson and Madison – spurred on by practical concerns of governing, pivoted to support an increasingly active, national government that created a National Bank, instituted a protective tariff to encourage the development of infant domestic industries, and pursued federally sponsored internal (infrastructure) improvements.

The constitutionality of these new departures was boldly defended and articulated in a series of landmark opinions by a Hamiltonian Federalist Supreme Court headed by John Marshall – appointed during the waning minutes of the Adams administration and now the only Federalist beachhead in the national government at a time of ascendant Jeffersonianism. Cribbing from Hamilton's Federalist #78, Marshall's audacious opinion in *Marbury v. Madison* (1803) ensured that the power of the federal courts to void unconstitutional legislation was written into the country's fundamental law. Marshall's opinion in *McCulloch v. Maryland* (1819) involving the constitutionality of the national bank struck a blow to strict constructionist understandings of the powers of the national government, and boldly stumped for a broad reading of that government's implied powers. At the same time, in a pincer movement, the Marshall Court blocked actions by the states that might have impinged upon those powers, such as in the steamboat monopoly case of *Gibbons v. Ogden* (1824). Evincing classic Hamiltonianism, the Marshall Court stood up for the rights of property and contract that formed the foundation for an emerging market-capitalist economy (*Fletcher v. Peck*, 1810; *Dartmouth College v. Woodward*, 1819). At the same time the ever-judicious Marshall took care to leave most day-to-day matters of social and economic ("police powers") regulation to state and local governments, where most of it, at this time, took place. *Barron v. Baltimore* (1833) reaffirmed that the rights protections of the Constitution's first ten amendments ("The Bill of Rights," whose addition had been demanded by the Antifederalists) were restrictions on the powers of the national government only. As such, for most of the nineteenth century, those asserting rights claims involving property (mostly), religious liberty, the freedom of speech, and criminal procedure would have to look not to the Bill of Rights but to the constitutions of their states.

While Marshall was writing the Federalist political and constitutional vision into the nation's fundamental law through bold acts of interpretation, the Federalist party itself fizzled out and died. John Quincy Adams might have been raised within the party of his founder father John, but as his political career advanced, he acted upon his own (highly) independent judgment, placing his individualized assessment above both party interests and loyalties, and local and sectional interests. Adams supported Thomas Jefferson's Embargo Act (1807), which decimated his home region of New England, as well as the latter's Louisiana Purchase (1803), which was likely to dilute the region's influence. For their part, Adams's Democratic-Republican Party opponents, including the Tennessean Andrew Jackson, from whom he took the presidency by a hair in 1824, were increasingly reimagining the political sphere as one not contaminated by party spirit but foundationally structured by it – as an affirmative political good.[1]

Jacksonian Democracy

As the country moved further into the nineteenth century, the nation's founders grew increasingly elderly and died. A new generation was rising, and new trends in political thought and action were afoot. The era's watchword was "democracy." Even the Federalists, who, to varying degrees, had been invested in a culture of deference, fed by the conviction that there were higher and lower sorts, that the better sort had a rightful claim to rule, and that social boundaries and manners were to be respected, were transformed by the spirit of the age. As time passed, however, a parade of foreign visitors to the United States from the late 1820s through the early 1840s who scribbled furiously in their notebooks – most famously Alexis de Tocqueville, Fanny Trollope, and Charles Dickens – were shocked by the mass populace's rejection of these norms and mores. Amazed and intrigued, they wrote of the easy familiarity of the Americans they met, who seemed imbued with a spirit of social equality that recognized few boundaries, proprieties, hierarchies, and manners. The Americans, they observed, approached everyone on familiar terms, and would not entertain the thought that some might be their superiors or their betters.

American Tories, who continued to believe that the country's high-minded elites held a rightful claim to its political leadership as manners and mores were democratizing, were appalled by Andrew Jackson's ascension to the White House (1828). A backwoodsman from the western frontier, Jackson was a hot-headed brawler and a dueler, with the bullets in his chest to prove it. Although a lawyer, "Old Hickory" had no formal education to speak of; the contrast with his predecessor, the scholarly, Harvard-educated John Quincy Adams, was especially stark. (A satirist had said that when President Jackson received his honorary doctorate from Harvard, where the speeches had to be delivered in Latin, Jackson blurted out "E *pluribus unum*, my friends, and *sine qua non*," and sat down.) Jackson had made his reputation as a ruthlessly effective army general and Indian fighter: he was the hero of the Battle of New Orleans in the War of 1812, and led attacks against the resident Seminole Indians in support of the Georgia militias that resulted in the American seizure of Spanish Florida.

While possessed of a political temperament, inclinations, and instincts, and some strong views on policy, the aging Jackson was no political theorist. That said, the "Jacksonian" political thought to which his name has been attached had been fashioned by his supporters, and they formed the Democratic Party around him. Not least among their ranks was Martin Van Buren, who, as the son of an upstate New York tavernkeeper, was an envious antagonist of the Hudson River valley's aristocratic Dutch elite. Van Buren played a major role in pioneering the modern political party system, with its imperatives concerning party-building, party discipline, and (strategically) expanded suffrage. He envisioned party as a national structure, a constructed coalition attentive to message control and political mobilization through subsidies and patronage. (It was Van Buren's New York ally William Marcy who had coined the phrase "To the victor belong the spoils.") Van Buren made getting out the vote a priority, and played a major role in the adoption of the recently invented (1831) presidential nominating conventions that drove the shift toward choosing presidential electors by popular vote.

Jackson's presidency (1829–1837) innovated in the realm of executive power. He wielded his presidential powers boldly and aggressively: "King Andrew I" demanded that his cabinet be directly accountable to him, and no one else. (The Whig Party's understanding was that, as government officials responsible for implementing congressionally authorized policies, these executive branch officials were answerable instead to Congress) Jackson exercised his veto power to an unprecedented extent. In all this, and his other actions, including his challenges to the presumptive authority of the Supreme Court to settle constitutional meaning, Jackson frequently appealed to his (popular) electoral mandate. He was an unconflicted slave owner, and, as an aggressive champion of westward expansion, an unapologetic prosecutor of Indian removal.

The spirit of the times was reflected in Jacksonian campaigns against economic, political, and social hierarchy and privilege. Appealing to the good sense and rightful claims to rule of the many – the common man – Jacksonian Democrats disdained men of preening elevation and refinement, and holier-than-thou professions of virtue. They lambasted the rich and powerful and those they excoriated as the country's monied interests, reminding everyone that ordinary Americans were the source of all political power, and that the common man's advancement and security should set the rightful direction of American politics and policy.

The Democrats fought against bids to rule – through what they often took to be underhanded and nefarious means – by self-appointed elites, would-be aristocrats, and special interests, the last of whom were perpetually endeavoring to secure grants of exclusive or monopoly power, and special privileges, to exploit the people for their own private gain and enrichment. Like Thomas Paine before them, while far from avoiding the problem themselves, Jacksonian Democrats were alive to the political truth that all power was liable to abuse.

They suspected that any new initiative undertaken by the federal government (especially) – which they frequently alleged surpassed its constitutional powers, which had been designed to secure the interests of ordinary Americans – was the result of extortion by special interests. They espied in these government programs elite cooptation and corruption, seeking special privileges via "partial [or 'class'] legislation." Although the era's Democrats were firm believers in property rights, the "commercial republic," and "the

> When an honest observance of constitutional compacts can not be obtained from communities like ours, it need not be anticipated elsewhere, and the cause in which there has been so much martyrdom, and from which so much was expected by the friends of liberty, may be abandoned, and the degrading truth that man is unfit for self-government admitted. And this will be the case if expediency be made a rule of construction in interpreting the Constitution.
>
> Andrew Jackson (1830)

release of energy" by small producers, they nevertheless set themselves in inflamed opposition to the concentrated power of a financial and corporate elite that, they insisted, crushed the common man under its heel.

Jacksonian democracy's backcountry pioneer settlers – who were hacking their way westward to stake their claims to abundant land – and its small freeholders, mechanics, laborers, and small businessmen in the country's growing cities may have been a bit unruly and uncouth. But, as they saw it, they were hard-working and patriotic – the backbone of the republic. The Jacksonian historian George Bancroft testified (1835): "If it be true that the gifts of mind and heart are universally diffused, if the sentiment of truth, justice, love, and beauty exists in every one then it follows . . . that the common judgment in taste, politics, and religion is the highest authority on earth and the nearest possible approach to an infallible decision."

Their fight against privilege may have been impassioned, but it was far from gloomy or pessimistic. Jacksonian Democrats were bursting with optimism about the country's future, and about the expansion of political participation and popular rule. This optimism was in full flower in the Young America movement of the 1830s and 1840s, led by the New York city newspaper and magazine editor John L. O'Sullivan. Carrying forward what had already become an American tradition, O'Sullivan and his compatriots crowed about American exceptionalism – about the country's unique "Manifest Destiny." The country would be led into this bright future by a cohort of vigorous, patriotic youth, who would spread across the continent through conquest and settlement, expanding the nation's scope, power, and influence. O'Sullivan's *Democratic Review* (1837) championed the Jacksonian outlook, attesting to its "abiding confidence in the virtue, intelligence, and full capacity for self-government, of the great mass of our people." As a corollary, it issued repeated warnings concerning consolidated power, including in government. After all, William Leggett, the political editorialist and editor of the Jacksonian *New York Evening Post* reminded his readers (1834), experience had shown "that this power has always been exercised under the influence and for the exclusive benefit of wealth. It was never wielded on behalf of the community."

The themes and touchstones of this political philosophy were brought to bear on the full succession of political issues and disputes of the day, including suffrage extension; westward expansion; the establishment and continuance of a National Bank committed to tight money and firm credit; contract rights; bankruptcy and imprisonment for debt; the constitutionality of federally funded infrastructure projects (internal improvements); and the protective tariff.

The Whig Vision and "the American System"

Taking their name from the revolutionary opponents of George III, deployed this time against the United States' own "King Andrew," the motley new Whig Party (c. 1834) were clearer about what they were against than for. Writing in the *American Review*, the Whig journalist George Colton worried about a disturbing "current of a wild democracy" loosed by the Democrats.

> The doctrine of political equality has been so perverted into a teaching of literal equality in endowments, competency, and political wisdom, that it is not easily understood how one head can be wiser than another, or more fit to govern. . . . But it is not strange that the people should believe the charlatans and knaves who take such pains to persuade them that they are as wise as they are free.

"What is needed more than anything," Colton continued, "is for the good and great men – the high-minded, honest, sensible and experienced men – to take hold of the politics of the country, and place themselves where they belong, at the head of the masses, to guide, teach, and save them." The Whigs nevertheless, in their own way, could not resist their opponents' democratizing spirit. The "Hard Cider," "Log Cabin" campaign of William Henry Harrison bid for the mass appeal of the common man. When considered alongside Andrew Jackson's strong pronouncement of a constitutional faith, and his uncompromising commitment to the American Union in face of truculent state resistance in the Nullification Crisis (1832), the common ground shared by the Whigs and the Democrats helped consolidate a new, post-founding American politics.

That said, to the extent the founding legacies were carried forward, Jackson's Democrats were recognizably the party of Jefferson, and the Whigs bore the clear imprint of Hamilton. John Quincy Adams, who started as a Federalist, became a National Republican, and then, finally, a Whig – where he would be joined by Henry Clay, Daniel Webster, and the rising Abraham Lincoln – provided a direct link from one era to the next. In his First Inaugural Address (1825), Adams extended and refined the Hamiltonian vision of a vigorously engaged, forward-looking national government. He conceived of the powers and duties of government not as necessary evils, but as great charters to be exercised actively and to their fullest to advance the public good and the national interest. While stipulating that the federal government could not, of course, transcend its constitutional powers, Adams enjoined the government to seize the initiative, and do as much as it possibly could, even in the face of popular criticism. "[T]o refrain from exercising [the federal government's powers] for the benefit of the people themselves," he declared, "would be to hide in the earth the talent committed to our charge – would be treachery to the most sacred of trusts." Adams insisted that an active national government was an engine that would drive the country forward to achieve the greatness that was its destiny.

To realize this optimistic vision, the Whigs supported a broad construction of national powers, especially the powers of Congress, which they took to be the federal government's pre-eminent policymaking branch. At the forefront of their objectives was to enlist the national government in promoting economic development. Kentucky's Henry Clay called the program "The American System" (1832), declaring that the "transformation . . . of the country from gloom and distress to brightness and prosperity, has been mainly the work of American legislation, fostering American industry." Animadverting against free trade ("It never has existed, it never will exist"), which he warned would lead to the United States' "re-colonization" by Great Britain, Clay proposed a high and mounting tariff to stimulate domestic manufactures, and to fill the federal government's coffers. Clay lent his full support to the National Bank, with an eye, among other things, to disciplining unreliable state banks and stabilizing the rollercoaster economy. He called, moreover, for an extensive program of federally funded infrastructure projects ("internal improvements"), funded by tariffs, and for the sale of public lands, to encourage trade and manufactures.

All of these policies were the subject of intense constitutional contention between the Democrats and the Whigs across the Jacksonian era. When John Marshall's opinion in *McCulloch v. Maryland* (1819) affirmed the constitutionality of the National Bank, Andrew Jackson's veto of its charter defiantly denied it. When congressional Whigs funded roads, canals, and bridges, Jackson vetoed the appropriations, provoking Clay to rise to their defense. In perhaps the most ominous face-off of all, as the tariff rates mounted, John C. Calhoun and his home state of South Carolina, speaking in the voice of an aggrieved (ostensibly) co-equal constitutional sovereign, declared it null and void.

The partisan contention over these measures was fed by simmering class resentments and sectional divisions. The South and West opposed the tariff, while the North favored it. Jackson framed the Bank debate as a battle between rich elites and the common man, lamenting that "[i]t is to be regretted that the rich and powerful too often bend the acts of government to their selfish purposes," and affirming that "the humble members of society – the farmers, mechanics, and laborers – who have neither the time nor the means of securing like favors to themselves, have a right to complain of the injustice of their Government." And this is to say nothing about the looming divisions over slavery, concentrated overwhelmingly in the South, and raised repeatedly as an issue as the country expanded westward. The Whigs and Democrats desperately instituted a succession of shaky, *ad hoc* deals and compromises on slavery, kicking the can down the road, doing their best to ignore, or provisionally transcend, divisions that seemed likely to not only sunder the nation's sections and parties, but also lead to all-out civil war.

Majority Rule and Minority Rights

The American political order is often casually described as "democratic." In describing it this way, people have several different things in mind. The US Constitution is premised on popular sovereignty: the bedrock principle that the source of government power stems from the people. Many of the United States' government institutions make decisions by majority vote, typically by elected representatives, but sometimes (as in the storied New England town meetings) of the people themselves. Americans have made much of their commitment to what liberal thinkers like Benjamin Constant and Isaiah Berlin have called, respectively, "active" or "positive" liberty. By this, they mean popular self-determination: the empowerment of the people to chart their own collective social and political course to advance their collective understanding of the common good.[2] At the same time, however, the problem of minorities – those who, by definition, tend to come out on the losing end of majority votes – has been at the forefront of American thinking about, and practice of, government. This problem was a major preoccupation of the US Constitution's most influential architect, James Madison. As noted in the previous chapter, the founding constitutional debates were suffused with concerns about the protection of minority rights and interests within a system premised upon popular rule.

The concern for minority rights and interests in a democracy is of special concern in diverse, pluralistic polities. In a heterogeneous polity, different groups – economic, sectional, social, religious, ethnic, national, linguistic, racial, sex- and gender-based, policy-seeking, partisan, and innumerable others which form and activate politically over time – possess and pursue different, and often diametrically opposed, interests. These are often mobilized, both affirmatively and aversively, in the pursuit of power – the right to rule. Different polities are constituted by different constellations of groups and interests, held and mobilized with differing levels of intensity. Some of those interests might be subsidiary, others important, and still others considered vital, with the group itself, as a sub-community, determining, subjectively, the significance of their shared interest. The political scientist Arend Lijphart distinguished between pluralist, and even deeply divided, polities and consensus polities, and noted their very different political and constitutional dynamics. Lijphart noted, moreover, that countries have diverged in the successes of their institutional architectures in dealing with these problems. Pluralist polities often strive for and arrive at arrangements for the guarantee for minority rights. This is not simply a matter of fairness and principle. It is also a matter of civic peace, and even of the future of the polity as a going concern. In deeply divided polities, where what the minority takes to be its vital interests are consistently defeated, violent resistance and, perhaps, secession and civil war are possible.

The American founders were well aware that the United States was a plu-ralistic polity. The continuance of chattel slavery, they feared, might render it a deeply divided one as well. The founders took the country's differences and divisions into account as best they could in fashioning the nation's con-stitutional architecture, most prominently, for instance, by giving states, regardless of population, an equal vote in the Senate.

By the very nature of its colonial genesis, American politics has raised vital questions about the relationship between parts and the whole. Each of the orig-inal thirteen colonies was connected directedly to the metropole in London, which had licensed them. None was formally connected to each other. As the colonies coalesced around a set of shared interests and grievances, and gradu-ally concluded that they constituted a political community separate from Great Britain, they joined together to form a common government. But for a long time the colonists' (and then Americans') primary sense of political loy-alty and obligation, of citizenship and belonging, remained with their states, which many continued to insist remained free, independent, and sovereign. (This understanding was clearly reflected in the nation's first national con-stitution, the Articles of Confederation.) The impetus for a new Constitution (1789) arose out of the practical problems, inadequacies, and debilities of this ordering. It was specifically designed to create a more powerful set of national institutions, and a more national political community. But, even with the adoption of the more national Constitution, the centrifugal pull of the nation's sub-polities remained strong. The de-centralizing, de-consolidating, and fis-siparous tendencies were, moreover, inflamed by innumerable political and constitutional controversies between the national government and the states, both bi-laterally and sectionally. These controversies implicated important questions concerning primary loyalties, responsibilities, and interests.

Contentions between the respective claims to self-government of the federal government and the states were prominently raised across the antebellum period by the disparate sectional and regional effects of an array of govern-mental decisions and public policies. Issues of minority rights – the power of minority political communities to protect what they consider their vital interests within the prevailing political order – prompted a succession of stands, statements, and articulations of new political theories. These included the Hartford Convention (1814–1815), called by New England Federalists angered by what they took to be the systematic advantages conferred by the Constitution on the South and West that had led to a persistent disregard of their interests by the Democratic-Republican administrations of Thomas Jefferson (especially his trade embargo) and James Madison ("Mr. Madison's War" – the War of 1812); the disputes over the protective tariff (leading to the Nullification Crisis of 1832); and then, catastrophically, the conflict over slav-ery (leading to Civil War, 1861–1865), a system failure that had been staved off in a whitewater political ride over the rapids of westward expansion and the acquisition of new territories and the admission of new states in which the slave or free status of the appended land was raised again and again.

The anti-"Tariff of Abominations" and pro-slavery South Carolina Senator John C. Calhoun's *A Disquisition on Government* (1851) was the era's most sophisticated reflection on the protection of minority rights and interests in a democratic polity. In an abstract theoretical treatise – but with the preservation of slavery clearly in mind – Calhoun argued that polities were comprised not of isolated individuals, but of groups with identifiable interests. Where the vital interests of a core political constituency were concerned, those who might lose out in a majority vote were entitled to retain a veto power that allowed them to protect those interests. To not afford them such protection, Calhoun insisted, would be to unjustly deny them their fundamental liberty, and to subject them to tyranny. For such a measure to be approved, Calhoun argued, the decision-making body should be required to assemble not just a simple "numerical majority" of the body, but rather a "concurrent majority," or the assembled approval of all vitally interested groups. Such a requirement, he noted, would be conducive to mutual accommodation and compromise.

> Laws, so far from being uniform in their operation, are scarcely ever so.
> John C. Calhoun (1828)

Calhoun's proposal went to the heart of the issue of the ultimate nature, cohesion, and even survival of a polity. This is because if a minority, especially a core minority, found its vital interests consistently trenched upon, it would be entirely appropriate for that minority to pause and reconsider its decision to remain a part of – rather than to exit – the political community. Calhoun was arguing that it was implicit in the decision to enter any social contract, including the American constitutional compact, that a core community's vital interests would be protected. Otherwise, that minority would have never agreed to be a part of that polity in the first place.

Calhoun suggested a constitutional amendment to implement his framework of government, appropriately protective of minority rights: a dual (sectional) presidency, with each of the two presidents holding the power to veto legislation that went against the interests of his section. Even without the novel proposed mechanism, however, the Constitution as it currently existed had provided an array of beachheads for minorities to dig into and protect their interests, whether in the states (federalism) and localities, in the different branches of the national government, or in the country's rights consciousness, and formal bills of rights. It was initially assumed that the political parties themselves were potentially fatal fissures. But, although things intermittently tended in the direction of partisan polarization, it seemed that in assembling a group of cross-cutting interests and cleavages, the party system for the most part had had the opposite effect: so far, at least, it had worked to knit the nation together. As slavery was gradually abolished in the North, and as it became even more vital to the South, as an abolitionist movement swelled, and as the nation moved westward, the parties themselves cleaved in half. After forcing out their anti-slavery elements, the Democratic Party became a pro-slavery bastion. The Whigs were torn to pieces over the issue, and a new anti-slavery party, the Republicans, arose out of their ashes. The divide was now stark, and geographically arrayed. Mutual suspicion and recriminations followed, and the nation fell into civil war.

Whether a system is premised on rule by the numerical or a concurrent majority, of course, there remains the question of who the "people" are who are entitled to a voice and a vote as full civic members of the polity. Calhoun did not provide any voice or role for the South's enslaved people. In both the North and the South, the antebellum US electorate was limited, with a few exceptions that changed over time in some places, to white adult males. That said, the era was nevertheless characterized by extensive democratization in the sense that the property requirements were gradually eliminated – an inclusive wave that made the American political order the increasing province of white male suffrage. In this regard, despite the above debilities, the United States was, in its time, a world leader.

The Sovereign Individual

In announcing their separation from Great Britain as portending "a new order of the ages," Americans found themselves even more actively pondering the question already posed before the Revolution by the upstate New York French-American farmer and writer J. Hector St. John Crèvecoeur (*Letters from an American Farmer*, 1782): "What then is the American, this new man?" Now, though, superimposed over that first question was a second: "What kind of country are we going to be?"[3] The simultaneousness of the intense inwardness of the former question, and the trumpeting outwardness of the latter, taken up individually and collectively, as an assumed destiny, gave rise to what we might call the anxiety of exceptionalism – a dynamic in which independence was not simply experienced, but willed.

Many Americans took the idea of independence, from Europe and its Old World ways, to involve much more than establishment of a new government: it would involve the invention *de novo* of a new democratic subject for an aspiring new nation. For some, any indication that America followed or borrowed traditional customs – such as English common law – was both a black mark and a spur toward innovation; the very notion of being "dependent" on Old World customs was an offense to their view of themselves as independent Americans. It was in this culture that Benjamin Franklin, the scientist and inventor – the lightning rod, bifocals – was a national hero and emblem; that David Dudley Field sought a replacement for hand-me-down English law via the legal Codification Movement; that Ralph Waldo Emerson's *The American Scholar* (1837) called for a genuinely American scholarship and literature; and that Walt Whitman, author of *Song of Myself* (1855), imagined new *Democratic Vistas* (1871).

A singular departure of the antebellum United States was the rise in claims on behalf of the sovereign self. These claims worried the line between politics and a refusal of politics. During this period at least, appeals to the sovereign self were less likely to involve claims either to antinomian individual autonomy or untrammeled license (along lines lately articulated in France by the Marquis de Sade) than claims of an alternative moral, social, and perhaps even political allegiance. These often stubborn or strident claims perpetually raised the specter of dissent, withdrawal, repudiation, and (individual) secession.

Individual integrity was the touchstone for the sovereign self. As such, compromise entailed corruption. If conventional understandings of politics are preoccupied with the bargains and compromises necessary to sustain group life as it confronts the realities of diversity and disagreement, claims on behalf of the sovereign self, disposed toward treating all (morally significant) compromise as rotten compromise, were anti-political.[4] As such, the politics of this version of Crèvecoeur's new man involved a deep skepticism toward institutions, and an iron will both to fully realize oneself as an individual and to live the dictates of that self, impervious to outside criticism and pressures to conform.

The New England Transcendentalists of Concord, Massachusetts – Ralph Waldo Emerson, Henry David Thoreau, Bronson Alcott, Margaret Fuller, and others – were initially weaned in the bosom of the region's perfectionist pietist Christianity. That Christianity, which in this period was associated most closely with the Unitarian Church, valorized moral purity and rectitude. The broader world was in many respects a sewer, and there was nothing these evangelists for the sovereign self abhorred more than dirty hands. The unremitting focus was the purification and cultivation of the self's true and singular soul – which Transcendentalists firmly believed was the only route to salvation.

In current parlance, the Transcendentalists were "spiritual but not religious." They are perhaps more accurately described as anti-religious, since they were the scourges of even the most liberal churches of their time. Ralph Waldo Emerson started as a Unitarian minister, but he attacked organized Christianity for privileging doctrine, ritual, and biblical literalism over moral and spiritual intuition. This culminated in his scandalizing address to the Harvard Divinity School (1838), in which, among other things, he preached that, although certainly admirable, Jesus was not the son of God any more than each of us are the sons of God. Attacked by traditionalists as a band of atheists and infidels, the Transcendentalists set out to forge a new anti-institutional, quintessentially American form of (zealous) spirituality. In this, they looked both outward (to German idealism and eastern religions) and inward in search of "The Divine Soul which inspires all men" (Emerson).

If a man was tossed out of a window when an infant, and so made a cripple for life, or scared out of his wits by the Indians, it is regretted chiefly because he was thus incapacitated for – business! I think that there is nothing, not even crime, more opposed to poetry, to philosophy, ay, to life itself, than this incessant business.

Henry David Thoreau (1863)

The Transcendentalists experimented in and lectured on themes of self-reliance, non-conformism (Emerson), and living simply and with integrity (Thoreau). As such, they vacillated between withdrawal from and engagement with the broader society and its economy and politics. In the former vein, drawing in part on Fourierist socialism, they founded free-standing utopian communities (Brook Farm, 1841–1847; Fruitlands, 1843–1844) – an impulse fascinatingly endemic to this era, and not unique to the Transcendentalists – and on Independence Day (1845), Henry David Thoreau moved into his cabin on Walden Pond (see *Walden; or, Life in the Woods*, 1854). In the latter vein, the Transcendentalists lambasted the shallow, commercial spirit of the age and of their fellow-countrymen, and the triviality of society. In time, they took stands on great national policies: against the Mexican-American War, and, most significantly, against chattel slavery.

In protesting the Mexican–American War, Thoreau refused to pay taxes that would go in part to support the conflict. In *Civil Disobedience* (1849) – an essay that would have a profound influence on Mahatma Gandhi, Bayard Rustin, and Martin Luther King Jr. – Thoreau argued that his refusal to pay his tax, for which he was jailed, was justified as a moral duty. In *A Plea for Captain John Brown* (1859), he defended the radical abolitionist whose ill-fated raid on the federal armory at Harper's Ferry, Virginia, aimed to ignite an armed uprising by enslaved Americans – a crime for which Brown was hanged. These defenses of disobedience of law and armed rebellion aggressively defended ostensibly anti-political acts, if we understand politics to involve ordinary institutional practices and rules in ostensibly functional polities. They were impassioned calls for a "contentious politics": politics by other means, or (as Malcolm X later put it) "by any means necessary." Always preoccupied with his integrity, ethics, and moral purity (among other things, he experimented with vegetarianism and labored to minimize his economic and ecological footprint), Thoreau was personally committed to non-violence. By contrast, John Brown's commitment to moral integrity in confronting one of the great moral evils sought to spark an uprising that would "purify this land with blood." This would not be the last time Americans faced the question of what methods are most appropriate to fight against the sometimes great injustices that are either advanced or tolerated by the ordinary politics of the American political system.

Although they were religious outsiders – to the extent that they raised questions about whether they were in any way "religious" – the Transcendentalists were not as different from the more mainstream evangelical Christians of their time as we might initially suppose. They were, after all, swimming in the stream of the (evangelical Protestant) Second Great Awakening (1790–1840), a spiritual mass movement with an emphasis on an inner light and individual conscience (see also Anne Hutchinson, Jonathan Mayhew, and Roger Williams), personal responsibility, and the forging of a direct, personal relationship with Jesus Christ.

The emotion-drenched spiritual revivals of the Second Great Awakening not only swelled the ranks of the United States' evangelical Christians, but also sparked the founding of a whole new slate of sects, theologies, and churches. The Church of Jesus Christ of Latter-day Saints (LDS/Mormons (Joseph Smith), the Shakers (Mother Ann Lee), the Adventists (William Miller), and the African Methodist Episcopal (AME) Church (Richard Allen) were all progeny of this movement. Some scholars have argued that it was the sheer diversity of faiths unleashed by this cascade of religiosity, and not any concern for religious influence in politics *per se*, that led to the wave of state disestablishments that took place between the founding and the 1830s.

This religious revival spurred individuals not only to look inward within their souls to seek salvation from sin, but, in anticipation of Christ's millennial return, also to purify the society in which they lived in preparation for the Second Coming. As for the Transcendentalists, these imperatives led in two different directions: inward and outward. The latter path became especially important in post-founding American politics, and has remained so, with varied intensity, ever since. Many evangelicals considered social reform a Christian duty and quietism a dereliction. As the passions of evangelical Christianity came to displace the Enlightenment rationalism and deism of the founders, social reformism – temperance, abolitionism, women's rights – developed into a consistent feature of American political life. While men were certainly involved in these movements, women took the lead in creating organizations calling for the repentance of sin and the moral purification of society through legal and social reform. Moral reform organizations tended to ally more with the Whig Party (and, later, the Republicans) than the Democrats. But their chief commitment was to cause and issue, rather than party. This was part of the dynamic that, in time, would lead to the destruction of the Whigs on the rocks of chattel slavery.

Anti-Materialism and Nature

The New England Transcendentalists preached a spirituality that transcended the material world, emphasizing, with affinities with eastern religions and philosophies like Hinduism and Buddhism, a non-dualism by which humanity and nature (and God and humanity) were one. The quest was to tap into this essential and transcendent unity of all beings – what Emerson (who had been studying the *Bhagavad Gita*) called "the oversoul" (1841) – by looking deeply into oneself, and finding there a microcosm of the universe.

Transcendentalists were especially critical of the rampant materialism, relentless pursuit of wealth, and idolatrous worship of success suffusing the bustling and building America in which they lived. Thoreau found the development of railroads troubling, and mocked the pretentions of the revolution in communications unleashed by the newly laid transatlantic cable, although, registering a partial dissent, Emerson professed a delight in originality and individual ambition promising technological transformation.

Thoreau was especially concerned with the move by his materialist society to dominate, if not destroy, the natural world, which he immersed himself in and celebrated. He urged his countrymen not to set themselves against nature, but rather to live with it in rich and meaningful harmony. He was a strong and early dissenter against the (Lockean) producer ethic and, as such, was the antithesis of Benjamin Franklin's cheerfully relentless industriousness, which counseled ambition, efficiency, and work, work, work. In this regard, Thoreau's *Walden, Walking* (1851) and *Life Without Principle* (1863), among other things, offer a sharp rebuke, and alternative, to Franklin's acclaimed *Autobiography* (1791) and Poor Richard's *Almanack* (1732). Better to commune with nature, cultivate your best self, Thoreau alternatively counseled. Spurn, he preached, the crass and shallow. Forget social climbing, distinguishing yourself, and getting ahead. Focus on the good, the true, and the eternal. Life, for Thoreau, was meant to be a deep and rich experience – to be lived fully, and enjoyed.

The Call of Moral and Social Reform

As noted above, the often intense personal reckonings concerning one's integrity and duty at the heart of Transcendentalism were, in a different form, also at the heart of the contemporaneous Second Great Awakening, which left a broad and enduring mark on American political culture. Unlike Transcendentalism, which bore the strong imprint of New England intellectualism, and a pronounced individualism affirmed by what was, after all, a small and elite group, the Second Great Awakening was a mass popular movement centered on the dramas of tent revivals and camp meetings resounding with shouting and swooning, expressing intense religious feeling and enthusiasm. These were fired by an apprehension, as explicated by a post-millennial theology, that the Second Coming would soon be at hand. Would you, as a Christian believer, be saved, and granted eternal life? Or would you, an impenitent sinner, be cast down into the pit of Hell for all eternity? The revivals and camp meetings offered participants an opportunity to join with others *en masse* in saving their souls by repenting of sin and purifying themselves, by recommitting their lives to Jesus.

Transcendentalism had struck a subtle balance between inwardness and outwardness on matters of moral integrity and commitment. Transcendentalists certainly kept an eye on the broader society, and often criticized and critiqued it. But, their writings aside, they were not engaged directly in politics. When they protested, as Thoreau did against the Mexican-American War, it was typically by showily washing their hands of any direct connection to the evil, serving, as they saw it, to preserve the state of their souls, rather than working cooperatively to change the world – although, to be sure, in so doing, they hoped to set an example for others. For many of the devotees of the Second Great Awakening, by contrast, the apprehension that the Second Coming would soon be at hand implied an imperative of readying society for that great return, and day of judgment. This entailed making a commitment not only to evangelizing for the faith, including abroad through the establishment of foreign missions (the American Board of Commissioners for Foreign Missions was established in 1810), but also to undertaking moral reform at home. As such, the Second Great Awakening played a major role in motivating the antebellum United States' storied succession of reform movements, including the abolitionist and temperance movements, and the movement for women's rights. (The latter was a concomitant development occasioned by the fact that so many women were involved in both of these former movements, and were often criticized for their unwomanly or "unnatural" involvement in the public sphere, if not outright discriminated against by some of the most prominent male abolitionist leaders.)

The era's reform movements blended Christian moral fervor (arising out of a pervading sense of sin and salvation), the sanctity of conscience, and the pre-eminence of higher (as opposed to lower, man-made, "positive") law. Reform politics was contentious "social movement" politics: its members, at least initially, were focused less on the ordinary politics of voting and elections and participating in society's *status quo* political institutions – women, of course, and most African-Americans, were barred from voting – than on confronting those institutions, which they accused of moral failure, if not evil. This was a politics of protests, meetings, manifestos, tracts, and demands. Moral reformers trained their opprobrium on a single issue or a closely related constellation of issues that they took to be egregious problems. And they closely identified personally with their commitment to and involvement in the crusade to remedy that evil.

Perhaps the first of the era's movements to achieve a critical mass was temperance, launched with the founding of the American Temperance Society (1820). Temperance movement activists, many of whom were women, were concerned with the dissipation, lost wages, and abuse caused by the (over) indulgence in intoxicating liquors. They looked forward to a society of sober men whose morals and sense of both Christian and social duty was not loosened by intoxication. As their name indicates, movement participants tended to call for the temperate use of alcohol rather than total abstinence. Some emphasized voluntarism or moral suasion, whereas others sought legal restrictions on the production, consumption, sale, and distribution of alcohol.

Opposition to slavery was not new to this period. White Protestant sects – Mennonites, Amish, Presbyterians, Congregationalists, and Quakers – and radical republicans had issued some of the first organized criticism of chattel slavery. From the nation's earliest days, a number of free blacks had spoken out against this evil. The condemnation continued in the antebellum era, initiating a vibrant tradition of black political thought and debate. Some of these thinkers, like David Walker, Martin Delany, Alexander Crummell, and Maria W. Stewart, had been born free. Others, like Henry Highland Garnet and Frederick Douglass, had escaped bondage. Their diverse origins were complemented by diverse, and often divergent, views about the nature of the challenges posed by slavery, and their country's pervading system of ascriptive racial hierarchy. Their varied diagnoses led them to focus on different imperatives, and forge contending visions concerning strategy and their collective future.

> Now Americans . . . was your sufferings under Great Britain one hundredth the part as cruel and tyrannical as you have rendered ours under you?
> David Walker (1829)

David Walker's *An Appeal to the Coloured Citizens of the World* (1829), the first sustained argument and attack on slavery in America by an African-American, launched the debate. The Bostonian Walker, who denounced both the barbarity of American Christians who perpetrated and tolerated slavery and the ignorance and hypocrisy of the purportedly learned and egalitarian Thomas Jefferson, played a critical role in sparking abolitionist fervor amongst whites and blacks alike. Walker demanded a genuine adherence by his countrymen to God's will and plan, in a way that realized His promise of liberty and equality for those God had created in His image.

Walker's shot across the bow launched a series of debates amongst black thinkers. Often starting from Christian foundations, some (like Walker) insisted upon appealing to their countrymen's common humanity, regardless of their race, and to the country's oft-professed – if egregiously unrealized – creedal political ideals. These appeals were often underwritten by an assumption that, notwithstanding the immense difficulties African-Americans would face there, the United States was, and always would be, their home.

These black thinkers were writing at a time when many whites, either out of sympathy, hostility, or some perplexing admixture of both, were calling for the repatriation of African-Americans *en masse* back to Africa through colonization. Other black political thinkers, however – including the pioneering black nationalists Delany, Crummell, and Garnet – called for the mass emigration of their people, either to Africa, to elsewhere overseas, or even to all-black districts that would be established on what was currently US territory.

Another divide opened between the more militant free black abolitionists, who called for direct – and perhaps violent – confrontation, and moderates like Douglass and Stewart, both of whom opposed violence on moral and pragmatic grounds. This latter wing of black thinkers advocated building alliances and winning new converts to their cause through publicity and moral suasion.

The evangelical Christian abolitionist Stewart also emphasized the importance of both intellectual self-cultivation and inward-focused spiritual and moral revival by African-Americans themselves. Like her formerly enslaved evangelical abolitionist compatriot Sojourner Truth, Stewart chided African-American men for their complacency over, if not complicity in, the denial of the rights of women, both generally and within the abolitionist movement. While they were sometimes seconded in this by men like Douglass, they were nevertheless prominently answered by some black men who vigorously defended the movement's patriarchal hierarchy, like the Presbyterian minister Garnet. Black abolitionists also clashed over the relative emphasis to be placed on slavery itself as a distinct phenomenon, or as a manifestation of a racial caste system equally prevalent in the ostensibly free North.

> Tell us no more of southern slavery; for with few exceptions, although I may be very erroneous in my opinion, yet I consider our condition [in the North] but little better than that.
> Maria W. Stewart (1832)

The abolitionist movement significantly ramped up in intensity in the 1830s. The white radical Massachusetts abolitionist William Lloyd Garrison was both a co-founder of the American Anti-Slavery Society (1833), which booked lecture tours for abolitionist speakers and provided assistance to free blacks and fugitive slaves, and a founder of the pioneering abolitionist journal *The Liberator* (1831–1865), which the Society widely distributed. Frequently shouted at and pelted with rotten eggs, if not tarred and feathered, the uncompromising Garrison demanded that churches, political parties, and governments in the North sever all ties with the slave-holding South. Garrison called on people to refuse to vote, to remove all their poisoned complicity in this evil.

But the escaped slave Frederick Douglass, author of the celebrated *Narrative of the Life of Frederick Douglass, an American Slave* (1845) and other memoirs and writings, was perhaps the country's most galvanizing abolitionist orator. While he began by working with Garrison, Douglass broke with him in 1847 over the latter's refusal to enlist pragmatic political means, strategies, and tactics in the anti-slavery struggle. Like Garrison and Thoreau, however, Douglass underlined the complicity of each and every American, North and South, in the perpetuation of this monumental evil. In a famed oration concerning the Fourth of July (July 5, 1852), Douglass took aim at a country annually celebrating its revolutionary commitments to liberty and equality: for the Negro, Douglass lectured,

> your celebration is a sham, your boasted liberty, an unholy alliance; your national greatness, swelling vanity; your sounds of rejoicing are empty and heartless; liberty and equality hollow mockery; your prayers and hymns, sermons and thanksgivings, with all your religious parade, and solemnity, are, to him, mere bombast, fraud, deception, impiety, and

hypocrisy – a thin veil to cover up crimes which would disgrace a nation of savages.

"The 4th of July is yours, not mine," he concluded.

Many women, black and white alike, including Frances Ellen Watkins Harper, Sojourner Truth, Harriet Tubman, Lydia Maria Child, Angelina and Sarah Grimke, Lucretia Mott, and Elizabeth Cady Stanton, were actively involved in the abolitionist movement. They were subjected to criticism and exclusions, from both outside the movement and within it. This led them, in turn, to recognize that, in important ways, as women, they were subject to the denial of the same natural rights that they were arguing had been refused to African-Americans on the basis of their race (and on two different grounds, as Sojourner Truth pointed out, in an early statement of "intersectionality," for African-American women). As with opposition to slavery, arguments for women's equality at this time were not altogether new: in the "age of revolutions," both Mary Wollstonecraft in England and Olympe de Gouges in France had published sophisticated appeals for women's equality. It was, nevertheless, a major new departure when proponents of equal rights for women led by Elizabeth Cady Stanton and Lucretia Mott met at a Women's Rights Convention in Seneca Falls, New York, and issued a landmark Declaration of Sentiments (1848) modeled on the Declaration of Independence, demanding that the United States fulfill its creedal promise, grounded in God-given natural rights, that "all men and women are created equal." They called for a full slate of equal rights under law for women, including the right to vote.

The birth of "first-wave feminism" is an illustration of the way that new understandings of exclusion on the basis of ascriptive identity can arise out of concrete political engagement in what at first might seem like unrelated campaigns for the civic inclusion of others. Black women active in the abolitionist cause needed no prompting to apprehend the parallel, and kindred, exclusions. But the white female abolitionists soon recognized that, as women, they were in a cognate position, facing their own form of discrimination and exclusion. Through these painful experiences, they arrived at a consciousness of a unique commonality of interests. They were joined by a number of prominent male abolitionists, including Garrison and Douglass, both of whom came to champion women's rights.

An "Empire of Liberty"?

If the United States claimed its independence in the "age of revolutions," when republican claims to liberty, equality, and fraternity filled the air, from Great Britain and France to the Haiti of Toussaint Louverture and the Venezuela of Simón Bolívar, it was also part of the "age of discovery," which flowed like a torrent into the "age of empires." Holland, Great Britain, France, Spain, and Portugal all had claims in the Americas and (with the exception of Portugal) on territory that, in time, would become US soil. The new United States was ambiguously, yet prominently, positioned within the tensions of these global directions and forces. The American Revolution was an anti-imperial revolt – an anticolonial "shot heard round the world" proclaimed in the name of self-rule and individual rights. At the same time, its universalizing liberal claims, reinforced by an exceptionalist sense of mission, seemed to many to both counsel and license expansion. From the beginning, settlers in the colonies were pushing westward, while demanding the support and protection of their governments in doing so. In taking the monumental leap – against his pronounced constitutional scruples – of making the Louisiana Purchase (1803) from France, which doubled the size of the country, Thomas Jefferson fulfilled his vision of securing "an empire of liberty." Jefferson then immediately commissioned the Lewis and Clark expedition (1804–1806) to explore the new territory.

The explorers started at the Mississippi River near St. Louis, and moved west along a northern route, ultimately trekking all the way to the Pacific Ocean in what is present-day Oregon. *En route*, Lewis and Clark consistently encountered and interacted on more or less friendly terms with the region's many indigenous tribes. While, with genuine curiosity, the scientifically minded Jefferson commissioned the expedition to collect information on the West's native population, his eventual successor, the bellicose Andrew Jackson, although sometimes expressing sympathy for the land's indigenous inhabitants and a friendly desire "to reclaim them from their wandering habits and make them a happy, prosperous people," did not fret much in getting down to the business of their removal – of getting them out of the way of the white settlers. Jackson and most others agreed that the settlers, by dint of their superior race, Christian faith (with its presumed evangelizing and civilizing mission), and industriousness, had a rightful claim to whatever land, in the name of civilization and progress, they were willing to take and productively use. This was done in contravention of treaty rights that had been secured earlier by the Indians (to say nothing of their implicit prior ownership of the land), and by forced resettlement or outright slaughter (disease spread by the settlers continued to claim many Indian lives as well). Jackson's successor James K. Polk provoked a war with Mexico on a pretext, seizing most of the land that today comprises Texas, Arizona, New Mexico, Colorado, and California. As such, the "empire of liberty" had a clear complexion: it represented the spread of white settler democracy.[5] The status of slavery in the West was hotly disputed before the Civil War. And the claims to – or refusal of – full civic membership by the (former?) Mexicans, and Native Americans then resident in the region, along with similar claims by later waves of Asian immigrants, although seemingly confirmed by laws and treaties, was qualified, if not blatantly disregarded, by settlers and their government alike. But there was little in this to distract those committed to the task, who saw themselves as helping the United States fulfill its divine destiny by expanding westward by whatever means necessary, as John L. O'Sullivan put it, as *the great nation* of futurity."

The impulse to expansion raised questions about the relationship between the American "empire of liberty" and the other countries in the hemisphere – especially, as designs on Canada faded, those to the United States' south in Central and South America. From one perspective, the Monroe Doctrine (1823), forged by President James Monroe's Secretary of State, John Quincy Adams, offered itself as a grand anticolonial statement. Made during a wave of national independence struggles by Central and South Americans in revolt against their Spanish and Portuguese rulers, this policy declared the United States' commitment to enforcing non-interference of European powers in the internal affairs of western hemisphere countries. On the other hand, in pursuing, sometimes quite aggressively, this ostensibly magnanimous and principled commitment, the United States became deeply entangled *itself* with the internal affairs of those countries, raising once again the paradoxes of the country's ostensible commitment to liberal universalism.

Labor: Work and Slavery

Whether through the influence of the Puritan concept of each person having a divinely ordained "calling," of Lockean liberal understandings of freedom and responsibility, or the operation of other concrete practical forces, the concept of work – labor – has been unusually important to American political thought. In the late eighteenth century, in his *Letters from an American Farmer*, Crèvecoeur was already observing that: "Here the rewards of [the American's] industry follow with equal steps the progress of his labor; his labor is founded on the basis of nature, *self-interest;* can it want a stronger allurement?"

But across the first half of the nineteenth century, the context in which Americans labored was rapidly changing. The age of what Emerson described as "our turbulent freedom" was defined by an economic revolution that saw the rise of mills and factories, and the building of railroads, against a backdrop of political transformations wrought by westward expansion, widening suffrage, the elimination of state religious establishments, and mass immigration. In the Panic of 1837, the United States suffered the greatest economic downturn in its history (a record until the Great Depression of the 1930s). This meant catastrophic bankruptcies and an altogether new phenomenon: mass unemployment of a kind alien to Crèvecoeur's eighteenth-century world of independent farmers. This cataclysmic downturn sent swarms of poor people into almshouses barely able to care for them. All of these developments challenged Crèvecoeur's assumptions concerning perpetual abundance and cheerful self-reliance. At the same time, nevertheless, those views maintained a strong hold on the American imagination.

There soon arose critics of the dogmas of industrial capitalism, and of the (faux?) Christian lapdogs who had justified its excesses and predations. In *The Laboring Class* (1840), Orestes Brownson, a protean and prolific thinker, writer, and activist who, over the course of his life, made his way from Transcendentalism to conservative Roman Catholicism, began by lambasting Christian teaching that served the interests of the rich and powerful by training the eyes of the country's exploited working class toward heaven, steering them away, he argued, from the real problem: the underlying capitalist system. Anticipating Karl Marx and Friedrich Engels's *Communist Manifesto* (1848), Brownson, attentive to the contemporaneous English Chartist movement (1838–1857), denounced the ways in which capitalism exploited its workers, which he adjudged worse than slavery. A critical issue for Brownson was the rise of a new class of those who worked not for themselves, but for another: that is, for wages. He, like others after him – including Abraham Lincoln – was profoundly troubled by the way that wage labor made one dependent on another, in a manner that represented the very antithesis of then extant liberal and republican understandings of freedom, and vitiated the free men's broader dignity and humanity. Under such conditions, Brownson declared, class warfare was inevitable. He looked forward hopefully to an ultimate showdown that would end with the establishment of a political and economic system premised not on exploitation and abuse, but on genuine freedom and social justice. At the time Brownson was writing, a grassroots working-class/ labor radicalism was erupting, in a few places at least. These new radicals, singing "chants democratic" (Whitman), were campaigning against the depredations of wage labor under industrial capitalism, and demanding concrete reforms, including higher wages, the end of imprisonment for debt, and the ten-hour workday. While this movement saw the hoped-for class solidarity fractured by racial, sex, and ethnic divisions, and nativism, it nevertheless gestured toward new possibilities in working-class republicanism.[6]

It was hardly lost on antebellum Americans that chattel slavery – the ownership of human beings by other human beings, who set them to forced labor – was related somehow to the broader concerns that positioned a commitment to the free, independent laborer at the heart of the American political imagination. If wage labor was an abomination, what about unpaid, forced labor? These conundrums and contradictions twisted many Americans in knots, although more and more of them were thinking their way through to perfect clarity . . . on opposed sides.

One path through the thicket was provided by ascriptive identity. Although it had existed in many forms and guises through the ages, "the peculiar institution" in the United States was based on the concepts of race and chattels (i.e. only Africans and those of African ancestry were enslaved, and the

enslaved were legally categorized as the "chattels," or property, of the owner).
The work done by ascription was bi-modal. On one side, it defined the category
of those whose dignity, humanity, and freedom were of concern by their
race (the ever-changing category of what came to be known as "whiteness" –
this, too, was there in Crèvecoeur from the start, when he said of "this new
man," "the American," that "He is either an European, or the descendant of
an European"). On the other side, it defined enslaved Africans and those of
African descent as wholly outside of this circle of concern, whether because it
considered them an inferior or naturally incapacitated class of human being,
or as non-human (property), pure and simple.

   In the eighteenth century, many (white) Americans reflexively equated
being American with being of (Western) European ancestry. That said, claims
that Africans and those of African ancestry were inferior or non-human were,
at least for respected thinkers, ventured not proudly, but tentatively and provisionally. Large slaveholders like Washington, Jefferson, and Madison were
uneasy with slavery: they sometimes privately denounced it as an evil, or
offered embarrassed apologies for it. (In practicing chattel slavery, Jefferson
said, the United States was holding the "wolf by the ears." He added, "I tremble
for my country when I reflect that God is just.") Many, including Jefferson, considered slavery a fact on the ground, to which there was no obvious remedy.
Given the conditions in which they had held these millions of people, to end
the institution, many of the more vexed slave owners believed, would itself
lead to calamity, both for those freed from bondage, and for the country's
free white population alike. (Many spent years considering the possibilities of
expatriation to Africa via "colonization" societies.) The best hope that these
slaveholder elites could realistically muster was that this manifest evil would
somehow gradually wither away and die.

   To say these slaveholder founders were haunted or embarrassed by chattel
slavery – while continuing to practice and profit by it – is not to say that they
believed in the equality of races. While expressing the hope that science might
prove blacks the intellectual, physical, and moral equals of whites, Jefferson
noted that his own observations on the "natural differences" between the races
suggested that that prospect was, alas, unlikely. Other prominent founders
challenged these views. In a letter to John Jay (1779) concerning the possibility
of enlisting black soldiers in the American Revolution, Alexander Hamilton
suggested that the apparent inferiority of blacks had nothing to do with
nature ("their natural faculties are probably as good as ours"), and everything
to do with the environment and context in which they were held.

   Beginning in the 1820s, however – not coincidentally, as abolitionist voices
grew stronger, and a series of violent uprisings by enslaved peoples rocked the
South (most alarmingly, the aborted Denmark Vesey Rebellion in Charleston,
South Carolina in 1822, and the Nat Turner Rebellion of 1831, in which
fifty-nine white Virginians were killed) – a new cohort of southern think-

ers, including the Christian ministers and theologians Richard Furman and James Henley Thornwell, the historian, philosopher, and political economist Thomas Roderick Dew, the attorney and mathematician Albert Taylor Bledsoe, and the scientists Edmund Ruffin and Josiah Nott, began to defend slavery, not as a necessary evil, but as (variously) divinely ordained, natural, rational, sensible, and, indeed, a positive good for both owners and the enslaved alike.

One argument enlisted in the defense of slavery was that freedom was meant for people capable of *independence*. There were classes of people, however, who simply lacked the capacity to live and act independently. These people, it was said, were naturally *dependent* – like children. A related set of paternalistic arguments went on to argue that the ownership of slaves entailed a set of corresponding moral duties of masters to feed, clothe, and shelter their slaves – the same moral duties a parent would have for a child.

Many of the most prominent arguments, including some of the most prominent paternalist arguments, however, looked at the question through the prism of work or labor, and the broader capitalist economic system. No one was more systematic in defending chattel slavery on these grounds than the Virginia-born sociologist George Fitzhugh, whose pro-slavery *Sociology for the South* (1854) and *Cannibals All!* (1857) were imbricated within an elaborated critique of capitalism, and the inhumanity of economic markets. Such markets, Fitzhugh emphasized, had been pioneered and practiced most ruthlessly, not in the plantation South, but in the industrializing, market-and-finance capitalist North. The permanent revolution unleashed by capitalism and the liberal, individualistic, political philosophy that underwrote it, Fitzhugh argued, had disastrously laid waste to all traditional and social orders and hierarchies, and destroyed the organic communities that made richly sustaining human lives possible. (On this, at least, Orestes Brownson – coming from the Left – and Fitzhugh – coming from the Right – adamantly agreed.) Fitzhugh pronounced the North's system of ostensibly "free labor" capitalism to be anarchic, and more unjust and exploitative than southern slavery. Indeed, he insisted, society faced a choice between social arrangements that were either all-slave or all-"free." Fitzhugh argued strenuously for the former – which, he elaborated, would involve the enslavement of whites (and others) as well. In his broad and deep sociological critiques, Fitzhugh called upon Americans – and the world – to repudiate liberal individualism and restore what he held to be a more human and humane feudal order. The only truly natural right, Fitzhugh explained, is the right to be taken care of. And the enslaved, he asserted again and again, are taken care of, from cradle to grave, in sickness and in health. They were embraced within the bosom of a paternalistic system that attended to their needs, both when they worked, and when they did not. In this way, Fitzhugh argued, slaves actually got to keep more of what they produced than did northern factory workers. In the exploitative capitalist North, by contrast, you either work or starve. As such, most people actually had a human right to

be enslaved. Conversely, a small number of others, with the gift for organization and command, had the high responsibility to enslave them. Fitzhugh
declared the South's enslaved population "the happiest people in the world."
In his "Mudsill Speech" (1858), South Carolina Senator James Henry Hammond
added to Fitzhugh's argument that southern slaves were better off than free
northern workers by explaining that it was a great law of society, on display
most enticingly in the slave societies of ancient Greece and Rome, that there
be a "mudsill": a class of workers who do the lowest and basest but necessary
kinds of menial drudgery and dirty work, which freed up society's highest and
most refined members to think great thoughts and do great deeds – to move
civilization forward. As such, far from hindering civilization and progress,
chattel slavery advanced it.

Conclusion

Many students of American political thought, especially those who place
surpassing emphasis on its stirring eighteenth-century revolution and its
remarkable founders, posit a continuity in the thought, institutions, and
political, social, and economic context that extends from the nation's founding to what came after, in some cases right down to the present day. But
it was already obvious – including to many of the founders who outlived
the country's founding moment, and into the 1820s and 1830s – that major
developments were afoot from the moment the Constitution's ink was dry.

While the Constitution was relatively clear in setting out the basic structures, powers, and limits on the national (and, to a more limited extent, state)
government(s), and in articulating a set of core principles that breathed life
into the polity as a going political concern, it was also famously succinct. On
a number of major issues – particularly where disagreements in the founding
generation were pronounced or where it was assumed that ongoing evidence
and experience would instruct – the Constitution set clarity aside in favor of
broad wording, vagueness, euphemism, and omission. It was this Constitution
that was carried forward into the turbulent new country and century.

Almost immediately, key questions were raised about the relative powers of
the national government and the states, informed by new agitation concerning numerical majorities and minority rights. Antagonistic political parties
formed premised on an expanding white male franchise which wreaked havoc
on the presumption of elite governance and presumed social hierarchies. The
cotton gin was invented, and global industrialization and trade revolution-
ized an economy, extensively rooted in slave labor, that had formerly been
structured around subsistence farming and financial speculation in land and
slaves, and a commercial republic of small-scale merchants and artisans. Wage
labor became the wave of the future. The country rapidly expanded westward,

altering the distribution of power in the institutions of the national government. Fresh claims were made on behalf of the sovereign self. An evangelical Christian religious revival contributed to a wave of new reform movements that set their sights on righting wrongs and remedying grave injustices, including the nation's original sin of chattel slavery.

This, too, was America – if not of the founding, then of five minutes later. And the founders who lived to see it knew it. They and their successors – and the many others, in a mass democracy who butted in – fought, sometimes bitterly, over how to negotiate the challenges of continuity and change confronting any governing order with dynamic political, social, economic, and moral aspirations. In this, nothing was proving so ominous as slavery, which soon would lead the southern states to declare their secession from the American Union to form their own independent country – a challenge answered by President Lincoln and the North, which refused to let them go.

Questions

1. Antebellum America is commonly described as an age of mass democratization. If that is the case, how consistent was this development with the principles and institutions of the country's founding era, and before?
2. Was the establishment and institutionalization of the United States' two-party system inevitable? Was it a good thing or a blight on the country's future?
3. Which of the major parties in this period, the Democrats or the Whigs, were the "conservatives" and which were the "liberals"? Do either of these parties have enduring legacies in the present day?
4. How useful is John C. Calhoun's proposal to protect minority rights through the mechanism of a concurrent majority? Is this theory hopelessly tarred by Calhoun's enlistment of it in defending chattel slavery? Or is it a mechanism that might be productively considered today to protect minority rights? If not, what other mechanisms might be better suited to accomplishing that task?
5. Are the introduction of celebrations of the sovereign self and uncompromising moral commitments well suited to politics? Or are they better understood as problems?

4

Secession/Civil War/Reconstruction

The country's westward expansion, greatly enabled by the coups of Jefferson's Louisiana Purchase (1803) and James K. Polk's ginned-up Mexican–American War (1846–1848), was broadly popular as contributing to the fulfillment of the country's "manifest destiny" and an "empire of liberty." Many Americans, nevertheless, harbored misgivings about the role of westward expansion in opening up new fissures in the growing division over slavery. Would the new territories and states be slave or free? That determination, they knew, would not only affect the internal affairs of those states, but also most likely tip the precarious balance of power between slave and free states in the core institutions of the national government: Congress, the presidency, and the Supreme Court. The slave South looked to westward expansion as an opportunity to consolidate and extend the slave power. The free North, by contrast, looked to westward expansion as a means of, first, quarantining slavery within its original borders, and then ultimately overwhelming it by the admission of new states pledged to "free soil, free labor, and free men."[1] By the 1850s, the country was on a collision course.

Race, Slavery, and Natural Rights

John Locke's theory of limited government by consent committed to individual freedom under the rule of law began by positing that the sovereign individual was the rightful owner of his own body. Locke, put otherwise, started by holding that the individual, as a human being, had property in himself. In his *Second Treatise on Civil Government*, he argued that an individual, acting of his own free will, applied his bodily labor to the land (free labor), in the process productively improving it. In so doing, he created new value (the labor theory of value, entailing a producer ethic). The productive Lockean liberal individual then endeavored to protect what now he had a rightful claim to as his "property." He did so via the consensual establishment, in cooperation with others in the same situation, of a government pledged to the protection of this fundamental natural right, together with those of "life" and "liberty." Given the widespread Lockean presumption that each person has the natural right to the property of his own body, and hence to the fruits of his own labor, the slavery question cut to the core of American assumptions and understandings of liberal freedom. From the beginning, in one way or another, Americans were confronted with this fundamental contradiction between the country's professions to liberty under law and the on-the-ground reality of chattel slavery.

There were those who made short work of the contradiction by immediately declaring it blatant and egregious. Whether on Christian or other grounds, including natural rights, they often stridently stipulated that slavery was morally wrong and contravened basic American principles concerning liberty and equality. While such views were articulated from the country's inception, including by a number of its founders, however, they did not constitute a movement.

The coordinated and concerted mobilization to rid the United States of slavery began in earnest in the 1830s, when a critical mass of abolitionists began unleashing a fusillade of arguments and demands. Appeals to natural rights to liberty and equality as pre-political rights which no just government could transgress and which any just government must protect had been central to the American Revolution, whose rhetoric frequently posited slavery (the concept) as the antonym of liberty. If men and women naturally loved *liberty*, abolitionists argued, were not America's enslaved peoples men and women as well? Other abolitionists emphasized the principle of *equality* (although liberty and equality, in this context, were not mutually exclusive). Equality arguments trained their attention on the ascriptive subordination of entire classes of people (blacks, women) as egregious violations of the natural rights principle that "all men are created equal."

Some advanced republican arguments that slavery degraded the slave and the master alike. Far from cultivating within him the civic virtues so important to a free, democratic polity, slavery schooled the slave owner in the habits of tyranny and oppression. Others made economic arguments that slavery was a backward and inefficient mode of production doomed to obsolescence unless it was artificially, and pointlessly, preserved. Frederick Douglass argued that slavery cultivated habits of laziness and idleness in masters that were insalubrious in an aspiring commercial republic.

Many abolitionists appealed to Christian convictions concerning brotherly love and affection – to a common humanity. They argued that slavery starkly transgressed both natural and divine law: as human beings, the enslaved, too, were made by and in the image of God. As such, tacit approval and support for slavery – complicity – was an abominable sin and shame. Echoing the strict Puritan insistence upon individual and communal moral purity – a moralistic sensibility still evident today in many American reform movements – calls went out to Christians to cleanse themselves of this blackest of sins.

> No man in America has ever stood up so persistently and effectively for the dignity of human nature, knowing himself for a man, and the equal of any and all governments. In that sense he was the most American of all of us. . . . He could not have been tried by a jury of his peers, because his peers did not exist.
>
> Henry David Thoreau, "A Plea for Captain John Brown" (1859)

(The call was heeded by the Christian zealot John Brown, whose raid on the federal armory at Harper's Ferry, Virginia in 1859 was meant as the first step towards launching an armed uprising by the enslaved Brown – who was soon tried and hanged – issued a fiery call to his fellow Americans "to purge this land with blood.") Many abolitionists warned ominously that, should the nation continue to sanction the enslavement of human beings, divine retribution would inevitably follow.

Humanitarian arguments by abolitionists challenged paternalistic accounts that had cheerily testified that the South's enslaved peoples lived in a Southern idyll. Sure, the slaves worked hard. But, it was said, they were well treated and had all their basic needs met. All in all, they had things pretty good – as recognized and appreciated by the happy, smiling, shucking, singing slaves themselves (whose lives they caricatured in story, song, and minstrel shows). Abolitionist writers hit back hard against these purported facts. In *Slavery As It Is* (1839), Theodore Dwight Weld published a devastating exposé of slavery by reprinting thousands of ads for runaway slaves, and otherwise documenting the institution's pervasive cruelty and inhumanity. Weld focused in particular on the traumatic breakup of slave families, which were also recounted in a wave of newly published slave narratives in which formerly enslaved people directly related their personal experiences of excruciating and barbaric cruelty, and, sometimes, of miraculous escapes. In his autobiographical *Narrative* (1845), Frederick Douglass wrote of the horrors of being brutally whipped. Sojourner Truth (1850), enslaved in New York's Hudson Valley, testified to the almost unendurable agony she had suffered when her beloved son was sold South. The former Virginia slave Henry "Box" Brown (1849) recounted the miraculous story of how he seized his own freedom by mailing himself in a box to abolitionists in Philadelphia. The melodramatic novel *Uncle Tom's Cabin* (1852) by Harriet Beecher Stowe, a white New England abolitionist from a family of prominent Christian ministers, was perhaps the most widely influential of all in conveying slavery's horrors to a mass audience: it was the bestselling novel in the nineteenth-century United States and, behind the Bible, the country's second bestselling book of any kind. *Uncle Tom's Cabin* tugged at the nation's heartstrings by humanizing enslaved people. Through the device of fiction, it invited its readers to enter into the hearts and minds of the novel's characters, and thus identify with them as they suffered slavery's monumental terrors and cruelties.

Slavery and Union

Those who believed slavery to be a crime against humanity held a spectrum of views on what should be done about it. Some, including Abraham Lincoln, called for quarantining the wicked institution within the states where it already existed. This position allowed them both to voice their conviction that slavery was profoundly wrong and to affirm their continued allegiance to the original constitutional bargain that had incorporated protections for the autonomy of the states in governing their "domestic institutions," including slavery. In one of his storied debates on the slavery question with Stephen A. Douglas in his losing campaign for a US Senate seat from Illinois (the Lincoln–Douglas Debates, 1858), Lincoln expressed his hope that this approach would place slavery "in the course of ultimate extinction." Others, however, took a more radical position demanding its immediate eradication. Some of these abolitionists were quick to agree with their more moderate compatriots that the original constitutional bargain had afforded critical protections for the chattel slavery. But, unlike the latter, far from implying any duty of fidelity, they held this fact to be a damning – indeed, fatal – black mark on the Constitution itself: in a July 4, 1854, rally sponsored by the Massachusetts Anti-Slavery Society where he was joined on the stage by Sojourner Truth and Henry David Thoreau, William Lloyd Garrison set fire to a copy of the Constitution, denouncing the wicked charter as "an agreement with Death and a covenant with Hell."

Today, many celebrate the abolitionists as far-sighted heroes and peerless moral champions. This is not how they were looked on in their own time by most Americans, however, even by many critical of chattel slavery. Abolitionists like Garrison were regarded as inflammatory troublemakers. Many took them to be hell-bent on flouting the Constitution, and destroying the Union. In his "Letter to the Public" in the first issue of *The Liberator* (1831), Garrison himself noted "that many object to the severity of my language." Given the nature of his cause, however, Garrison defiantly declaimed, "I will be as harsh as truth, and as uncompromising as justice. On this subject, I do not wish to think, or speak, or write, with moderation. . . . I am in earnest – I will not equivocate – I will not excuse – I will not retreat a single inch – AND I WILL BE HEARD."

In this, Garrison plainly succeeded: the abolitionist movement found itself at the center of an array of political vectors and vortexes concerning the status of slavery within the broader political and constitutional order. The slavery question, for instance, was implicated in broader political debates arising out of the country's sectionalism. It was said that the Constitution had been adopted to secure the common good, without regard to special or particular interests. Thomas Jefferson's embargo (1807), instituted in response to abuse of American shipping and sailors on the high seas by Britain and France in their ongoing global war, had provoked a fierce backlash by New England Federalists – heavily involved in and dependent on international trade. Further provoked by President Madison's even more draconian embargo during the War of 1812, the New England States, meeting at the Hartford Convention, seriously considered seceding from the Union. Subsequently, and even more ominously, the South contended that its economic interests were being systematically disregarded by federal policy decisions involving the Bank of the United States, federally sponsored internal improvements, and the tariff. Without a means of protecting those interests through mechanisms like John C. Calhoun's proposed concurrent majority, politicians like Calhoun and Jefferson Davis of Mississippi were starting to suggest that it might not be in their states' interest to continue as members of the federal union.

Southern thinkers often framed these issues as implicating questions of the nature of and fidelity to the original constitutional compact. At the heart of these understandings was the theory that the Constitution was properly conceptualized as a compact among sovereign states. This compact theory of union had been continually and vigorously challenged from the beginning by the likes of John Marshall, Daniel Webster, and others, who advanced an opposed "one people" theory of an indissoluble union entered into by one singular, sovereign political body, acting collectively as "We the People." As sectional antagonisms heated up over an array of issues, articulations of the compact theory of union grew louder and more adamant. One of the major claims was that the original constitutional bargain had provided express protections for chattel slavery. The rival "one people" versus "compact" theories of union were soon drawn into the question both of who gets to judge whether the Constitution was being honored when the federal government either acted or failed to act, and, if it was held to have been dishonored, who was authorized to do something about it. This context and framing meant that the growing sectional tensions over slavery were contested not simply on the grounds of the rightness or wrongness of slavery *per se*, but also as disputes over regional and sectional interests, and the respective constitutional powers of the national government and the states.

Article I of the Constitution had created a national government of enumerated powers, with all residual powers lodged in the states. This meant that most of the day-to-day powers of governance in the United States, including the "police powers" to issue regulations concerning health, safety, and morals, and broad legal control over "domestic institutions" (including crime, families, property, contracts, civil injuries – torts – and other such matters), were reserved to the states. While it may have seemed clear to some – certainly to the Federalists – that, pursuant to a constitutive act of "We the People," the sovereign power of the new nation was lodged squarely in the national government, it seemed equally clear to others that, in the end, and on many issues of major significance, sovereignty (still) ultimately resided in the states.

Although it never used the word, the Constitution plainly envisaged slavery: the Constitution's scheme of representation in Congress counted "free persons . . . three-fifths of all other persons." What we call the Fugitive Slave Clause stated that "No Person held to Service or Labour in one State, under the Laws thereof, escaping into another, shall . . . be discharged from such

Service or Labour, but shall be delivered up on Claim of the Party to whom such Service or Labour may be due." The Constitution had also approved the continuation of the slave trade until 1807 ("the importation of such persons as any of the states now existing shall think proper to admit"). Without this provision, the slave trade's future would have otherwise been left to Congress.

President Jefferson's embargo, internal improvements, the Bank, and the tariff all led to serious constitutional disputes, often with a strong sectionalist tinge. In one way or another, these ultimately played themselves out, and were resolved. Instead of being fought and settled through ordinary – if, at times, tense – political bargaining like these other issues, however, sectional contention over slavery only got worse over time, since the stakes were repeatedly raised, and the ante upped, with every new demographic, economic, and geographic change, as the country expanded westward. It was hoped the Missouri Compromises (1820/1821) would quell contention over slavery, as had other hard-fought bargains and settlements concerning the embargo or the tariff. But instead the slavery issue heated up. In this regard, the moral denunciations hurled by the abolitionists at the South didn't help. In addition to resenting the charges of barbarism directed their way, southerners were concerned that the abolitionists were launching a full-scale assault on their constitutional rights, and, to make matters worse, with their talk of moral and natural rights, inciting their slaves to perhaps murderous revolt.

These tensions were implicated in the fugitive slave question. Beginning in the 1820s, but more extensively in the wake of the Supreme Court's decision in *Prigg v. Pennsylvania* (1842), northern and western states began to enact "personal liberty laws" that made it harder for southern slave owners to recapture what they regarded as their escaped chattels. These laws enraged southerners, who considered them a flagrant violation of their constitutional rights. When the Fugitive Slave Act of 1850 was passed to try to reinforce (as southerners saw it) the original bargain on this matter, it was northerners' turn to be outraged: the new law actually required them (and the federal government) to directly assist in the recapture of runaway slaves, personally implicating them in what they took to be a great evil, leading to the passage of even more draconian personal liberty legislation across the North and West. The ongoing expansion westward repeatedly raised the question of the status of slavery in each newly acquired territory and newly admitted state. Contention over the constitutional status of slavery led to the founding of the new Republican Party, and the political ascendency of the ex-Whig, now Republican, Abraham Lincoln.

Abraham Lincoln's Political Thought

The Springfield, Illinois, lawyer Abraham Lincoln was neither an abolitionist nor a thoroughgoing egalitarian. Although his views evolved over the course of his life, Lincoln began with the firm ascriptive conviction that African-Americans were socially and culturally inferior to white people. He opposed race mixing, and was horrified and disgusted by the possibility of racial amalgamation: he believed whites and blacks should be kept apart. These views informed Lincoln's opposition to the spread of slavery to the country's newly acquired western territories and states. Like Lincoln, many white Americans looked to this land as a place where poor but ambitious whites could migrate and start anew as independent men productively mixing their labor with the land to better their condition. These views were also behind Lincoln's early support for the repatriation of blacks back to Africa. The intensely ambitious politician, moreover, believed – rightly – that the overwhelming majority of white Americans basically saw things the same way. Despite all this, Lincoln was nevertheless adamant from the outset that African-Americans were human beings, and that that meant something. Under Lincoln's understanding of Lockean liberal premises, as human beings, African-Americans were entitled to the full recognition of their natural rights and, in turn, to equal (positive) legal and constitutional rights. Among their natural and constitutional rights was the right to work freely, and to secure the fruits of their own labor – to earn their own keep by the sweat of their brow.

Lincoln's complexities have made him a singular figure in American history. Ever since his assassination by a southern sympathizer after his issuance of the Emancipation Proclamation (1863) and only days after Confederate General Robert E. Lee's surrender to Union General Ulysses S. Grant at Appomattox Courthouse, Virginia (1865), sealing the Union's victory in the Civil War, Lincoln has entered history as much myth and symbol as ordinary man. Born in a log cabin on the backwoods Kentucky frontier, and self-educated by reading the Bible, Shakespeare, and Plutarch by lamplight, he is taken as personifying the Lockean liberal up-by-your-own bootstraps, self-made man success stories that seem hard-baked into the American mind. Martyred by his assassination (and elegized by perhaps the country's greatest poet, Walt Whitman, in "When Lilacs Last in the Dooryard Bloomed," 1865), at the moment the Thirteenth Amendment (1865) he championed ended slavery, Lincoln is also mythologized as a Christ-like figure who died redeeming the nation's sins. Others, by contrast, have cast him, variously, as a shrewdly opportunistic politician who vacillated on slavery and harbored the same racist sentiments common in his time, or as a ruthlessly millennialist moralizer, a radical egalitarian, a would-be dictator, and an authoritarian, big-government centralizer.

Lincoln first made a name for himself nationally during his aforementioned losing campaign for the Illinois US Senate seat (1858) against Stephen A. Douglas, where he displayed prodigious talents as an eloquent yet plainspoken orator, and showed himself to be a major voice on the slavery question. In accepting the Republican Party's nomination for the Senate seat, Lincoln was convinced that, as an institution, slavery required expansion in order to survive. As such, he was convinced, the slave power aimed to make slavery national. But, borrowing from the Gospels, Lincoln boldly declared that "A house divided against itself cannot stand." Seven remarkable campaign debates with Douglas on the constitutional status of slavery propelled Lincoln into the national spotlight, and ultimately underwrote his bid less than two years later for the Republican nomination for President (1860).

Over the course of these debates, Lincoln proclaimed a hatred of slavery, which he pronounced in patent violation of the natural rights that Jefferson, borrowing from Locke, had declared in the creedal Declaration of Independence (1776) that governments were instituted among men to protect. That great charter of liberty and equality, Lincoln emphasized, reaffirmed abstract universal truths "applicable to all men and at all times" that had provided the foundation for the American Revolution – even if, given the tragic compromises the founders had been forced to make in light of the on-the-ground realities, the country had yet to fully realize those revolutionary ideals. Countering Chief Justice Roger Brooke Taney's notorious claim in *Dred Scott v. Sanford* (1857) the year before, Lincoln insisted that the natural rights language of the Declaration had been meant to apply, without regard to race, to all human beings.

At the core of the slavery issue as Lincoln understood it was the inherent dignity of labor. We are all commanded by nature to labor, and, as such, the earth rightly belongs to the rational and the industrious. Slavery was objectionable in the first instance because it allowed some to be idle while they robbed others of the fruits of their labor. Lincoln additionally argued that labor was inherently dignified. The abomination of slavery perversely recast it as something low and degraded. The nobility of free labor gave men the opportunity to better their condition through the acquisition and productive use of property. By this dignified industriousness, men could successfully compete in the "race of life" by working their way up from the humblest of conditions, to prosper and, perhaps, even become rich. All men, black or white, were entitled to this great chance as a fundamental human right.

As the country's political economy was changing in disorienting ways around him, Lincoln acknowledged that men might begin in a dependent state – working for wages for another. But (dependent) wage labor should and would be only a temporary condition – a way-station on the road to self-employed independence. The promise of America was that no man was set in a fixed, dependent position: for those who worked, the economic trajectory of freedom and equality pointed indubitably upward. God meant for men to rise. Slavery set itself in opposition to this plan.

However monstrous an injustice slavery was in the eyes of God – Lincoln

> The prudent, penniless beginner in the world, labors for wages awhile, saves a surplus with which to buy tools or land, for himself; then labors on his own account another while, and at length hires another new beginner to help him. . . . If any continue through life in the condition of the hired laborer, it is not the fault of the system, but because of either a dependent nature which prefers it, or improvidence, folly, or singular misfortune.
> Abraham Lincoln (1859)

wondered whether the bloody war was a sign of divine retribution – far from calling for its abolition in the states where it already existed, as protected by state laws and the federal Constitution, the careful lawyer Lincoln insisted simply, but firmly, that, henceforth, it not be extended one inch further. Nothing in the original constitutional agreement, the foundation of the indissoluble Union that he cherished, Lincoln maintained, required any more than this.

> [A]n increasing hostility on the part of the non-slaveholding States to the institution of slavery, has led to a disregard of their obligations. . . . [T]he constituted compact has been broken and disregarded by the non-slaveholding States, and the consequence follows that South Carolina is released from her obligation.
>
> South Carolina Ordinance of Secession (1860)

Having expressed these convictions before and during his campaign for the White House, Lincoln was elected in a sectional four-way split, in which he won only 39% of the popular vote, and did not receive a single southern vote in the Electoral College. Upon his election, seven states in the deep South almost immediately seceded from the Union, and four others soon joined them. Targeted from the moment of his election for assassination, Lincoln had to take great care in making his way from Illinois to Washington, DC, where he was sworn into office on March 4, 1861. On April 12, 1861, South Carolina fired on the US fort in the harbor in Charleston. The "War Between the States" had begun.

Lincoln declared the South's would-be secession unconstitutional, and refused to allow it, casting the Civil War as a war not to end slavery but for the preservation of the Union. He reminded Americans, not least in the opening lines of his Gettysburg Address (1863), that the nation was both older than the Constitution and perpetual. In seceding, the southern states had recurred to both the compact theory of Union and Calhoun's theories concerning the rights of political minorities. In his First Inaugural Address (1861), Lincoln acknowledged that the Constitution was ambiguous on the key constitutional disputes that had divided the states, like the status of slavery in the territories. Given that ambiguity, he reasoned, either the majority or the minority view must prevail. Lincoln declared Calhoun's theory of the right to a minority veto a recipe for minority rule. This was an affront to the foundational principles of democracy. It was, moreover, a recipe for anarchy, as it would embolden a diverse, and perhaps endless, succession of political minorities to thwart the political majority's duly considered will. Ambiguities notwithstanding, what the Constitution had clearly envisaged, Lincoln insisted, was that slavery would be protected in the states where it already existed. Despite his fervent moral objections to slavery, Lincoln attested, he would hold fast to the terms of the constitutional compact. Beyond that, however, the national government had the power, and the duty, to enforce the policy on the matter that it had determined to be both best for the country and most consistent with its most cherished values. Lincoln thought this was a fair position. He understood it as manifesting a willingness to meet the Slave South halfway. The South thought otherwise: fired by years of anxieties, fears, and warnings, and genuine concerns about demographic and geographic change portending a new balance of power in the national government, the region was in no mood for this sort of reassurance, or any sort of compromise over what its white denizens held to be their fundamental rights as property-holding individuals, and as states.

Lincoln did not scruple in doing what he believed necessary to save the Union. His wartime presidency repeatedly raised questions about the role of emergency or necessity in potentially altering the limits on government – and especially executive – power. As President under exigent circumstances, Lincoln stretched the meaning of the Constitution: he declared martial law, expanded the size of the army without congressional approval, and suspended the writ of habeas corpus. Answering charges by northerners and southerners alike that many of his wartime measures entailed egregious constitutional transgressions, Lincoln offered a sophisticated, step-wise response. The rebellion threatened the nation's very survival, he noted. As such, the rebellion was a menace to each and every law enacted under the nation's authority, including the fundamental law of the Constitution. Yes, he may have violated some laws, he conceded, but when he did so – when he had no other choice but to do so – he did so to the minimum extent possible. And he did so, not out of selfish or partisan motivations, but with the nation's preservation as his first and only consideration. "Are all the laws but one to go unexecuted and the government itself go to pieces lest that one be violated?" This, Lincoln submitted, failed the test of common sense. It failed to meet the threat to the very survival of the country which, by the oath he had sworn to "preserve, protect, and defend" the Constitution, he insisted he had the high responsibility to ensure.

A New Birth of Freedom? Equality and Union after Slavery

The Union victory in the Civil War and the subsequent military occupation of the South raised fraught questions of both the moment and the future. Having seceded from the Union and announced the creation of a new, independent country, and having attacked and waged war on the United States, and then been resoundingly defeated, what now would be the political and constitutional status of this reconquered region? The issue was extensively and bitterly debated. In the firm control of the fiery anti-slavery Radical Republicans, Congress was often at loggerheads with a White House that was initially occupied by Abraham Lincoln, but then, following his assassination, by the intransigent and inept southern Unionist Andrew Johnson, whom Lincoln had chosen to balance the ticket.

Both Congress and the White House agreed that the national government would formally abolish slavery by constitutional amendment (the Thirteenth), everywhere and forever, a denouement in which the conquered South acquiesced. Beyond that, however, nothing was clear. The initial debates over Reconstruction focused, first, on the political and constitutional status of the defeated confederate states, and, second, on the conditions for their reincorporation into the United States.

A number of Radical Republicans insisted that in announcing their secession from the Union and in waging war on the United States, the southern states had forfeited any of their claims as states, and had reverted to the status of conquered territories. As such, they were now rightfully under the total control of their military occupiers, who were free to reorganize them into new states on whatever terms seemed most fit. Others essentially accepted the geographic continuity of the southern states, but neither the legitimacy of their treasonous governments, nor the civic status of the traitors who had led or supported them. Going forward, the federal government – with the Congress, and not the President, in the driver's seat – had to firmly control this region, either directly or through the establishment of loyal state reconstruction governments. At the forefront of Congress's concerns under the Joint Committee on Reconstruction – which was dominated by Republicans, and led by Thaddeus Stevens – was the status of the four million formerly enslaved people who, as Stevens underlined, had been liberated "without a hut to shelter them or a cent in their pockets." Stevens declared that: "This Congress is bound to provide for them until they can take care of themselves. If we do not furnish them with homesteads, and hedge them around with protective laws; if we leave them to the legislation of their late masters, we had better have left them in bondage." What followed in the period we call Reconstruction (1865–1877) was a wave of ambitious legislation that endeavored to assume these responsibilities: the establishment of the Freedman's Bureau providing extensive direct aid such as food, clothing, health care, work, legal assistance, and schools; the Civil Rights Act of 1866 guaranteeing basic rights to make and enforce contracts, sue and be sued, give evidence in court, and inherit, purchase, lease, sell, hold, and convey real and personal property, without regard to race; the Enforcement Acts (1870–1871) giving the federal government criminal enforcement powers to prevent state and local discrimination in voting, office-holding, jury service, and other denials of the equal protection of the laws on account of race; and the Civil Rights Act of 1875 outlawing racial discrimination in, among other things, privately owned public accommodations, transportation, and places of amusement. The agrarian reform/land redistribution that Stevens hinted at – for example, the provision of homesteads (the "forty acres and a mule" promised by Union General William Tecumseh Sherman in Special Field Order No. 15 of 1865, approved by Abraham Lincoln) – saw fledgling, but soon aborted, beginnings.

All of this met staunch resistance from the white South, including from the white Tennessean in the White House, setting Reconstruction on a path to a succession of pitched battles both between the national government and hostile elements of the white South and, at the national level, between Congress and the President. One understandable but problematic desire expressed by many, including Lincoln, after the end of chattel slavery and the carnage of war was to return to normal as quickly as possible. This, in effect, meant military withdrawal, and the return to home rule by the southern states. As a practical matter, this entailed leniency to the formerly disloyal, and a quick return to their ordinary civic and political status. It soon became apparent, however, that upon the return of that status, white southerners intended to re-establish white supremacist rule: almost immediately, they enacted the notorious Black Codes (1865–1866) instituting restrictions on movement requiring written authorization to be present in a public place; established mandatory and coercive (black) youth "apprenticeship" programs; aggressively enforced criminal prohibitions against "impudence" (e.g. swearing, insufficient deference to white people), idleness (unemployment), and vagrancy (being in a public place with no apparent purpose), which were used to enlist African-Americans in a "convict" labor system; and adopted contracts for work that left blacks perpetually in debt, and thus effectively conscripted in a system of perpetual debt peonage (the basis as well for the South's emerging sharecropping, tenant farmer agricultural system). Violence and terror, both informal and organized (the Ku Klux Klan, 1865), visited swift retribution on any blacks who sought to exercise even their (ostensibly) newly protected civil and political rights, or who in any way stepped out of line socially.

These efforts to re-establish white supremacy and, indeed, return southern blacks to slavery in everything but name were undertaken in open defiance of the principles of Reconstruction, including Radical Reconstruction. This resistance, in turn, provoked a federal response with additional legislation designed to meet the challenge. Most of those efforts ran headlong into President Johnson, who vetoed, among other things, the Freedman's Bureau Act and the Civil Rights Act of 1866; revoked Special Field Order No. 15; and acted (in the teeth of congressional legislation meant to prevent it) to remove holdover members of his cabinet from the Lincoln administration, whom he deemed too favorably inclined to blacks, and to the Reconstruction Congress, and insufficiently aligned with his preferences. Johnson's vetoes, in turn, sparked their own backlash, including the election of a landslide, veto-proof Radical Reconstructionist Congress. This ended with Johnson's impeachment. While the vote to remove him from office fell one vote short, from then on he was effectively sidelined. The office of the presidency was taken out of the picture until the more sympathetic Republican head of the Union Army, General Ulysses S. Grant, was elected as Johnson's successor (1869–1877).

As the bid for "restoration" fueled by a white supremacist southern nationalism played out, some of the major lines of contention were constitutional. The argument was that the actions taken by the federal government in pursuit of Reconstruction transcended the national government's constitutional powers and trenched upon the rightful constitutional authority of the states. These objections appealed to "the Constitution as it was." The argument was that, while the Thirteenth Amendment had banned chattel slavery, it otherwise left intact the basic structures of American constitutional government – including the wide scope afforded to the governments of the states. Slavery aside, southerners insisted, nothing essential had changed. By these lights, states remained free to pass whatever laws they wanted concerning property, contracts, labor, crime control, voting – or most any local police powers regulation free from federal supervision or interference.

Northern Republicans insisted they had the constitutional authority to pass the Reconstruction program. But they recognized that that program had undertaken some novel departures for which the constitutional authority was arguable. In response, they spearheaded the addition of two additional amendments to the Constitution. While the Thirteenth Amendment (1865) had abolished "slavery" and "involuntary servitude" ("except as a punishment for crime whereof the party shall have been duly convicted"), it did not provide sufficient authority to meet the rearguard resistance already emerging in the white South. Accordingly, the Fourteenth Amendment (1868) provided that: (1) "[a]ll persons born or naturalized in the United States" were citizens of the United States, and of the states in which they lived; and that (2) "[n]o State shall make or enforce any law which shall abridge the privileges or immunities of citizens of the United States"; "nor shall any State deprive any person of life, liberty, or property, without due process of law"; "nor deny to any person within its jurisdiction the equal protection of the laws." Concerned about the future political power of both the new freedman and those who would defend their fledgling status as free and equal citizens, the Fourteenth Amendment additionally, first, provided that all persons be counted as full persons (rather than, for slaves, as three-fifths of a person) for purposes of representation; second, reduced representation when the right to vote of free male inhabitants was denied or abridged; third, stripped those who had engaged in insurrection and rebellion from holding federal offices (i.e. among other things, from serving in Congress); and, fourth, forbade the assumption or payment of "any debt or obligation incurred in aid of insurrection or rebellion against the United States, or any claim for the loss or emancipation of any slave." The Amendment added that: "The Congress shall have the power to enforce, by appropriate legislation, the provisions of this article." The Fifteenth Amendment (1870), in turn, provided that "The right of citizens . . . to vote shall not be denied or abridged . . . on account of race, color, or previous condition of servitude," and gave Congress similar powers to enforce its provisions.

These Civil War (or "Reconstruction") Amendments raised vexing questions about the degree to which the fundamental rules and nature of the political order had been altered by the national cataclysm. Many historians and constitutional scholars argue that, after the Civil War and the adoption of the Civil War Amendments, the United States henceforth lived under what was, in essence, a new constitutional regime or order – one that was more national, less de-centralized, with new mechanisms put in place for rights protection that fundamentally altered those that had been theorized by the eighteenth-century founders and had formed the axis of discussion in the Federalist–Antifederalist debates over the Constitution's adoption. Some argue, moreover, that the processes unleashed by the war and its aftermath, and the new government powers – indeed, responsibilities – outlined in the Civil War Amendments fundamentally altered the relationship between the national government and the states, elevating the powers and respon-sibilities of the former at the deliberate expense of the latter. The matter remains unresolved to this day, and is often, sometimes subtly, at the core of many contemporary constitutional theories and debates.

These were not purely abstract debates. As had been the case in the immedi-ate aftermath of the adoption of the initial Constitution in 1789, arguments over what the Civil War meant, and promised, concerning government powers and the country's creedal principles were soon implicated in a succession of real-world political controversies and campaigns. Although slavery had been officially abolished, the struggle between claims of white supremacy versus racial equality and, in close relation, the claims of the constitutional powers of the states (to reinstate white supremacy) and the national government (to overturn it) continued through Reconstruction, on into the twentieth century and, arguably, right down to the present. In other areas one degree removed from the race question, however, new understandings of liberty, equality, democracy, and the powers of government had been unleashed, and soon took flight.

A succession of reform movements appealed to the moral and political ideals that had become so central to the Civil War. In his great speech at Gettysburg mourning the battle's Union dead, to take a prominent instance, Lincoln described the nation as having been "conceived in liberty, and dedi-cated to the proposition that all men are created equal." Expressing the solemn hope that the Battle of Gettysburg's "honored dead . . . shall not have died in vain," Lincoln called upon the nation to re-dedicate itself to its revolutionary principles, with the hope "that this nation, under God, shall have a new birth of freedom; and that government of the people, by the people, and for the people, shall not perish from the earth."

Among the first to appeal to the war as having initiated "a new birth of freedom" were advocates of women's rights, many, if not most, of whom had been staunch abolitionists and, even long before the war, as we have seen, had named and set themselves against what they took to be the kindred denials of natural rights to liberty and equality on the basis of race and sex. The Fourteenth Amendment provided in abstract terms for birthright citizenship, and guarantees for citizens' privileges and immunities. It also promised to all persons national guarantees for fundamental rights to life, liberty, and property, and the equal protection of the laws. But, in a development that infuriated feminists, for the first time (in its provisions for the apportionment of representatives) the Constitution expressly described certain of its guarantees as applying exclusively to males. While abolitionist women had demanded that the proposed Fifteenth Amendment include a prohibition on ascriptive denial of the right to vote on account of sex, moreover, it provided only that "The right of citizens ... to vote shall not be denied or abridged by the United States or by any State on account of race, color, or previous condition of servitude." Because of these failings, some feminists opposed the ratification of these two amendments on principle. But others, including Frederick Douglass, had practical concerns. This was "the negro's hour" (ignoring, as some pointed out, that half of the manumitted African-Americans were women), Douglass argued, and adding such controversial language at this critical moment would be dangerously counterproductive. For many of the era's feminists, this denial was a rank injustice. Appealing to universal principles of natural rights enshrined in the Declaration of Independence, as reaffirmed by Lincoln, and vindicated by the Union victory in the war, women's rights advocates launched a campaign demanding the right to vote.

Declaring "my sex are entitled to the inalienable right to life, liberty and the pursuit of happiness," Victoria Woodhull began lobbying Congress on behalf of women's suffrage. "[O]ur laws are false to the principles which we profess," she insisted. Woodhull went on to compare the oppressions, exclusions, and disparate treatment of women in the United States to slavery and tyranny – declaring them, indeed, "a tyranny *more* odious than that which, being rebelled against, gave this country independence." Legally barred from voting on the grounds of her sex, Susan B. Anthony, who, with others, had founded the National Women's Suffrage Association (NWSA) in 1869, insisted on casting a vote in the presidential election of 1872 (in which Ulysses S. Grant was re-elected). Anthony was criminally prosecuted. During her trial, in defiance of the judge, who struggled to maintain order in the courtroom, she delivered an incendiary speech to the jury denouncing her exclusion for "trampl[ing] underfoot every vital principle of our government. My natural rights, my civil rights, my political rights, are all alike ignored. ... I am degraded from the status of citizen to that of a subject." For good measure, in Thoreau-ian defiance, she added that "I shall never pay a dollar of your unjust penalty." The following year, citing natural differences between women and men that justified consigning them legally and politically to separate spheres, the Supreme Court turned away a Fourteenth Amendment challenge to an Illinois law barring women from practicing law.[2]

Other reformers looked to the "new birth of freedom" hailed by Lincoln at Gettysburg as entailing a recommitment to republican liberty, to "government of the people, by the people, and for the people." This meant to them that the people, acting together in their sovereign capacity as civic equals, were possessed of the power to enact legislation that would obliterate concentrations of economic power that had reduced ordinary people to the positions of subservience and dependence. In such an order, rather than being treated as civic equals, they were being illegitimately ruled and exploited. In this, the Granger (or farmers') movement led the way, squaring off against the consolidation of monopoly power by railroads, banks, and grain elevators.

The very first case in which the Supreme Court interpreted the Thirteenth and Fourteenth Amendments involved neither the rights of African-Americans nor the powers of the federal government to advance them, but rather Louisiana's establishment of a butcher's monopoly in New Orleans. In the *Slaughterhouse Cases* (1873), a Supreme Court stuffed with Lincoln and Grant appointees divided sharply over the implications of both the Civil War and its attendant amendments. Speaking through Justice Samuel Miller, the Court's majority upheld the Louisiana economic regulation on the grounds that, constitutionally, even after the war and ratification of the new amendments providing national guarantees for basic rights, the states still had a wide berth to exercise their police powers as they saw fit to promote health, safety, and morals in service of the broader public interest. The Civil War and the amendments, Miller explained, were about "the freedom of the slave race, the security and firm establishment of that freedom, and the protection of the newly-made freeman and citizen from the oppressions of those who had formerly exercised unlimited dominion over him." Any more expansive holding in cases involving constitutional rights claims more generally would transform the Supreme Court – after all, a national government institution – into "a perpetual censor upon all legislation of the states." Those who, in the aftermath of "events, almost too recent to be called history, but which are familiar to us all," had framed the Civil War amendments, the Court's majority were convinced, had aimed to protect the former slaves, not to work a revolution in the structure of American government.

The Court's dissenters strenuously disagreed. For Justices Stephen Field, Joseph Bradley, and Salmon Chase, the Civil War and the Civil War Amendments had not emphasized the republican, democratic claims of popularly elected state legislatures (and their city government subdivisions, like New Orleans) to legislate to advance the public interest. They were aimed at hemming in the scope of the legislative and regulatory powers of states and localities by providing newly vigorous legal protections of individual rights. Among those rights, the dissenters insisted, were the rights of butchers "to pursue a lawful and necessary calling." As the *Slaughterhouse* dissenters saw it, the Civil War had worked a substantive and procedural revolution in rights protection. From here on out, the federal courts were charged with aggressively policing rights violations. And if that meant more power to courts generally vis-à-vis legislatures, and more power for the national government (via the rulings of the federal judiciary) vis-à-vis the states, then so be it. The war had plainly had these radical implications. To read the Fourteenth Amendment to favor elected majorities in the states facing challenges under-written by constitutional rights claims would be, Justice Field thundered, to render that Amendment "a vain and idle enactment, which accomplished nothing, and most unnecessarily excited Congress and the people on its passage." The Fourteenth Amendment, Field concluded, had placed fundamental rights "under the guardianship of National authority."

This divide on the Court assumed a growing significance as the country entered a period of popular and social movement mobilization that called upon state legislatures (and, later, as the populist, labor, and progressive movements formed, upon the federal government) to curtail the abuse of consolidated economic power and (as they saw it) to re-establish a level playing field that was more consistent with the country's professed commitments to individual liberty and civic equality. Just three years after *Slaughterhouse*, the Supreme Court began hearing a series of "Granger Cases" addressing constitutional challenges to a succession of rate regulations on railroads and grain elevators enacted across the Midwest at the behest of America's farmers. Looking hopefully to the dissents in *Slaughterhouse* for protection, the newly regulated businesses argued in *Munn v. Illinois* (1877) – a case assessing the constitutionality of rate regulations that Illinois had imposed on a privately owned monopoly grain elevator in Chicago – that the Fourteenth Amendment had charged the federal courts with voiding state laws that violated fundamental rights, and that the Illinois law was (as Justice Field, dissenting again in *Munn*, put it) "subversive of the rights of private property." "If this be sound law," Field warned, "all property and all business in the State are held at the mercy of a majority of its legislature."

The Court's majority, however, speaking through its new Grant-appointed Chief Justice Morrison Waite, set out a general rule of judicial deference to legislative majorities in a democracy. "Every statute is presumed to be constitutional," Waite explained. "The courts ought not to declare one to be unconstitutional unless it is clearly so." Here, Waite reasoned, the monopoly grain elevator, although privately owned, was a business "affected with a public interest" – it was being "used in manner to make it of public consequence . . . [affecting] the community at large." As such, it was subject to regulation "for the common good." While such regulation might certainly go too far, Waite concluded, the rightful remedy was to be found in the legislature, and not the courts.

As the country transitioned from Reconstruction into the late nineteenth-century "Gilded Age," much of its emerging politics was adumbrated in these two Supreme Court opinions. In the next few years, the arguments of Justices Fuller and Waite lost out and the argument initially expressed in dissent by

Justice Field ended up commanding the Court's majority. This meant that, on the grounds that it violated the economic liberties of business owners, including their private property rights, the Supreme Court began to move aggressively to void legislation often passed at the behest of reformers not only to regulate monopolies, but also to improve working conditions and provide protections for organized (union) labor. Among these new regulations were laws concerning workplace health and safety, minimum wages, and maximum hours, and, in time, rights to organize. Outside the Court, these struggles between reformers seeking to regulate business in the public interest and conservatives resisting those reforms, both politically and constitutionally, set the tenor of much of the era's political contestation and thought, and, indeed, in many respects, set the terms of the political debates between progressives/liberals and conservatives that have structured American politics ever since.

Conclusion

Major strands of the political thought of the late nineteenth and early twentieth centuries were shaped by the Civil War, and can be understood as a form of contestation over the war's legacy – one that has continued to this day. Where constitutional powers and authority were concerned, did the Civil War fundamentally alter understandings of the rightful powers of the national government vis-à-vis the states or, for that matter, understandings of the legitimate powers of republican governments, taken as the agent of the sovereign American people, to advance the common good? Did it change American understandings of the importance and nature of Lockean liberal individual rights, or the rights of those who, on the ascriptive basis of their membership in an identifiable group, class, or caste, were subject to civic subordination or exclusion? Was the constitutional thought of the ante- and postbellum periods largely continuous? If so, in what sense? In all this, where does Reconstruction fit? Was it a brief, anomalous interlude? Or, before being cruelly abandoned – or thwarted – by white supremacist southern "redeemers" (and northern Republicans who grew weary of the effort, and moved on to other things), was Radical Reconstruction the instrument of the true and highest objectives for which the Union had fought the Civil War?

Looked at from a slightly different angle, what did it mean to abolish chattel slavery? What did it mean to treat all people as genuine equals, and to afford them full civic membership? How would those questions be addressed, not simply philosophically, but as matters of law and government policy? The Republican Party was (mostly) in control of the federal government from Reconstruction through the end of the nineteenth century. Some have argued that the party's increasing commitment to business interests and free market capitalism was a departure from its Civil War commitments to Enlightenment liberal principles of liberty and equality, and republican solicitude for those subject to economic and political subordination. Others, however, have noted a fundamental consistency in the party of Lincoln. In the policies and programs they advanced and opposed, and in the constitutional understandings they enforced, these others have argued, late nineteenth-century Republicans manifested a sustained commitment to the party's founding free labor ideology as carried forward into a new time, and a changing political-economic context. What was chattel slavery, after all? It was a denial of the right of ownership of one's own body – the foundational principle of Lockean liberalism – and the attendant denial of the right to work freely, and support one's self and family by one's free labor, by the sweat of one's brow. Does this not imply a commitment to private property rights, individual liberty, and, indeed, free markets? And, as such, aren't defenses of these principles a direct legacy of the abolition of slavery and of the noblest and best understanding of the Union cause in the Civil War?

Others looked at the abolition of slavery differently. For some, Lincoln's insistence that the war was being fought to vindicate the founding proposition that "all men are created equal," and that the triumph of the Union would occasion a "new birth of freedom," was understood as having elevated the principle of equality, at long last, to its rightful place in the nation's creedal firmament. African-Americans and women's rights advocates read the meaning of the war aspirationally: as introducing a project whose republican promise was full civic membership and equality for those who had been cruelly and hypocritically denied it. From then on, those suffering illegitimate classification, exclusion, subordination, and repression have appealed to the promise of the Civil War by invoking (variously) the principles of the Declaration of Independence, or of Lincoln, or the thwarted promise of a would-be powerful national government newly pledged to enforcing equality, or the constitutional guarantees of the Civil War Amendments, including the Fourteenth Amendment's guarantees of due process and the equal protection of the laws. The Civil War, in this sense, provided the foundations for later campaigns for civil rights and civil liberties, and for a purposive, activist national government which involved, in the nature of things, a demotion of the constitutional powers of the states.

The national government's commitment to Reconstruction began to flag in 1877. By the early 1890s, after an extended period in which white southern "redeemers" had fought the new order tooth and nail, white supremacist rule was re-established in the South. While the legal discrimination was generally less formal, African-Americans were widely discriminated against in the North as well. Women's rights efforts had been dismissively turned back. But farmers' and laborers' movements focused on unequal economic power were ascending. Before long, a new generation of activists campaigning for women's rights and the rights of African-Americans would take the stage, demanding not only the right to vote, but also a "Second Reconstruction."[3] The modern Left–Right polarities of American politics were beginning to form.

Questions

1. Did the South have the right to secede? How do we know when a part of a would-be polity has a legitimate right to secede from another?
2. At the end of the Civil War, there was a major push for agricultural reform that would have seized and redistributed southern land, and allotted "forty acres and a mule" to the recently freed slaves. Should we lament the failure of these efforts? Do they have any relationship to current debates about reparations for slavery?
3. Did the Civil War change the constitutional structure of the United States in fundamental ways that we could rightfully say involved the founding of a new "regime"? If so, does the eighteenth-century American founding have the same authority and relevance after the Civil War that it did before it?
4. Did the basic creedal principles like liberty, equality, and democracy mean something different after the Civil War than before it?
5. Is it useful to speak of the United States as having a single, unbroken, and continuous political, constitutional, and ideational trajectory? Or are these things better thought of as discontinuous and fractured? Might the US political experience be characterized as comprised of a succession of distinctive "regimes" or "governing orders"?
6. Did the outlawing of slavery implicitly promise new guarantees for the rights of women, queer people, or the unborn?

5

Industrial Capitalism, Reformism, and the New American State

The gargantuan scale of the changes to America's political economy in the late nineteenth century was apparent to anyone living through them. Suddenly, everything was bigger: it was a new age of mass production (steel), mass transportation (railroads), and mass consumer society (department stores). Operations on this scale profoundly affected the way Americans experienced the world, socially, economically, and politically. Wage labor, which Lincoln had assumed would constitute a brief interlude of dependency on the road to personal economic independence, became the permanent condition of most Americans. The ordinary business of life – purchases and sales, borrowing and lending (production and consumption, finance) – no longer consisted of personal transactions, entered into across the table from someone one knew and was known to, but was now conducted with large corporate entities across great distances, with little knowledge of or concern for the local community and the individual. Americans began consuming mass-produced products, and getting their information and notions from national news sources and other purveyors of information whose sky's-the-limit goal was to grow their profits by expanding their markets. Time itself was altered by the rise of continent-spanning corporate-administrative entities. Before, time had been set locally, pegged to the sun's rising and setting in a particular place. This caused problems for the newly national railroads, which not long after driving the "golden spike" at Promontory Point, Utah (1869), celebrating the completion of the transcontinental link, successfully lobbied for an official, nationally standardized system of days, hours, minutes, and seconds.

These developments brought the matter of power – private power – to the political fore. In American political thought up to this time, the question of individual liberty was discussed as if the chief threat to individual independence were government. As such, the chief method of preserving individual liberty was to place limits on government (especially national government) power. But these understandings now seemed out of joint with how many Americans were experiencing the world. In the new political economy, workers felt ruled most immediately by their employers, who enlisted them *en masse* in factories, paid them in wages, and hired and fired them at will. (If they lost their jobs – unlike the self-sufficient, yeoman farmers of Jefferson's idyll – they would literally have nothing to live on.) Farmers – seasonal, and perhaps perpetual, debtors, whose fates rose and fell with the vagaries of the weather and world markets – now lived at the mercy of far-away banks and the railroads that transported their crops to market in the nation's distant cities, with little concern for their personal trials, tribulations, and ways of life: farm families, for railroads, were little more than abstract notations in ledgers tallying profit and loss. Before long, an increasing number of farmers were either forced by agricultural consolidation or pulled by economic opportunities elsewhere to abandon rural life, and to move to the country's booming urban centers, where they, too, would now join the armies of (dependent) wage workers. It is not surprising that, in this unfurling world, farmers and laborers began to apprehend that the chief threat of concentrated power in their lives came not from government but from the nation's large-scale business corporations. And it began to occur to them, and a growing host of political thinkers and politicians, that government might actually be the one institution with enough "countervailing power" (as the mid-twentieth-century liberal economist John Kenneth Galbraith would put it)[1] to meet this challenge. Under these new conditions, a government with an expanded regulatory and administrative remit might be enlisted on behalf of the people to re-establish conditions of *de facto* individual freedom and independence. Talk of a newly empowered and centralized American state was now in the air, and on the table. Its aim would be not to crush liberty, but to expand it.

In the late nineteenth century, the concentration of economic power had a face: John D. Rockefeller, oil; Andrew Carnegie, steel; J.P. Morgan, banks; and Jay Gould and Cornelius Vanderbilt, railroads. Being a "captain of industry" was not a line for those with scruples: while it can't be denied that they got things done, great industries were forged through brutality, ruthlessness, kickbacks, collusion, and bribery, bedeviling clear lines between "free markets" and the drive for monopoly, oligopolistic, and oligarchic power. Once the markets were cornered, and the competitors eliminated, the choices available to smaller purchasers and consumers were constrained, and the prices they were charged were inflated.[2] A side-effect was the creation of what some considered obscene fortunes, opening up gaping inequalities of wealth and power.

People took sides. Were these buccaneering tycoons builders, producers, and heroes? Or were they thieves and villains – "robber barons"? Did their ascendancy portend a bright future or a dystopian nightmare? The conservative Henry Adams skewered the corrupt and degraded world they had made in his novel of Washington DC, sarcastically entitled *Democracy* (1880). Was this "Golden Age," as the novelist and humorist Mark Twain mocked, actually more like a "Gilded Age"?[3] Others, however, rose to the defense not only of these captains of industry but also of the abundant and efficient new world they heralded – if their sentimental and misguided opponents would only keep out of their way.

Restraining Government: The Philosophy of *Laissez-Faire*

The Yale University sociologist William Graham Sumner not only defended, but also celebrated the rising corporate fortunes that epitomized the Gilded Age. A pioneer in the new "social sciences," Sumner began with empirically observable facts. Only a few years earlier, the English naturalist Charles Darwin's *On the Origin of Species* (1859) had sparked a scientific revolution by positing that the diversity of the world's living creatures – including human beings – had emerged through a millennia-long process of natural selection. (In the process, among other things, Darwin had mounted a direct challenge to the account of human origins in the Book of Genesis.) A biologist, Darwin did not posit any relationship between his theory of natural selection and the powers of government. Almost immediately, however, his self-styled followers – most prominently, the English evolutionist and sociologist Herbert Spencer – did. Spencer posited that human society operated on the competitive, Darwinian principle of the "survival of the fittest." Following Spencer, American thinkers began to see this process at work in the revolutionary economic and social changes taking place in the late nineteenth-century United States, especially when it came to the era's new hierarchies and inequalities.

> No man can acquire a million without helping a million men to increase their little fortunes all the way down through all the social grades.
> William Graham Sumner (1906)

"Competition," Sumner declared in *What Social Classes Owe to Each Other* (1883), "is a law of nature." Sumner began with an empirical observation: in the competition for wealth, some – the fittest, most talented, and hardest-working – succeed and grow rich. Along the way, he further observed, the achievements of these wealthy, successful few redounded to the benefit of the many, whom they hired (and thus provided with livelihoods), and for whom they produced their products. In this competition, others – the less fit, less talented, and less hard-working – fared less well. Some were impoverished. Sumner declared this not to be a sign of dysfunction – as claimed loudly and insistently by a swelling chorus of "humanitarians, philanthropists, and reformers" who were calling upon the state to fight concentrations of economic power, income inequality, and other alleged "social problems" – but in keeping with the laws of nature.

The world as Sumner saw it – some called it *laissez-faire* capitalism – was not only natural, but good, since its commitment to minimizing the powers of government and allowing nature to takes its course maximized individual liberty. It afforded self-directed liberal individuals the freedom to strive, take risks and chances, pursue happiness, and rise. In this world, "Every man and woman in society has one big duty. That is, to take care of his or her own self." Government was there to serve a small set of limited, if essential, functions: "peace, order, and the guarantees of rights."

Sumner lamented the arrival on the scene of swarms of self-righteous "amateur social doctors" concerned with social justice and a growing list of purported social problems. These "quacks," he complained, were hell-bent upon raining on this parade. Sumner summarized their designs in a formula: "A and B decide what C shall do for D." A and B were the officious humanitarians and reformers, D is a poor man losing out in the competition of life, and C – whom Sumner famously dubbed "The Forgotten Man" (a term enlisted in American political rhetoric ever since) – is the "honest, sober, industrious citizen . . . paying his debts and his taxes," minding his own business and supporting his family. It was this "Forgotten Man" whose hard-earned income was being siphoned off through taxes to support society's shiftless losers.

Sumner was concerned not only about "C" but also about the baleful effects of big government. When governments grow, Sumner sniped, watch your wallet. Governments tend toward plutocracy: those who wield government's coercive levers end up advancing not the common good but their own private interests. Government employees wield whatever power they are given to do the bidding of the highest bidder – typically the rich and powerful. As such, Sumner warned, laws and regulations would be corrupted by "jobbery" – what economists today call "rent-seeking" – by people in and around governments, who would extract surplus benefits for themselves. The only way to minimize jobbery and prevent plutocracy – rule by the wealthy, which Sumner strenuously opposed – was to sharply limit the powers of government to the bare essentials. (Today we would call Sumner a "libertarian.")

Sumner was an academic formulating a systematic argument about the nature of society and the proper role of the state. Perhaps the greatest popularizer of *laissez-faire* capitalist ideals in this era was the Scottish-born industrialist and philanthropist Andrew Carnegie, a "self-made" man who apparently personified the "industrial virtues" that Sumner celebrated. A penniless immigrant, Carnegie started working at age thirteen in a textile mill for a pittance and rose, by mass-producing steel, to become the world's wealthiest man.

Carnegie was Sumner's equal in celebrating all-but-unregulated industrial capitalism ("not only beneficial, but essential for the future progress of the race"), and those who, through hard work and rare talents, succeeded in building things and amassing great wealth. Insisting on "the sacredness of property" and denouncing socialism, Carnegie did Sumner one better not only by fighting to build a major industry, but also in violently crushing efforts of workers at his Pittsburgh steel plants to unionize and secure better wages and working conditions. Carnegie proudly fought against the moves by these ingrates to take away one iota of his freedom as a property owner and producer.

Unlike Sumner, however, Carnegie also harbored strong convictions about the Christian duties and civic responsibilities of men of great wealth. In a reflection, perhaps, of his native Scots Calvinism, rich men, Carnegie insisted, should live modestly and responsibly, and not bask in obscene luxury. (He condemned the "conspicuous consumption" of his time, critiqued at length by Thorstein Veblen's *The Theory of the Leisure Class*, 1899.) While they might pass a moderate inheritance on to their heirs, the wealthy should practice Christian stewardship. Carnegie was perhaps the most prominent proponent and practitioner of philanthropy in American history: he gave vast amounts to cities and small towns across the United States to build public libraries, and to colleges and universities. He funded the construction of public performance spaces (such as New York's Carnegie Hall), and institutions promoting world peace (such as the Carnegie Endowment for International Peace). Such philanthropy was aimed at providing the preconditions for individuals to acquire knowledge, improve their character, and cultivate their better selves. Consistent with his views on Christian stewardship and philanthropy, Carnegie called for confiscatory estate and inheritance taxes: if the rich man had failed in his duties of stewardship (Carnegie condemned "the selfish millionaire's unworthy life"), it was the job of government to take his money, and turn it to "the common good." "The man who dies . . . rich dies disgraced," he famously pronounced.[4]

Carnegie further differed from Sumner in his republican concern that vast inequalities of wealth would tend to fray "the ties of brotherhood" that "bind together the rich and poor in harmonious relationship." In this regard, the worldly Carnegie understood the economy as, fundamentally, a *political* economy. He worried that the formation of stratified antagonistic classes would lead to a society where "mutual ignorance breeds mutual distrust," and the glue of a sense of common purpose, interests, and identity that binds a political community together would become unstuck. That his proposed prophylactic involved a paternalistic appeal to the Christian duties of society's richest men did not detract from the sincerity, at least, of this concern.

Sumner considered God to be the first mover who had created the harshly competitive natural world. For Carnegie, as for the oil baron John D. Rockefeller (another great philanthropist), God was apprehended, it seemed, through the Puritan doctrine of the elect. In *The Protestant Ethic and the Spirit of Capitalism* (1905), the German sociologist Max Weber observed that Puritan theology had posited that God gave every individual a purpose in his or her working life, for which the Almighty had endowed each of us with special talents and abilities. It was our Christian duty to devote ourselves fully to that "vocation" or "calling" during our time on earth. As such, Weber observed, worldly success in one's vocation was taken by the godly as an outward sign that one was in God's good graces, and saved. Accordingly, Carnegie, Rockefeller, and others like them understood themselves to be living godly lives as capitalists and industrialists: they were doing what God had put them on this earth to do, and doing it well – to the benefit, both materially and spiritually, of themselves, their country, and the world. The obverse of this was that they apprehended government initiatives to restrain them as all the more outrageous – as perversely aimed at thwarting God's will, and their economic freedom, which, looked at in this way, were essentially the same thing.

Conservative Critics of Industrial Capitalism and Liberal Modernity

Sumner's prickly outrage about the legions of humanitarians, philanthropists, and social doctors – proponents of social justice – who presumed to identify a long list of (specious) social problems and then proposed ostensible solutions at least reflected an awareness of new trends in American social and political thought. When, in *The Psychic Factors of Civilization* (1893), the Brown University sociologist Lester Ward expressed exasperation with the prevailing view that "[t]his vast theater of woe is regarded as wholly outside the jurisdiction of government," he was presaging an efflorescence of new thought that would, in time, dethrone the prevailing *laissez-faire* understandings, paving the way for the creation of the modern American social welfare, regulatory, and administrative state.

While Ward and those Sumner derided as "humanitarians" were laying the foundations of modern progressivism and liberalism, it is worth noting that not all of the era's "conservatives" were on board with Sumner's celebration of the rise of *laissez-faire* industrial capitalism. A group of wealthy, white, Anglo-Saxon New England Republicans concerned about mass immigration and urban machine politics deserted Maine's Republican Senator James G. Blaine for the conservative Democrat Grover Cleveland in 1884 in the hopes of securing anti-corruption reforms (like civil service laws) and promoting anti-patronage politics. While these "mugwumps" shared Sumner's concern about government corruption, they would answer this challenge not by campaigning against government power *per se*, but by pressing to return the levers of government to the "best" people – whose virtue and sense of high responsibility and duty promised "good government." Perhaps the most notable exemplar of the strain was the Harvard historian (and scion of the revolutionary Massachusetts dynasty) Henry Adams.

Of all the mugwumps, Adams meditated most deeply on the arrival of industrial modernity. After a brooding visit to France's spectacular Romanesque Abbey at Mont St. Michel and Gothic cathedral at Chartres, and an immersion in medieval Christian theology, Adams reflected on the profound way in which medieval Christianity had formed western civilization's distinctive world-view. Medieval philosophy and its aesthetic fruits (like Gothic architecture) apprehended a world imbued with God's will and superintended by His plan. "Three things are necessary for the salvation of man," Adams quoted from Saint Thomas Aquinas (*Two Precepts of Charity*, 1273): "to know what he ought to believe; to know what he ought to desire; and to know what he ought to do." These were inherent teachings of Jesus, and prescribed by his

(Roman Catholic) Church. The force of these teachings was conveyed in the image of the Blessed Virgin that, Adams argued, had once unified western culture in the thirteenth and fourteenth centuries. Adams explained how he had been wrenched from this profound and placid vision by moving from the medieval wonders of Mont St. Michel and Chartres to the bustling Paris Exposition, which exemplified the modern industrial age's radically different spirit. Modernity kneeled not before the Blessed Virgin but before the dynamo. Modern humanity worshipped scientific and technological progress. The electric generator had replaced the Church as the foundation for western civilization, with, in Adams's estimation, profound, and profoundly disorienting and disturbing, consequences.

Adams's nostalgia was shared by the likes of the Harvard philosopher George Santayana and, in time, "New Humanists" like Paul Elmer More and Irving Babbitt (*Democracy and Leadership*, 1924), whose influence helped form the political thought of T.S. Eliot and Russell Kirk and, as such, of the traditionalist vein of modern American conservatism. Adams's sense of dispossession and lament for the decline of a Christian West succumbing to post-Christian values was also voiced in a cruder, more simplistic, and more dogmatic form by a new Christian dispensation: fundamentalism. In contrast to Adams's brooding lament – Adams proposed no solutions – fundamentalist Christians seized upon a last-ditch remedy: an uncompromising return to biblical literalism. Laboring under a profound sense of siege unleashed by the new historical biblical scholarship and Darwin's theory of evolution by natural selection (along with a host of other modern developments), they turned to the Bible *tout court* as a means of restoring order in a time of chaos, certainty in a time of doubt, and rightful authority in a time of prideful rebellion.

This critical conservative reaction to industrial modernity, especially in its Fundamentalist Christian guise, introduced a new line of thought into US politics, one that had a special purchase on the country's intellectual and geographic peripheries. While robust, this thought often resided outside of the national consciousness, as it was outside the precincts of national political power. It nevertheless broke through to the surface every now and then, sometimes spectacularly, as in the Scopes "Monkey" Trial in Dayton, Tennessee (1925), involving the (staged) prosecution of a public school teacher for teaching Darwin's theory of evolution, or in intellectual statements like the Nashville Agrarians' localist, anti-industrial, and anti-liberal manifesto *I'll Take My Stand: The South and the American Tradition* (1930). By the time this thought moved the center of American politics in the late twentieth century as a powerful precinct of the Reagan-era Religious Right, however, it was largely shorn of its critique of capitalism: although there are exceptions, the mainlines of modern conservatism, in a "fusionist" vision, uneasily – and, in many ways, inconsistently – married a Lockean liberal pro-capitalist libertarianism with a variety of traditionalist-minded, anti-modernist religious conservatisms.

Reformist and Revolutionary Critics of Industrial Capitalism: Ideas

Given the social disorientation and sometimes abysmal conditions unleashed by the emerging industrial corporate capitalist order, the proponents of *laissez-faire*, notwithstanding their deep pockets and immense power, found themselves increasingly on the defensive. In the industrial revolution's birthplace in England, the visionary romantic poet William Blake had written hauntingly of his country's "dark Satanic Mills" (1804). After an apprenticeship at his father's company in Manchester, Friedrich Engels, the wealthy son of a German industrialist, had chronicled the millworkers' miseries in *The Condition of the Working Class in England* (1845). Together with Karl Marx, the two published the stirring *Communist Manifesto* (1848), which enjoined: "Workers of the World, unite! – You have nothing to lose but your chains!" Marx and Engels saw industrial capitalism starkly dividing the world into two opposed classes, capitalists and workers, who were, essentially, at war. They called for worldwide revolution – for the overthrow of capitalism, and the establishment of a dictatorship of the proletariat. The next stage would be the establishment of socialism, and then communism, portending a state of peace and brotherhood, free from conflict and oppression, where even the state – currently allied with capital – would be superfluous, and could at last wither away.

Marx and Engels's *Communist Manifesto* and Engels's *The Condition of the Working Class in England* (which was translated into English by the progressive reformer and civil rights activist Florence Kelley in 1885) were read by American audiences. Despite this, Marxism only gained momentum in the United States after the Bolshevik Revolution (1917), which was celebrated by home-grown radicals like John Reed, and radical immigrants like Emma Goldman – an anarchist who was at first enchanted and then disillusioned by the Russian Revolution. (Goldman was stripped of her citizenship and deported to Soviet Russia during the World War I-era "Red Scare.") Before the Bolshevik Revolution, most radical responses to the rise of industrial capitalism in the United States were found in the domestic immigrant communities most directly affected by its harshest conditions.

Pre-figuring late twentieth-century interventions by Arthur Laffer ("The Laffer Curve") and Steve Forbes (the "flat tax"), some came peddling nostrums that intrigued because they at least diagnosed and confronted the problem. One of the most alluring to working-class contemporaries was the single tax on land proposed by Henry George in *Progress and Poverty* (1879). Drawing upon English economist David Ricardo, George insisted that the era's grossly unequal wealth distribution stemmed from the illegitimate appropriation by privileged, non-producing, and monopolistic landowners of economic rents rightfully belonging to the nation's laboring producers. God-given land in

its initial, unimproved state, George observed, had once been almost universally available to be productively worked. Given recent industrial capitalist
miseries, in a context in which material progress was doing little to alleviate
massive poverty, George called for subjecting unimproved land to a single
common tax which would provide all the funding government needed to
institute programs to bridge the gap between rich and poor, and advance the
common good.

In *Looking Backward* (1889), Edward Bellamy, like Marx and Engels, focused
on what he took to be the inevitable class conflict between labor and capital:
Bellamy called the labor problem "the Sphinx's riddle of the nineteenth century." Instead of joining the authors of *The Communist Manifesto* in prophesying
class war, however, he imagined a future world miraculously – and peacefully –
transformed. *Looking Backward* was a futuristic (social) sci-fi fantasy, constructed
along the lines of Washington Irving's Rip Van Winkle (1819), which imagined
an American colonist in the Catskill mountains who drifted into a twenty-year
slumber, missing the American Revolution. Bellamy sent his young protago-
nist Julian West off to sleep only to arise in Boston in the year 2000. Much to
West's amazement, the Boston of the future is utterly conflict-free, living in
a beneficent fug of harmoniously shared interests. A Dr. Leete debriefs West
on all that had happened during his slumber, and explains this new America.
Over time, Leete explains, everyone came to appreciate that it was best to live
according to the rule (as Marx had earlier described it) "from each according
to his ability, and to each according to his need." In the Boston of 2000, there
was no money, no poverty, no crime; there were no markets, no wars – indeed,
there was no politics. "[T]he nation guarantee[d] the nurture, education, and
comfortable maintenance of every citizen from the cradle to the grave." All the
modes of production were owned in common, for the common good. Society
had simply evolved in this felicitous direction by unanimous consent, after
sustained deliberation of what would be best for all.

Like Henry George's *Progress and Poverty*, Bellamy's utopian dream was a
bestseller that inspired hundreds of fan clubs and discussion groups. Late
nineteenth-century radicals were calling for revolution. Late nineteenth-
century utopians closed their eyes and imagined the era's problems
miraculously solved. A growing cohort of thinkers, however – neither revolutionaries nor utopians, but reformers who accepted the basic premises of
the social, economic, and political system, but were disturbed by many of
its consequences – began looking not to global solutions, but at incremental
changes, pragmatic adjustments, and targeted public policies. In a meliorist
spirit, they proposed revisions, improvements, and reforms.

In this, William Graham Sumner's scourge Lester Frank Ward led the way. A
botanist and paleontologist by training, the sociologist Ward lit into Sumner
by going straight to the latter's starting premise concerning the "laws of
nature." Of course, Ward conceded, the natural world was a brutal and com-

petitive place, where the battle went to the strong. (Ward, too, was a disciple of Darwin.) But, then again, Ward asked, *so what?* The fatalistic conclusions Sumner had drawn from his observations of the natural world, where fur flew, guts spilled, and blood spurted, simply did not follow. Did that mean that all we could do was passively sit on our hands and take in this sanguinary spectacle? Meeting Sumner's insistence that "practical anarchy" was the only reasonable response to this will to power and bloodbath, Ward lambasted his "baseless prejudice" and "instinctive hostility" to government. Society was suffering from "great and serious evils" – "underpaid labor . . . misery and squalor . . . diseases . . . and premature deaths." As noted above, Ward rejected the contention by *laissez-faire*'s proponents that government was proscribed from countering these evils. This, he argued, made no sense. Yes, the "natural" state of the world was that, in the absence of intervention, the strong would prevail, and the weak would be crushed. But, Ward countered, "[t]hese much-talked-of laws of nature are violated every time the highway robber is arrested and sent to jail." "It is utterly illogical," he continued, "to say that the aggrandizement by physical force should be forbidden [as Sumner, like most everyone, did] while aggrandizement by mental force or legal fiction should be permitted."

Human beings, Ward affirmed, had indeed evolved by the processes of natural selection. This meant that they had highly evolved minds. They could think in sophisticated ways to master nature, and turn it to their own advantage. Why shouldn't highly intelligent human beings adjudge these social problems unacceptable, and enlist their impressive minds to find effective means of addressing them? And, while government action might not always offer a solution, why should those studying social problems commit *ex ante* to removing government policy from their toolkit?

A seminal thinker of the contemporary discipline of public policy, Ward was frustrated by the prevailing terms of his era's political debates, which pitted *de facto* anarchists (Ward meant libertarians, or proponents of *laissez-faire*) denouncing government as a thieving racket against socialists cleaving to a naïve faith that government was the answer to all our social and economic problems. By these lights, Ward said, one side was positing that government was *never* the answer to our problems, and the other that it *always* was. Actually, he argued, there was no deep principle at stake. The most sensible thing would be to think practically about problem-solving. Society should enlist experts trained in the new social sciences to gather evidence and study specific social and economic problems. These experts would then give their considered advice about whether government might be enlisted in either solving the problem, or at least improving the situation. If, in their considered, apolitical judgment, it could, they would then offer advice on what might be the best way for it to do so. As such, government would take up these issues on the basis not of some *a priori* principle, but of an informed and dispassionate assessment of whether "judicious regulations" might be effective. In advancing these views, which set aside radical or revolutionary frameworks and ambitions, Ward helped found "modern" or "reform" (as opposed to "classical") liberalism.

Notably, Ward's theory of government conferred considerable authority on a new class of social scientists and public policy experts enlisted in the civil service. Ward, it should be said, was ambivalent about democracy, especially in the form it was then being practiced in the United States. He contrasted the informed and public-spirited government by expert to the "puerile gaming spirit" of partisan politics. He confessed that, as a replacement for brawling, tribal politics, he would "substitute something more business-like," devoted to "the real interests and necessary business of the nation."

Ideas in Action

Resistance in a very different voice issued from the rural South and Midwest: populism. Sumner and Ward were academic theorists. The populists were either farmers or politicians in the real-world fight who represented agricultural constituencies, evincing an admixture of "liberal-Left" and "Right" that belied ideological classification. Southern and Midwestern populists spoke directly to genuinely aggrieved people, in this case to those who had been the apple of Jefferson's eye, the (ostensibly) virtuous, proudly independent yeoman farmers, now being exploited – crushed – by distant forces that seemed utterly beyond their control: railroads, banks, and other corporate entities operating on a large scale in global markets on which the small freeholders had become dependent, and who were now stripping them of their livelihoods, dignity, and freedom.

Farmers were debtors: they borrowed against the promise of future earnings from their crops, which were at the mercy of declining prices and mercurial weather. When they were unable to repay their loans, banks foreclosed, seizing their homes and farms, driving them off the land, imperiling their families, and hollowing out their communities. They were at the mercy of monopolies, who dictated terms to them from big cities at great distances: the monopoly railroad that happened to pass closest to their land; the grain storage elevators in hubs like Chicago that bought their crop and brought it to market. These monopolies colluded. Through special privileges like government land grants conferred by legislators whom they had showered with deals, discounts, cash, and gifts, they extracted everything they could from those with little power to object. Far from Jefferson's independent yeoman ideal, farmers were now pawns in someone else's game.

The bewilderment about how, as farmers, they had been transformed from the nation's backbone to its mark was reflected in the more unsavory traits of many populists. These populists were brimming with conspiracy theories, and were quick to alight upon scapegoats. While they were losing their livelihoods, weren't "vile hordes of Mongolian coolies" (Chinese immigrant laborers) flowing into their country and thriving, suggested Minnesota's Ignatius Donnelly in *Caesar's Column* (1891)? And who, exactly, were the men in the far-away cities calling in their loans and foreclosing on their farms? "[T]he real government is now, a coterie of bankers, mostly Israelites" (Jews) on Wall Street and in London – "the money power" – bent on enriching themselves while fleecing the good Christians who had founded and built this country. Far away, wealthy, and sometimes foreign-born, non-Christian elites were dividing what had once been a great nation of free, independent men into "two great classes – tramps and millionaires." Real Americans wanted their country back. At the Omaha Convention, the National People's Party Platform (July 4, 1892), which nominated James Baird Weaver for President, declared, "[W]e seek to restore the government of the Republic to the hands of the 'plain people,' with which class it originated." Citing the Declaration of Independence as their touchstone, the populists proclaimed that "We assert our purposes to be identical to the purposes of the National Constitution." As the evangelical Christian Nebraska populist William Jennings Bryan, a three-time Democratic Party nominee for President, put it in his legendary "Cross of Gold" Speech (1896), "It is the issue of 1776 all over again."

There is considerable debate about whether the populists were nostalgists howling for a return to a vanished agrarian past or far-sighted seers who offered real possibilities for a more republican, egalitarian, and democratic future. Some of the uglier anti-semitic and anti-immigrant convictions within their ranks notwithstanding, the late nineteenth-century populists are typically accounted part of their era's reformist Left. Recognizing the power in numbers that could be leveraged by agricultural producers, leaders of regionally based farmers' alliances like Charles Macune pioneered farmers' cooperatives and proposed a sub-treasury plan that would augment the credit available to hard-put and otherwise dependent debtors. Some populists spurned ethno-centrism and forged inter-racial coalitions. Facing exclusion, others established their own independent organizations like the Colored Farmers' National Alliance and Cooperative Union. In demanding that power be restored to common people, populists were fervent proponents of democracy – including direct democracy: they spearheaded state adoption of the initiative and referendum process whereby the people directly (as opposed to their bribed and corrupted legislatures) could make their own laws; the direct election of US Senators (instituted by the US Constitution's Seventeenth Amendment, 1913); the secret ("Australian") ballot; civil service reform (professionalized government oriented toward the general public good); the creation of an independent Federal Reserve bank, which, in addition to providing much-needed economic stability, reclaimed from private banks the power to direct the country's economic destiny; and called for the nationalization of the railroads. While many populists – like the majority of Americans of their time – were noxious when it came to race, alienage, or ethnicity, they were nevertheless fervent proponents of equality: of the idea that one person is just as good as another – although, in a Jeffersonian vein, they tended to valorize the humble farmer, as Bryan, "The Great Commoner," suggested, as the most indispensable businessman of all. Populists demanded a more powerful and proactive government that, while not straying beyond its appointed functions, would serve as a battering ram against concentrations of private power to liberate the common man. Maintaining that "Wealth belongs to him who creates it," populists demanded a progressive income tax; the free coinage of silver to expand the money supply (then tethered to the gold standard); boycotts of industries hostile to organized labor; a maximum hours law for government workers; and an end to corporate welfare and union-busting private security forces. No one was more contemptuous of the "idle" rich financiers who profited by simply shifting money around for their own fun and profit, while actually producing nothing.

> There are two ideas of government. There are those who believe that if you will only legislate to make the well-to-do prosperous, their prosperity will leak through to those below. The Democratic idea, however, has been that if you legislate to make the masses prosperous, their prosperity will find its way up through every class which rests upon them.
>
> William Jennings Bryan (1896)

In 1896, migrating populists seized control of the Democratic Party from its tight-money, business-friendly leaders, and, in a stunning convention at the Chicago Coliseum, nominated William Jennings Bryan for President. While Bryan lost a succession of presidential campaigns to the pro-business Republicans before the Democrats threw in the towel and nominated their own pro-business conservative, Alton Parker, many of the policy positions the populists had championed in their Omaha Platform were adopted by progressive politicians in both parties during the Theodore Roosevelt (1901–1909) and Woodrow Wilson (1913–1921) administrations. These new departures, in turn, set the foundations for Franklin Delano Roosevelt's New Deal (1933–1939), and for twentieth-century liberalism.

The road from populism to progressivism to liberalism was not built by farmers alone, but in coalition with the (largely urban, and often immigrant) labor movement. The American labor movement in this period was itself divided by major conceptual disagreements about how workers should be understood, economically and politically. Reformists assented to capitalism and to its underlying liberal individualist paradigm, banding together not to challenge the system's fundamentals – which many believed to be futile – but to demand fair wages, reasonable hours, and safe working conditions within it, to re-establish their status as free and equal rights-bearing individuals under modern industrial conditions. Radicals within the labor movement, by contrast, saw more possibilities and mounted a head-long challenge to capitalism and to its liberal individualist underpinnings. Hope, class solidarity, and class action, they were convinced, offered the only viable route to lasting change. In contradistinction to the reformist craft (or trade) unionism of the new American Federation of Labor (AFL) (1886), the industrial unionism of the Knights of Labor, the Industrial Workers of the World (the IWW or "Wobblies"), and the Congress of Industrial Organizations (CIO) organized workers not according to skill, trade, or industry, but according to their membership in the country's – indeed, the world's – working class (what the Wobblies described as "One Big Union").

At this time, collective action by workers was all but illegal: efforts to organize unions or otherwise press demands were considered criminal conspiracies against the property rights of business owners. When workers formed, or even talked about forming, unions – which they did because they were often working long hours under dangerous conditions, six days a week, without job security, compensation for injuries, or retirement plans – they were fired. *union formation* By the late nineteenth century, a labor movement was coalescing to fight back. The struggle was monumental, strewn with violence, including bombings, sabotage, massacres, and a succession of paralyzing targeted and general strikes.

One of the labor struggle's defining episodes, the Haymarket Affair (1886), when a peaceful rally in Chicago for an eight-hour work day descended into a violent conflict between political radicals and the police, inspired the immigrant anarchist Emma Goldman, among others, to take up the cause with a vengeance. In cross-country speaking engagements drawing huge crowds (some curious onlookers simply wanted to see the fiery female orator in the flesh), in her journal *Mother Earth*, and other writings, "Red Emma" both explicated and argued for anarchism. Men and women were enslaved, she said, by religion, by property, by the state, and by society. Invoking Emerson and Thoreau, Goldman demanded nothing less than the total liberation of individual human beings from all forms of domination and oppression. In this quest, nothing – no tradition, faith, custom, habit, or rule – was sacred. As Goldman hectored and enjoined, other anarchists – including Goldman's partner, Alexander Berkman – acted. Under the sway of Russian anarchists Bakunin and Kropotkin, who advocated *l'attentat* – targeted assassination – Berkman shot and stabbed Henry Clay Frick, the CEO of Carnegie Steel, in his Pittsburgh office, nearly killing him. Bombs were planted at the home of top US government officials. In Buffalo in 1904, the pro-business conservative President of the United States, William McKinley, was assassinated by an anarchist.

Eugene V. Debs drank from the springs of the era's radical anti-capitalism during his rise from a teenage Terre Haute, Indiana, railroad worker and railway union activist to a nationally celebrated agitator, orator, and five-time Socialist Party candidate for President. Debs began as a populist and Democrat. Only when he was jailed for leading a national railway worker strike that paralyzed the country's transportation system (1894) did he pause to study Laurence Gronlund's *The Cooperative Commonwealth* (1884), Edward Bellamy's *Looking Backward*, and the writings of Robert Blatchford and Karl Kautsky, which transformed him into a socialist. Before Gronlund, socialism in America had been mostly identified with the early nineteenth-century Owenite and Fourierist utopian communalist experiments of New Harmony (Indiana), Brook Farm (Massachusetts), and Oneida (upstate New York). Ignited by his studies, Debs – like Daniel De Leon, a one-time follower of Henry George and founder of the rival Socialist Labor Party – rejected demonstration communities and communes and called for direct engagement. The new radicals re-centered American socialism on the labor problem under industrial capitalism, emphasizing the imperative of revolutionary class struggle through industrial unionism. Like his erstwhile fellow Hoosier Abraham Lincoln, Debs could not help but observe "the change in the status of the worker, who, from an independent mechanic or small producer, was reduced to the level of a dependent wage worker." While Lincoln had been optimistic that wage labor would be only a temporary way-station on the road to stand-alone independence, Debs, living decades later, saw that wage labor was becoming the permanent condition of most American workers, with stand-alone independence nowhere on the horizon. Although he initially welcomed reformist help in fighting for shared goals like better wages, hours, and working conditions, he became convinced that these goals, even if achieved, would merely take the edges off a fundamentally exploitative economic system. Over time, Debs became increasingly critical of reformists who had taken their eye off the ball, losing sight of "the true nature of the struggle": wage workers had been reduced to the status of material inputs and factors of production. The only solution was "to overthrow the capitalist system of private ownership of the tools of labor, abolish wage-slavery and achieve the freedom of the whole working class and, in fact, all of mankind." Drawing upon Emerson, Thoreau, and John Brown, and appealing to great predecessor dissenters, including the American revolutionaries George Washington, Samuel Adams, and Thomas Paine, and to the example of Jesus Christ, who, Debs noted, had "aroused the ill will and hatred of the usurers, the money changers, the profiteers, the high priests, the lawyers, the judges, the merchants, the bankers – in a word, the ruling class," he called for the collective ownership of the means of production.

Within the labor movement, Debs was in competition with Samuel Gompers, an immigrant cigarmaker from New York City's Lower East Side, and the Founder of the AFL. Radicals baited Gompers and other "trade [or "craft"] unionists" with the charge that they were weak and compliant, submissive supplicants of the powers-that-be. Gompers was not interested in talking about revolution, and he did not organize workers as a class. But, that said, he was nevertheless highly confrontational, organizing, rallying, and calling strikes and boycotts, for which he was repeatedly jailed. "I have my day dreams, and build my castles in the air, and sometimes allow my mind to run riot," he confessed. "[B]ut when I want to be of some service to my fellow workers," he affirmed, I "get down to terra firma and help them in their present struggle." "It does not require any elaborate social philosophy or great discernment to know that a wage of $3 a day and workday of eight hours in sanitary workshops are better than $2.50 a day and workday of twelve hours under perilous conditions," he ventured. The class-minded Daniel De Leon might have mocked the AFL's organization as a federation of craft or trade unions as the "American Separation of Labor," and denounced it (as did Debs) as a conciliating surrender and retreat from the systemic and structural possibilities of class unity, but Gompers was convinced that it represented the best achievable path forward.

These at times bitter divisions between reformers and revolutionaries in the labor movement set the template for a broad array of future struggles by subordinated and subaltern – or, alternatively, discriminated against and equality-seeking – groups, including feminists and civil rights and gay rights activists, among others. Like the late nineteenth-century labor struggle, these poles would structure a succession of movements, pitting proponents of class consciousness, solidarity, and structural change against pragmatic, professedly "non-ideological" reformers who largely accepted the current system, but undertook often aggressive fights to claim their fair and rightful share. These antagonisms on the liberal-Left often resulted in dramatic splinterings, schisms, and breaks that added to equally bitter rifts over strategies and tactics. Some were committed to deploying the repertoires of "contentious [social movement] politics," like direct action, including deliberate lawbreaking (including civil disobedience).[5] Others insisted that such disruption was counterproductive, and stumped for more mainstream forms of political engagement in electoral politics, including working for pragmatic coalitional alliances with established political parties.

From Pragmatism to Progressivism

While the Left was calling for revolution, others, following Lester Ward's lead, began rethinking paradigms in more pragmatic, if nevertheless transformational, ways. One word on everyone's lips was "publicity": exposure. Shining a light on modern conditions themselves, many believed, would demonstrate that society's problems were self-evident, and make a *prima facie* case for addressing them. Investigative journalists writing for mass-circulation magazines – "muckrakers" – wrote gripping accounts of scandalous working conditions and collusion and corruption in major industries like oil, steel, and railroads. Jacob Riis photographed the poverty and slum life on New York's Lower East Side in *How the Other Half Lives: Studies among the*

Tenements of New York (1890). At *McClure's Magazine*, Ida Tarbell laid bare the ruthless criminality, corruption, and collusion that had built the country's most powerful oil company, John D. Rockefeller's Standard Oil of Ohio.[6] In *The Shame of the Cities* (1904), Lincoln Steffens exposed the corrupt politics of urban political machines. In a book that Jack London called "the Uncle Tom's Cabin of wage slavery," *The Jungle* (1905), Upton Sinclair, who later ran for office first as a socialist and then as a Democrat, for Governor of California (1934), provided a lurid, lightly-fictionalized account of Chicago's rancid meatpacking industry – in which ground rats (and maybe a few lopped-off human appendages) went into the hopper with the pork and beef on its way to American dinner tables. These exposés of industrial capitalism, political bossism, and money in politics – naming and shaming – sought, with barely concealed outrage, to ring down the curtain on secrecy and silence: from now on, since they now knew, everyone was complicit.

More systematic fact-gathering on social conditions was undertaken by the new social sciences. The modern study of sociology, economics, and political science emerged from the German-inspired research universities then being established in the United States, including Cornell (1865), Johns Hopkins (1876), and the University of Chicago (1890). These were complemented by new work undertaken at large public-service-oriented state land-grant institutions like the University of Wisconsin, which bid to turn higher education away from the more religious and humanistic liberal arts toward the problems of modern science, and the scientific study of society. Where, with notebooks in hand, the muckrakers questioned, poked, and probed, these social scientists collected data, tested hypotheses, and proposed theories of how society worked, to get a handle on cause and effect, with the goal of ameliorating, if not solving, social problems.[7]

Sunlight is the best disinfectant, declared the progressive Boston lawyer (and future Supreme Court Justice) Louis Brandeis, who had a foot in both camps. The brief he filed in the Supreme Court in *Muller v. Oregon* (1908), prepared by Josephine Goldmark, research director of the National Consumer League (founded by Florence Kelley), presented two pages of legal citations, and over one hundred pages of social science evidence justifying the need for the Oregon maximum hours law for women, whose constitutionality was at issue in the case. Reams of new empirical evidence underwrote a cascade of reform legislation, much of it enacted at the state level, that sought to improve public health, safety, and working conditions, as well as ambitious new programs in the regulation and administration of politics, business, and markets.

The burgeoning "progressive" movement was fed by diverse sources, each with its own understandings. While social scientists started from positivistic and secular scientific frameworks and premises, and muckrakers from a sense of outrage and injustice, denizens of the "social gospel" movement like Washington Gladden, Samuel Batten, George Herron, and Walter Rauschenbusch (*Christianity and the Social Crisis*, 1907), and those associated with the Federal Council of Churches, many of whom were Christian ministers and theologians, rooted their calls for social reform in post-millennialist understandings of sin and righteousness which enjoined the godly to rid the world of social evil in anticipation of the Second Coming. Their touchstone was the life of Christ: these progressives asked, "What would Jesus do?" They asked it not just of individuals, but, more broadly, of society and its institutions. As best we can, they insisted, we must institute the Kingdom of God in our common world, here and now. While the work of muckrakers was often dark and disturbing, the social gospel was often inspirational and uplifting: it appealed to the allure of a better day under a genuinely Christian social order.

While this movement was overwhelmingly Protestant, a number of prominent Catholic thinkers also joined the campaign for relief, regulation, and progressive reform. In his encyclical *Rerum Novarum* (1891) – "Rights and Duties of Capital and Labor" – Pope Leo XIII rejected both communism and *laissez-faire* capitalism, lending the Church's support to labor unions and government regulation committed to the dignity of workers and promoting the common good. Under the influence of *Rerum Novarum*, which drew on the Catholic natural law tradition, Monsignor John Ryan, a Minnesota-born professor of moral theology at the Catholic University of America raised on prairie populism, championed economic and social justice, becoming a prominent supporter of President Franklin Roosevelt and his social welfare programs, earning the sobriquet "Monsignor New Deal."

> The spiritual force of Christianity should be turned against the materialism and mammonism of our industrial and social order.
>
> Walter Rauschenbusch (1907)

At about the same time, a loose group of American philosophers known as the pragmatists were undertaking a major intellectual project that would, in its own way, help pave the path to social and political reform. Pragmatism started with critique. The philosophical foundations of western political thought set by the ancient Greeks, the pragmatists observed, had posited in advance a set of transcendent ideals and truths held to exist entirely out of time. Classical Greek philosophy then built its understandings of reality backward from those posited *a priori* ends or essences. The pragmatists did not argue that such ideals or essences did not exist. They argued, rather, that there was no means of either apprehending or applying transcendent principles to human needs and problems that, ultimately, had not been imbued with the real-world purposes or practical problems faced by contemporary people, alive in a particular historical moment. Those people could not help but understand those principles, ideals, and transcendent truths with an eye to who they were at that instant, where they wanted to go, and who they wanted to be. If one were not mesmerized by the auras and sanctity surrounding those posited abstractions and essences, both in the abstract and as they were invoked in contemporary society to justify *status quo* traditions, assumptions, rules, and theories of government, one could discern the all-too-worldly uses to which these purportedly transcendent ideals were being put.

The more forbidding work of the pragmatists, like that of Charles Sanders Peirce, addressed questions involving epistemology, language, and other recondite philosophical conundrums. But some of the work was applied, and broadly influential. William James explored the dynamics of individual psychology, including the ways people's psychological drives, needs, and emotions (including their religious passions and beliefs) shaped their apprehensions of the world around them. John Dewey of the University of Chicago and Columbia University was perhaps the most politically engaged pragmatist philosopher. Dewey directly addressed what he took to be the insalubrious sanctification of the *status quo* political order by ideal or essentialist theories concerning the (so-called) laws of nature, and "human nature" more generally. Starting from these, he observed, political theorists had posited an alleged nature and purpose of "the state." This, in turn, had been used to legitimate currently extant institutions, positing fixed conceptions of government's powers and limits. Condemning "intellectual atavism," Dewey argued that our understandings of the possibilities and limits of government were corseted both by a misdirected belief in unvarying universal truths and ends, and by habits, customs, traditions, and passions and emotions that had been justified *post hoc* by reference to allegedly transcendent principles and ideals, sometimes in service of very low and partial interests. Dewey called for the reclamation of human agency – of humanity's power to make its own world, and to live well within it.

Dewey went on to explicate what members of a political community should do to become masters of their own destiny as a genuinely democratic people. A truly democratic polity required a certain kind of citizen, formed by a certain sort of education. Evincing the spirit and skepticism of modern science, that citizen would learn to question all received ideas, assumptions, customs, habits, institutions, traditions, and rules, examining them critically and rationally, to arrive at informed conclusions about which made sense, and were useful, and hence good and worth keeping, and which were either pointless or pernicious, and thus were better off being sloughed off and discarded. As such, Dewey was perhaps the United States' most influential theorist and real-world champion of academic freedom (he was a co-founder of the American Association of University Professors in 1915), and a seminal proponent of modern civil libertarian understandings of the freedom of speech.

For Dewey, a genuinely democratic "public" did not yet exist in the United States. It had to be cultivated through education in new habits of inquiry and critique, and civic spirit. With an appropriate civic education, the members of the public could navigate their way through the shoals of unreason reinforced not only by religious dogma and the "precipitates of the past," but also by the early twentieth century's pervasive, inflammatory, and propagandistic mass media, including "the triviality and 'sensational' quality of so much of what passes as news."

Dewey was a major theorist of the possibilities of establishing a self-directing republican political community under modern conditions. In his optimistic search for the "conditions under which the Great Society may become the Great Community," he emphasized that "[f]raternity, liberty and equality isolated from communal life are hopeless abstractions." The public would find its self and its voice in sustained engagement and communication with each other over *res publica*: public things. "Regarded as an idea," Dewey wrote in *The Public and Its Problems* (1927), "democracy is not an alternative to other principles of associated life. It is the idea of community life itself."

The intellectual framework forged by the pragmatists had a radiating real-world influence. It elevated the normative claims made for majoritarian democracy in American public life – and in the rulings of a new generation of American judges – while demoting claims on behalf of counter-majoritarian checks, limits, and restraints (with the notable exception of protections for the freedom of speech). The majorities whom the progressives, under pragmatist influence, championed were decidedly not untutored masses of the ignorant, impassioned, or unreasonable, but well-educated, public-spirited republican citizens engaged in a perpetually unfolding process of informed experimentation in solving their collective problems and advancing their shared ideals. These were the majorities to be formed by a radically reimagined system of public education, where (as Dewey, writing as American history's most influential educational theorist, explained) rote memorization (including of Bible verses and didactic moral parables) would be jettisoned, and schools would place a new and surpassing emphasis on practical, problem-focused learning, critical thinking skills, and civic education (modelled in projects based on cooperative and collaborative group work).

Pragmatism in Politics and Government

Pragmatism entered the bloodstream of American politics through the work of engaged "public intellectual" journalists and other professionals like Herbert Croly and Louis D. Brandeis, who became close advisors to a rising cohort of progressive politicians: Croly was associated with Theodore Roosevelt, and Brandeis with Woodrow Wilson, both of whom shaped rafts of innovative government policy during their rise, and as Presidents of the United States. Both Oliver Wendell Holmes Jr., who was appointed to the Supreme Court by Theodore Roosevelt, and Brandeis, who was appointed by Wilson, imported these views onto the Supreme Court. There, Holmes and

Brandeis emphasized the imperative in most cases of deference by judges to legislatures; the understanding that the Constitution provided wide scope for legislative and (via the delegation of powers) expert experiments in regulation and administration aimed at addressing social problems; and the conviction that legal and constitutional analysis was led astray when judges were blinded by a slavish adherence to transcendent philosophies of natural rights and the role of government, which reinforced the *status quo*, frustrating society's ability to recognize and meet importunate challenges and problems.

Perhaps the most heralded statement of the vision for a "new republic" was Herbert Croly's *The Promise of American Life* (1909), a reflection on the fate of American commitments to liberty, equality, and democracy under the new social, political, and economic conditions of the late nineteenth and early twentieth centuries. Rather than, like some progressives, repudiating the founders as false friends of their professed ideals, Croly credited their ideals as noble and sincere. Nevertheless, he contended, under new conditions, their theories of individual rights and the legitimate powers of government were now barriers to their realization. Thomas Jefferson was a case in point. A paladin of liberty, equality, and democracy, Jefferson had also championed limited government, states' rights, localism, and a constitutional strict constructionism that rejected any flexibility concerning the powers of government to meet currently desired ends. These may have been congruous in Jefferson's own time, but in Croly's – characterized by massive accumulations of wealth and the consolidation of private power – the ideals and the means to their realization imagined by Jefferson were now incongruous: they were a recipe for passivity in the face of pressing social imperatives, undercutting America's capacity for flourishing and achieving its ideals. A passive and neutral national state was prostrate before the systematic entrenchment and reinforcement of power and privilege – a denial of the Lockean liberal equality of opportunity in which Jefferson had fervently believed. For average Americans in his time, Croly insisted, "It is as if the competitor in a Marathon cross country run were denied proper nourishment or proper training, and was obliged to toe the mark against rivals who had every benefit of food and discipline." An ideology of overwrought individualism, moreover, was frustrating the American people's sense that they might come together as a community, imagine a greater "national interest," and reclaim their rightful collective powers as sovereigns in command of their destiny. Croly called for a "square deal" for the American public – for the leveraging of the powers of the national government to write new rules that offered the possibility of a more just and democratic social, economic, and political order, to achieve (it was said of his thesis) Jeffersonian ends through Hamiltonian means.

Theodore Roosevelt, who unexpectedly ascended to the White House when President McKinley was assassinated by an anarchist, lent his energy, charisma, and leadership to a progressivism informed by Croly's "New

Nationalism." Roosevelt leveraged the nation's new anti-trust laws to break up concentrations of economic power, while introducing expert regulation of concentrations worth maintaining because of their useful economies of scale. He championed the passage of broad disclosure laws, and launched public investigations to shine a spotlight on the internal workings of corporations so that the public might better understand corporate behavior, and the nature and extent of corporate influence. "[L]aws should be passed to prohibit the use of corporate funds directly or indirectly for political purposes," Roosevelt demanded. He additionally pushed for regulation promising safer and healthier working conditions, as well as laws aimed at equalizing the power relations between labor and capital by establishing legal protections for organized labor. Roosevelt brought the nation's natural resources and treasures under public stewardship in the broader national interest. In the wind-up to his crusading third-party "Bull Moose" run for the White House (1912), Roosevelt's *The New Nationalism* (1910) downplayed appeals to Jefferson and Hamilton in favor of appeals to Abraham Lincoln and the Grand Army of the Republic (then still in living memory, and, not incidentally, a powerful political constituency) – those who had made the supreme sacrifice to save the Union, "the last best hope on earth" for the realization of human liberty and equality. "When I say that I am for the square deal," Roosevelt attested, "I mean not merely that I stand for fair play under the present rules of the game, but that I stand for having those rules changed so as to work for a more substantial equality of opportunity and of reward for equally good service." This was set within an overarching vision of a national community: "We are all Americans," Roosevelt explained. "Our common interests are as broad as the continent."

An alternative, more southern-inflected progressivism was offered in the Democratic Party by the Kentucky-born (although Boston-based) Louis D. Brandeis, and the Virginian Woodrow Wilson. The contrast between Wilson's "New Freedom" and (New Yorkers) Croly and Roosevelt's "New Nationalism" was sometimes subtle, and ultimately may have made little practical difference. But the Jeffersonian (and, in some respects, populist) tilt to the New Freedom was more rooted in rural, localist suspicions of distant, concentrated power as wielded by political and economic elites.

Whereas the New Nationalists were more likely to recognize some of the benefits – if not the inevitability – of some concentrations of economic power, and thus advocate regulating as opposed to smashing it, in a collection of writings on banking and finance entitled *Other People's Money* (1914), Brandeis categorically denounced the "the curse of bigness," and, like the rural populists of yore, called on government to break it up. Like the later Jefferson, Brandeis became a strong proponent of the broad democratization of all institutions – whether governmental or private – that exercised inordinate powers over the individual. And, like Jefferson, Brandeis understood democracy to be premised upon egalitarian republican presuppositions holding that, in a true community, citizens would meet in the public sphere as genuine civic equals – although in practice the two progressives either ignored (Brandeis) or stridently opposed (Wilson) the claims to full civic inclusion of African-Americans.

In *The New Freedom* (1913), Wilson, a Princeton political scientist, posited a misfit between the institutions established by the US Constitution and modern conditions which, he argued, the founders, had they been around today, would have acknowledged and addressed. In his earlier academic writings, Wilson had argued that the country would be better served by jettisoning its eighteenth-century Constitution, which was premised on the fragmentation of governing power through the separation of powers and federalism. In its place, he called for the adoption a British-style parliamentary system in which governing power would be efficaciously unified, and democratically accountable and responsive. Wilson championed an expansion of the powers of (expert) administration – which, during the mobilization for World War I, his administration would employ to an unprecedented extent. Later, however, he abandoned his call for a new Constitution, and argued instead for a more flexible and adaptive (Darwinian) understanding of governing possibilities under the nation's extant foundational law. It was high time for average Americans – not the commercial and industrial elites favored by Hamilton – to reclaim their right to self-government and, indeed, their liberty. "Freedom to-day," Wilson affirmed, "is something more than being let alone." To achieve these ends, "[t]he program of a government of freedom must in these days be positive."

Croly, Roosevelt, and Wilson provided peak political leadership, and a national political focus. But the progressive movement was large, sprawling, and fractious, with a rich variety of theorists and leaders at the local, state, and national levels. Progressives shared a sense that conditions had changed in critical ways that had caused a bewildering array of new social problems that the country was forced to confront. They believed that this would require a more active role for governments. And they believed that the prevailing dogmas concerning what the nation's founders supposedly wanted, and what the Constitution they had framed had supposedly required, in conjunction with the low, selfish, "gaming spirit" of party politics and unprecedented concentrations of wealth, were standing in the way of necessary reforms, and the possibility of effectively meeting the challenges of their day.

Some progressives placed an overriding faith in the possibilities of public-spirited administration and regulation by a well-trained, presumptively apolitical, cadre of expert civil servants. Others were more focused on the activation of broad-based and well-informed participatory democracy, which a number of them believed was not only the best form of government for Americans, but also an ideal worth working to establish, even if by the (ostensibly benevolent) application of force, worldwide, (Many progressives, like Theodore Roosevelt, were ardent champions of American empire.) Progressives often blended these diverse commitments in their own distinctive ways. They pioneered municipal government and electoral reform, modern academic social science, civil rights (the NAACP), modern professional social work, mothers' pensions, poverty relief, child welfare initiatives, the consumer movement, and new theories of education, of public opinion research and media criticism, and modern theories of ethnic and cultural pluralism.

While the progressive reformist fever transforming American government and politics was a casualty of World War I, progressive legislation contin- ued to be enacted even under a succession of more conservative Republican presidents – Warren G. Harding, Calvin Coolidge, and Herbert Hoover – across the 1920s. With the stock market crash that sparked the Great Depression (1929), the reformist troika of farmers, industrial labor, and urban middle-class professionals (lawyers, academics, clergy, social scientists, social workers, and free-floating reform-minded journalists and intellectuals) who had coalesced earlier to form the progressive movement not only united, but also, in a series of electoral landslides, moved once again to the forefront of the country's public life, claiming political power at virtually every level of American gov- ernment. In the 1930s and 1940s under President Franklin Delano Roosevelt – now flying under the banner of [modern] "liberalism" – this governing troika would set the country's intellectual and political agenda for the next half- century, and, in many respects, to the present.[8]

The New Pluralism: Ethnicity, Nationality, and Race

If these late nineteenth- and early twentieth-century developments were not transformative enough, the country's demographics were rapidly changing as well: the country was experiencing an unprecedented influx of immigrants from unfamiliar places – people of very different races, ethnicities, religions, and cultures. Between the 1880s and the Immigration Act (1924) – which, following the more targeted Chinese Exclusion Act (1882), imposed sweeping immigration restrictions that lasted until 1965 – Italians and Irish, Germans and Scandinavians, Eastern European Jews and Slavs, and the Chinese arrived in America in droves. (Those who came in through New York were greeted by the newly constructed Statue of Liberty – built 1875–1886 – which soon became a symbol of American openness and pluralism.) Many of these new immigrants were impoverished, illiterate, and did not speak English. They were not "white" (although the category "white" shifted across time, accord- ing to the vagaries of ascriptive classifications signaling membership and exclusion). Some were not Christians, and many who were were Roman Catholics or Eastern Orthodox, arriving in a heretofore *de facto* Protestant country. The population doubled between 1860 and 1900. Tracts like Madison Grant's *The Passing of the Great Race* (1916) raised concerns about an alien invasion and sounded alarms about replacement by the unassimilable – by those who shared neither the Anglo-Saxon race, nor its traditions, culture, and political values. Who then, indeed, were these *new* new men?

Widespread anxiety about ethnic, national, and racial pluralism was fed by the conviction that freedom – individual liberty under law – had a history, and that history was English. The sources of this belief were not obscure. The United States had emerged from a group of British colonies whose understandings of political authority and its limits were both genealogically English and forged in reaction to English political developments. Magna Carta; the development of English common law; the Protestant Reformation and the Church of England's split from Rome; the Petition of Right; the Glorious Revolution; the English Bill of Rights; and the formation of dissenting Protestant sects like Baptists, Methodists, and Quakers demanding rights of conscience and religious liberty – all these underwrote the lifeworld within which Americans had established their ideas, institutions, and conceptions of freedom. The nation's founding had been widely understood to be the latest chapter in the great story of the progress of Anglo-Saxon liberty – a relatively new description that masked even England's (to say nothing of Great Britain's or the United Kingdom's) diversity. Many Americans took this tradition and trajectory to be existentially menaced by the arrival *en masse* of this new class of immigrants. Did these people believe in the liberty we cherished? Were they even capable of understanding it?

Such concerns were hardly unprecedented. There had been deep uneasiness in the late eighteenth and early to mid-nineteenth centuries about, first, immigrants from revolutionary France, and then waves of Irish Catholics, the latter of whom helped spur the formation of the nativist Know-Nothing movement (1855–1860). Similar concerns were implicated in the country's continental expansion. Jefferson imagined westward territorial expansion as laying the foundations for an "empire of liberty." But the pioneer settlers starting from the east coast were well aware that the West, like the eastern seaboard before it, was already occupied by broadly dispersed aboriginal populations, and, further west, by Mexicans. While the native American "Indians" fascinated some like the artist George Catlin and the naturalist George Bird Grinnell, and the Spanish Catholic Mexican culture was honored by others, the most hard-charging considered these peoples a nuisance and an obstacle. The debate was over whether they should be absorbed and assimilated, removed and quarantined, or exterminated.

By the late nineteenth century, the formerly Mexican territories in the West had been conquered. But the aboriginal Indians remained. In *The Winning of the West* (1889), the rising Theodore Roosevelt nodded half-heartedly at humanitarian concerns many had voiced about their fate, before lashing out at the "false sentimentality" surrounding the matter. "It is ... a warped, perverse, and silly morality," he impatiently asserted, "which would forbid a course of conquest that has turned whole continents into seats of mighty and flourishing civilized nations."

Americans who advocated US imperial expansion at this time, like Roosevelt, Josiah Strong, Albert Beveridge, and others – whether on the North American continent or abroad – rarely minced words. There was no need to read between the lines to suss out ascriptive racist, nativist, ethno-nationalist, and expansionist convictions: civilization was confidently distinguished from barbarism, civilized peoples from savages, Christians from infidels, and the morally, physically, scientifically, and technologically superior from the backward and benighted, white from dark.

Civilized, white, Anglo-Saxon Christian peoples, it was said, had demonstrated their superiority by their manifest achievements and their military triumphs. With their energy, industry, and ambition, the Anglo-Saxon race had proved immensely productive and generative. The nomadic Indian tribes wandered the prairies in ways that were indistinguishable from their ancestors: they wasted their time doing, and improving, nothing. The world's other backward peoples were simply variants on this same theme. Thankfully, the Anglo-Saxon in America, this race of "energetic, restless, and courageous men," cheered Josiah Strong, had a "genius for colonizing." Albert Beveridge explained that he was fully justified in seizing land, and even whole countries, abroad if he could make better use of their land and natural resources, to say nothing of their peoples. This vision was underwritten, if not rationalized, by a diverse array of ideologies, from white supremacism to cultural humanistic tutelage (Shakespeare! Beethoven!), Christian evangelism, Darwinian theories of survival of the fittest, and hopes for the spread of Lockean liberalism, whose promise of the ownership of property, and a passion for progress, improvement, and individual rights, was intertwined with a theory of the state of nature and natural rights that sought to justify the colonial expropriation of North America from its indigenous peoples.

At the same time, some of these same ideologies led others, including members of the Anti-Imperialist League (1899), to strenuously *oppose* US colonialism, most prominently during the Spanish–American War of 1898 (in which the United States seized Cuba, Puerto Rico, the Philippines, and Guam). Echoing earlier criticism (by Abraham Lincoln, among others) of the Mexican–American War, the United States' anti-imperialist resistance condemned the country's imperial land-grab as a trumped-up military adventure aimed at illegitimate conquest, and an affront to the principles of popular sovereignty that were purportedly a core part of the American Creed. The libertarian William Graham Sumner warned that foreign conquests would soon come home to roost in ballooning military budgets, jobbery, and tax hikes.

From its earliest white settlement, the country had oppressed people and then justified that oppression by defining them as racially different or inferior. Civil War-era emancipation (1865) had ended at least inter-generational, race-based chattel slavery. But given the persistence of racism and white supremacist politics, and the degree to which state and society alike could be marshaled brutally to enforce those politics against African-Americans, and suppress any concerted resistance – to say nothing of the depredations wrought by generations of racialized bondage – the actual civic status of the approximately four million formerly enslaved people in the aftermath of this racial trauma remained an open question, as it does to this day.

The bid by the victors of the Civil War to guarantee liberty and equality to the country's formerly enslaved peoples met with strenuous resistance in the South, where most African-Americans of necessity continued to live. That white supremacist opposition was met with gradually waning force from the national government until the end of Reconstruction (1877), when, in the aftermath of the negotiated settlement of a disputed presidential election, active federal supervision of the South involving race was almost entirely withdrawn.

The national government pull-back was reinforced by Supreme Court rulings that, while setting a basic floor that prevented openly avowed legal discrimination on the basis of race, provided a roadmap for state and local governments for circumventing the laws and denying African-American civil rights. In the *Civil Rights Cases* (1883), the Court struck down the Civil Rights Act of 1875 (which had targeted discrimination by private entities) on the grounds that it had exceeded Congress's constitutional powers. A new "Jim Crow" apartheid system of legally enforced segregation (1890) was soon sanctioned by the Supreme Court (with a lone dissent) in *Plessy v. Ferguson* (1896). In the second decade of the twentieth century, the by-then largely defunct hooded white supremacist terrorist group the Ku Klux Klan was essentially refounded, and its redemptionist escapades celebrated, in the D.W. Griffith film *The Birth of a Nation* (1915), based on *The Clansman*, a 1905 novel by Thomas Dixon Jr. Griffith's account of white southern heroism, black incompetence, buffoonery, and complacency, and northern perfidy took root in the "lost cause" stories told in history books and American popular culture alike. In the "redeemed" Jim Crow South, blacks seen as stepping out of line – such as by being taken by whites as insufficiently deferential to ascribed racial hierarchies, of not "knowing their place," or being accused (often falsely) of preying upon white women or of committing crimes – were hauled out of police custody (often with police collusion), nooses wrapped around their necks, and hanged from trees, their swinging corpses set ablaze. Lynchings were celebrated as festive public occasions, drawing laughing, cheering crowds, and memorialized in picture postcards sold at drugstores. Racial violence – commonly sparked by instances when whites perceived blacks as having stepped out of their appropriate role or place – ignited white racist pogroms in which, in a few instances (e.g. Tulsa,

Oklahoma, 1921), thriving African-American neighborhoods were burned to the ground. Broad and vague statutes criminalizing loitering and unemployment were deployed to round up black workers and enlist them in convict labor systems to pick cotton or do hard labor on chain gangs, reinstituting slavery by other means. The southern African-American blues and gospel traditions (exemplified in songs like "Sometimes I Feel Like a Motherless Child," "Nobody Knows the Trouble I've Seen," and "Dark Was the Night (Cold Was the Ground)"), which became the basis for much of twentieth-century American popular music, memorialized, and sought respite from, these dire conditions. While not setting up quite as blatant and systematically legalized a white supremacist order, racial segregation in housing and work and other areas was informally enforced in the North as well. Racially restrictive real estate covenants, discriminatory lending (including redlining), racialized exclusion from labor unions, refusals to rent, sell, hire, and associate, and innumerable acts of informal discrimination provided an estimable counterpart to the Jim Crow South. In the North, however, crucially, blacks could vote. World Wars I and II, moreover, created an unslakable demand for industrial labor in northern factories, and the geographic push and pull sparked "the Great Migration" of millions of African-Americans from the South to northern cities, widespread racial discrimination notwithstanding, where new political and cultural opportunities beckoned.

In this context, the landscape of conspiracy against, indifference to, and support for African-American civil rights was both complicated and fluid. Consistent with its class-based understanding of the labor struggle, the labor movement's left flank, including the socialist Eugene Debs, the Industrial Workers of the World, the Knights of Labor, and the Communist Party, was outspoken in its commitment to racial equality. What mattered on the Left was working-class unity in fighting exploitative capitalism – not race, sex, nationality, or religion, all wedges, it was said, capitalists drove to fracture working-class solidarity. Important elements of the populist movement worked to build cross-racial coalitions. Reformers, meanwhile, mounted aggressive campaigns against particular injustices, such as Ida B. Wells-Barnett's anti-lynching campaign.

Apparent fluidity sparked new thinking. While some of the antebellum era's leading abolitionists like Frederick Douglass were still on the scene, a rising cohort of black thinkers were reconstituting the debate. Booker T. Washington, W.E.B. Du Bois, and Marcus Garvey alighted upon a set of themes that still frame debates about racial justice, civil rights, and American liberty, equality, and democracy: Americanism versus black nationalism (and pan-Africanism); integration versus separatism; accommodation versus

> In the past ten years over a thousand colored men, women and children have been butchered, murdered and burnt in all parts of the South. . . . Those who commit the murders write the reports, and hence these lasting blots upon the honor of a nation cause but a faint ripple on the outside world. They arouse no great indignation and call forth no adequate demand for justice. The victims were black, and the reports are so written as to make it appear that the helpless creatures deserved the fate which overtook them.
>
> Ida B. Wells-Barnett (1893)

confrontation; and repudiation versus redemption. At the same time, the philosopher Alain Locke heralded the intellectual and cultural arrival of the "New Negro" in a flourishing black literary and artistic "Harlem Renaissance" in New York City's pre-eminent black neighborhood.

Born into slavery and educated at tidewater Virginia's Hampton Institute (founded in 1868 by a bi-racial group of Christian missionaries to provide vocational and technical education for freed slaves), Booker T. Washington argued, vehemently and controversially, for self-help. It can be perilous to speak definitively about the essence of Washington's actual (privately held) views. This is not because he did not write and speak firmly and clearly, but because, like most black political thinkers operating in harsh, and perpetually shifting, political contexts and conditions, his public voice was sometimes circumspect, and strategic. Like many politicians, moreover, who are conscious of their different audiences, Washington tailored his arguments accordingly. The views of black political thinkers of this era also understandably changed in important ways over the course of their lifetimes, shaped by their ongoing reflections and experiences. Perhaps because Washington's call for "uplift" harmonized with the broader currents of his era's liberal individualist American political thought, then prominent both generally and within the post-Civil War Republican Party – to which African-Americans were deeply loyal – Washington became one America's most famous public figures.

> I believe it is the duty of the Negro – as the greater part of the race is already doing – to deport himself modestly in regard to political claims.
>
> Booker T. Washington (1895)

Washington's own life exemplified the path he preached. As recounted in his bestselling autobiography *Up from Slavery* (1901), once freed, he decided that he would not bemoan his lowly position, wallow in racial resentment, or issue intransigent demands. He would have no truck with labor unions or radical politics. What he would do was set his nose to the grindstone, work hard, and pull himself up by his bootstraps. Washington succeeded, founding a university committed to his philosophy: Alabama's Tuskeegee Institute (1881), where African-Americans were given the building blocks they needed to begin their own journey of uncomplaining hard work and achievement. Along the way, Washington won renown as a "spokesman for his race" who bent the ears of the rich and powerful, including Andrew Carnegie, John D. Rockefeller, and Presidents William Howard Taft and Theodore Roosevelt. Washington argued (most succinctly in his *Atlanta Exposition Address*, 1895) that America was a great land blessed by economic and political freedoms. While harboring no illusions about racial bigotry and discrimination, he argued that once it had lanced the boil of slavery, the United States could at last live up to its genuine promise as a place where the ultimate measure of men and women (regardless of race) would be worldly achievement. Over time, hard work and merit would be recognized and rewarded. Given his gospel of work and success, it is no wonder that Washington secured hefty donations from wealthy northern businessmen like Carnegie and Rockefeller, men who had also started from nothing, and built their vast fortunes, industries, and institutions through relentless labor and vaulting ambition. (These wealthy white philanthropists bankrolled the establishment of many of the United States' historically black private colleges and universities, like Spelman and Morehouse, while other historically black public universities were funded by Republican-sponsored federal land grants.) Criticizing blacks who were demanding social and political equality – although he favored both, and insisted on the right to vote – Washington argued that broader civic and social equality would not come through "artificial forcing," but through the application of the "industrial virtues" that William Graham Sumner had championed. "No race that has anything to contribute to the markets of the world," Washington insisted, "is long in any degree ostracized."

W.E.B. Du Bois came from a different world, possessed of a different temperament and talents, and arrived at very different opinions. Born in the relatively tolerant and nearly all-white mountains of western Massachusetts, the bookish Du Bois was possessed of a piercing and capacious intelligence that was immediately recognized by his white neighbors, who raised the money to send him to Nashville's historically black Fisk University, where he was stunned by the brutality of southern racial oppression. He went on to graduate school at Harvard, where he was the first African-American to earn a Ph.D.

Du Bois's broad and extensive personal and political odyssey and accomplishment defies easy summary: having renounced his American citizenship and joined the Communist Party, he died an exile in Ghana during President John F. Kennedy's administration (1963). In addition to serving as a university professor who wrote a seminal history of Reconstruction, a pioneering sociological study of the Philadelphia Negro, and a profound socio-cultural-political reflection on "the souls of black folk," Du Bois was a driving force behind the Niagara Movement and the founding of the (bi-racial) National Association for the Advancement of Colored People (NAACP) (1909), which forged the modern civil rights vision and program. Later, he moved decidedly to the Left, penning important anticolonial, pan-Africanist, and black nationalist statements.

The Souls of Black Folk (1903) was, among other things, a landmark work of cultural imagination that sought to define no less than the position and predicament of African-Americans in the country of their birth, where their ancestors had been brought, via the barbaric Middle Passage, in shackles and chains. "Between me and the other world there is ever the unasked question," Du Bois attested, in a moment of sustained interiority, "How does it feel to be a problem?" Du Bois told of the moment as a child when he first came to realize that, because of the color of his skin, he had been consigned, even by the well intentioned, to an alternate world, "shut out . . . by a vast veil." "Why did God make me an outcast and a stranger in my own house?" he queried the heavens. As a result of this strange position of living in "a world which . . . only lets him see himself through the revelation of the other world," however, the American Negro was "gifted with a second-sight," a sense of "his twoness," as an American and a Negro, that yielded a "double-consciousness, this sense of always looking at one's self through the eyes of others, of measuring one's self by the tape of a world that looks on in amused contempt and pity." The result was that the American Negro could not attain a "true self-consciousness" – a sense of a true and unified self. He was not only psychologically but also culturally fragmented and fractured – torn asunder in the deepest regions of his psyche, beset by a "longing . . . to merge his double self into a better and truer self," but in a way in which "neither of the older selves [would] be lost." The issue transcended the personal, Du Bois explained. There was no "America" or "United States" in any meaningful sense – economic, political, historical, social, or cultural – without the black person, the black body, and the black experience. "[T]he Negro problem," as such, posed "a concrete test of the underlying principles of the great republic."

One of the major purposes of the essays in *The Souls of Black Folk* and in the civil rights conclave in Niagara Falls, Canada, that gave birth to the Niagara Movement was to oppose and offer an alternative to what Du Bois dismissively dubbed Booker T. Washington's "Atlanta Compromise" and "The Tuskeegee Machine" – Washington's "programme of industrial education, conciliation of the South, and submission and silence as to civil and political rights." Snidely describing Washington as "the most distinguished southerner since Jefferson Davis," Du Bois set himself against "Mr. Washington's cult," so in tune with the Gilded Age's grotesque materialism, commercialism, and gospel of success that he despised. To this, Du Bois outlined an alternative that insisted upon political power, civil rights, and first-class liberal arts educations for African-American youth.

Du Bois denounced Washington's contention that the black man's "future rise depends primarily on his own efforts." This, Du Bois complained, "has tended to make the whites . . . shift the burden of the Negro problem to the Negro's shoulders," and has allowed them to "stand aside as critical and rather pessimistic spectators, when in fact the burden belongs to the nation, and the hands of none of us are clean if we bend not our energies to righting these great wrongs." In a founding statement of the civil rights movement published in the NAACP's influential magazine, *The Crisis*, Du Bois (its editor) called for political mobilization for a confrontational program that would litigate, legislate, and promote social integration among the races to expand economic opportunity, promote public education (generally, and for "the talented tenth" black elite), cultivate black culture, and legally enforce civic equality. Spurning conciliation and accommodation, Du Bois demanded full civil, political, and social rights.

Even the foundational opposition between Washington and Du Bois, however, did not exhaust the choices on offer to black Americans in this fertile moment. While not the first black nationalist, or the first black to advocate for a return to the African homeland, the Jamaican-born, London-educated, and Harlem-based Marcus Garvey's Back to Africa Movement, spearheaded by his Universal Negro Improvement Association (UNIA), preached a distinctive version of black pride, black culture, black nationalism, and black repatriation.

In retrospect, in mapping this moment of African-American political thought, we might be tempted to place Marcus Garvey on the Left, Washington on the Right, and Du Bois in the middle. The deeper one delves, however, the less plausible this classification becomes. Garvey, as it happens, admired Booker T. Washington and he was contemptuous of both Du Bois (whom he dismissed as a "mulatto leader") and the NAACP. What Garvey admired in Washington was his commitment to self-help and self-determination, and his insistence that blacks not depend on whites, from whom Garvey expected (and asked for) nothing. Garvey despised Du Bois's integrationism. A separatist, Garvey had no desire to move beyond race, or look outside the black community. The white and black races were different, he affirmed: each constituted its own separate nation. (Here, Garvey agreed with the Ku Klux Klan, with whom he had cordial discussions.) Garvey was a pan-Africanist. He believed that those of black African ancestry all over the world were "one in blood." Celebrating "the pride and purity of race," Garvey denounced race-mixing, which "destroy[ed] the Creator's plan by the constant introduction of mongrel types." "Surely the time has come," he announced in *The True Solution to the Negro Problem* (1922), "for the Negro to look homeward" to Africa.

Garvey's vision appealed to a large segment of American blacks, particularly in New York City, where he fronted efforts to transport willing subscribers to Africa on his Black Star shipping lines. Ensnared in a flurry of corruption charges, however, Garvey was deported to England, effectively ending his American sojourn. It would be a mistake, however, to see him as a failed or fringe figure. His efforts to found a mass movement among American blacks was uniquely successful for its time. Garvey, moreover, had a profound influence not only on the development of the Rastafarian religion in Jamaica (despite the fact that he had no personal involvement with it), but also on the Reverend Elijah Muhammad's Nation of Islam, the political philosophy of Nation of Islam minister Malcolm X (whose parents had first met at a UNIA meeting), the political thought of the Black Power, Black Pride, and Black is Beautiful movements of the 1960s and 1970s, as well as the prominent radical black self-defense organization the Black Panthers.

Sex and Gender

The civic status of women raised related but distinctive questions about ascriptive hierarchies and civic membership. While at least white women benefited from the perquisites of their race, even they, by virtue of their sex, were considered outside the ambit of full civic equality. Although not the first time women protested their status, feminism's post-bellum "first wave" achieved a critical mass, and culminated in the adoption of the Nineteenth Amendment (1920), guaranteeing women the right to vote.

First-wave feminists raised issues that would define both feminism and other movements against subordination and exclusion and for full civic equality. One involved liberalism's foundational separation of the public and private spheres, with the "political" (parties, elections, voting, and legislating) attributed to the former, and the non-political "private" (cooking, cleaning, child-rearing, socializing, and recreation) consigned to the latter. Many first-wave feminists were coming to appreciate that, given their ascriptive position and status, hewing to familiar lines demarcating separate private and public spheres would be difficult: matters like sex, marriage, and the household were highly political.

Much of women's exclusion and subordination was justified by an essentialism holding women to be naturally ill suited to participation in public life. In her satire "If Men Were Seeking the Franchise" (1913), Jane Addams, the progressive reformer active in the settlement house movement (with Julia Lathrop, she founded Chicago's Hull House), temporarily set aside the question of the attribution of a set of female characteristics to women's essential "nature." But, Addams archly wondered, why were we ignoring men's natures, instead of asking whether it justified *men's* exclusion from public life? Given their bellicosity, vengefulness, and congenital obsession with sports, rankings, prizes, and money, and given men's deplorable insouciance about cleanliness and indifference to children, should they really be entrusted with the vote and allowed to hold public office? For her part, Victoria Woodhull, the advocate for the freedom of sexual intimacy outside of marriage ("free love"), spurned essentialist understandings of female modesty and domesticity, declaring to an audience of over three thousand people at New York City's Steinway Hall (1871) that "I have an *inalienable*, *constitutional*, and *natural* right to love whom I may, to love as *long* or as *short* a period as I can; to *change* that love *every day* if I please, and with *that* right neither *you* nor *any* law you can frame have *any* right to interfere."

While Emma Goldman wrote broadly about the deformations to the human soul wrought by domination and oppression of any kind, estranging human beings from their true natures and their all-but-limitless potential, Charlotte Perkins Gilman penned more personal accounts of oppression's psychic toll. In *The Yellow Wallpaper* (1892), Gilman portrayed a woman succumbing to mental illness while essentially imprisoned in her home by her husband – a credentialed medical doctor and man of science – ostensibly for the sake of her health. In her utopian novel *Herland* (1915), Gilman imagined three friends on a scientific expedition in the Peruvian jungle who stumble upon an all-female society. As in *Looking Backward*, the men in the group (especially) bombard the inhabitants of this strange new world with questions. Among its most notable features, they learn, is the complete erasure of the border between public and private. Gilman pursued this theme further in *Women and Economics* (1898) and *The Home: Its Work and Influence* (1903), where she asked how contemporary society might be restructured to make women's equality possible. The assignment of the responsibilities of cooking, cleaning, and child-rearing to women, Gilman argued, had all but precluded their full civic equality. Gilman rejected gendered understandings of these household tasks, and called for their collective assumption by society.

Conclusion

While it contained none of the epochal "constitutional moments"[9] like the American Revolution, the Civil War, or the subsequent Great Depression/ New Deal, the late nineteenth and early twentieth century was nevertheless a major turning point, with a revolutionary impact on how future Americans would understand and practice politics. Industrialization, urbanization, mass and radically pluralistic immigration, and the transportation, communications, and organizational revolutions raised unprecedented challenges and problems on a grand scale, prompting a cascade of questions concerning the role of government and the metes and bounds of membership.

The era's conservatives, holding sacrosanct a negative understanding of individual liberty, fought to hold the line, insisting upon a sharp – and, arguably, even sharper – separation of the public and private spheres, and a highly circumscribed role for government, whatever the economic, political, and intellectual pressures to abandon those commitments. Proto-progressives like Lester Ward, however, began to reimagine an involved activist government mobilizing scientific/social scientific expertise as an instrument for addressing, and potentially solving, social problems, which they refused to regard as "natural" and inevitable.

Waves of successive reform movements, including the insurgent populist, labor, and progressive movements, and an unprecedented cohort of radical anarchists, syndicalists, communists, and socialists all demanded action, either within the system or outside it. Fundamental questions about the nature of the polity were raised not only about the role of government but also about the terms of political membership. The nation continued to expand, both geographically – and now, imperialistically, outside the continental United States – and in its ethnic/religious/racial composition. Was it the same nation? Could it be? Should it be? African-Americans and women, moreover – who were present from the very beginning and had questioned and then aggressively challenged the terms on which they had been included all along – began to find an unprecedented public profile for their campaigns, portending new thinking about equality under the rubrics of feminism and civil rights.

Questions

1. How useful or appropriate is it to think about political ideas like liberty, equality, and democracy separate from material, real-world, social, economic, and political developments? Do these societal changes alter the meaning and implications of these ostensibly "timeless" political-philosophical principles, suggesting new understandings, for example, of the role of public institutions like government, or private institutions like the family?
2. Are (inordinate?) concentrations of private power the proper concern of government?
3. Can more government ever mean more freedom?
4. Can the study of society ever be approached as a natural science like chemistry or physics, neutrally and dispassionately, in a "value-free" way, without regard to any underlying moral or ethical theory?
5. Can government experts – bureaucrats – ever, or consistently, act in politically neutral ways to dispassionately advance the public interest?
6. Are there "natural" laws concerning economics, politics, sex/gender/ sexuality, and race? If so, is it folly – or dangerous – to interfere with them?
7. Do pragmatism and progressive political thought counsel abandonment of those natural laws? For good or for ill?
8. Is wealth inequality a political problem or an economic necessity?
9. Which is more "Christian" or "godly": capitalism or socialism?
10. How useful is the concept of the "self-made" man, who succeeds by "pulling himself up by his bootstraps"? Are "industrial virtues," republican virtues, and liberal virtues compatible?
11. Is radicalism or reformism more appealing, whether in its underlying political understandings or its proffered political strategies? Do you consider radicalism dangerous or necessary? Do you consider reformism evasive or practical?
12. Is political partisanship a good or a bad thing?
13. Is increasing racial, ethnic, and religious pluralism good or bad for society? Does it portend good or ill for a polity?
14. Is a rise in populist sentiment good or bad for a polity? Is populism inherently "liberal" or "conservative"?

6

The New Deal Liberal Order:
Collapse, Culmination, or "Great Exception"?

By the second decade of the twentieth century, the old order had been under sustained intellectual and political assault for decades. Populism, progressivism, and a host of radical parties and movements had forged transformative understandings of the role of government and the relation between the public and private spheres. Although their paths to power had been quirky, two progressive presidents had made it to the White House, and made the most of it. Propelled by clear visions and possessed of remarkable capacities for executive leadership, both Theodore Roosevelt (1901–1909) and Woodrow Wilson (1913–1921) were brimming with policies, initiatives, decisions, and paths. They, and other movement actors, were already changing the basic structures of American government.

The country's first expert independent regulatory commission, the Interstate Commerce Commission (ICC), which focused on railroads, had been created as far back as 1886. But the Wilson administration continued along this path, launching both the Federal Reserve (1913) to apolitically steer the nation's monetary policy, and the Federal Trade Commission (1914) to police monopolistic policies and set rules of fair competition in economic markets. Four "progressive" amendments to the Constitution had been ratified. The Sixteenth Amendment overruled a Supreme Court decision to authorize a federal income tax aimed at financially shoring up an increasingly proactive and engaged federal government; the Seventeenth Amendment paved a path for ordinary voters to get around state legislatures that were ostensibly captured by big money by instituting the direct, popular election of US Senators; the Eighteenth Amendment struck a blow for women and families, rational and sober living, and democratic deliberation by the prohibition of alcohol; and the Nineteenth Amendment accomplished the same objectives by other means by giving women the right to vote.

If, as the progressive Randolph Bourne pithily decreed, "war is the health of the state," the mobilization for World War I under Wilson drilled the US government into tip-top shape. During the war, the federal government assumed the management of railroads and mines, set food prices, and, to pay for it all, hiked the top statutory income tax bracket to an unprecedented 94% (with an effective tax rate for the top 1% of 40–50%). (The income tax that the Supreme Court had struck down as unconstitutional in 1895 had been 2% on incomes

137

over $4,000, which, at the time, comprised the top 1%.) Given global trends –
the Bolshevik Revolution (of which the progressive Lincoln Steffens declared,
"I have seen the future, and it works"), the appearance of Fabian Society (1884)
democratic socialism in the longstandingly liberal Great Britain, and even
German conservative Otto von Bismarck's support for the establishment of a
social welfare state to stave off popular discontent and diminish the appeal
of radicalism – many took the turn toward active, interventionist, meliorist
government to mark an inevitable trend, an evolution that was part of a
historically determined path of progress.

World War I complicated the situation in diverse ways in Europe. In the
United States, with, arguably, an exceptional political culture undergirded
by different constitutional institutions and political thought traditions, the
trajectory was also complicated. Where Wilson had been a visionary with
grand ambitions for American (and, in some ways, world) government, his
successor, the conservative Ohio Republican Warren Harding, promised a
"return to normalcy." During the 1920s, a succession of Republican presidents
– Harding, Calvin Coolidge, and Herbert Hoover – rolled back taxes and cut
federal regulations. At the same time, the *status quo ante* had hardly been
restored, and Republicans and Democrats joined to continue the (patchwork)
construction of modern activist government. While agriculture struggled, the
general economy boomed, a mass consumer culture flowered, and at least
the most aggressive reform agendas stalled. As President Coolidge famously
declared, celebrating what he took to be the national ethos, "The business of
America is business."

And then the stock market crashed (1929). The ham-handed responses in
Washington – in which the government initially did the opposite of what most
contemporary economists believe should be done under such circumstances
by championing individual austerity and government passivity, and instituting a draconian protective tariff – helped sink the United States, and then the
world, into the greatest economic cataclysm in world history. In the Great
Depression, the stock market lost two-thirds of its value, industrial production
fell by nearly a half, and almost a quarter of the workforce were unemployed.
Many on the Left were convinced that they were finally witnessing capitalism's end times, an eventuality they had long prophesied. The rolls of the
Communist Party swelled. It was the reformist liberals, however, who were
swept into power. The Democratic opposition, in quick succession, won control of Congress (1930), the White House (with the election of Franklin Delano
Roosevelt in 1932), and then even larger majorities in Congress. President
Roosevelt was repeatedly reelected for an unprecedented – and, eventually, via
the Twenty-Second Amendment (1951), outlawed – four terms. The Democrats
also secured overwhelming majorities of the nation's governorships and state
legislatures.

As the Nazis seized power and war loomed, reformist New Dealers, socialists (led by Norman Thomas), communists (under Earl Browder), and others on the Left, who often feuded with each other about what to do at home, quieted their disagreements and united as part of a patriotic, anti-fascist "Popular Front" (1935–1939). The Molotov–Ribbentrop (Hitler–Stalin) Pact (August 23, 1939), which paved the way for the German invasion of Poland a few weeks later that started World War II (September 1, 1939), ended this brief period of Left–liberal unity. A few die-hards, like the great African-American singer Paul Robeson, drawn by the party's universalist hopes and aspirations, commitment to the interests of the working class, and stand against racial injustice, remained stalwart communists. Many others, however, turned in their membership cards. A sectarian anti-Stalinist Trotskyist Left formed under the leadership of James P. Cannon, Martin Abern, Max Shachtman, and others. Their one-time membership in the party during the Popular Front period would come to haunt many former communists during the Cold War, particularly during the "McCarthy era" (1950–1954), when, following the "loss" of China to Chairman Mao Zedong's communist insurgency (1949), and the outbreak of the Korean War (1950–1953), many American communists and ex-communists were fired from their jobs, or blacklisted. A liberal anticommunist civil libertarian resistance championing freedom of speech and academic freedom formed.

On December 7, 1941, Imperial Japan, allied with Fascist Italy and Nazi Germany, attacked the American military base at Pearl Harbor, Hawaii. In a dramatic appearance before Congress, President Franklin Roosevelt sought and secured a declaration of war. The United States had entered World War II (1939–1945).

The New Deal

The guillotine of the Great Depression fell on the watch of the business-worshipping Republicans – not just Herbert Hoover, but a decade's worth of business-friendly Republican stewardship. The conservatives' response to the cataclysm was, essentially, to take some ameliorative measures, but to hold fast to the *status quo* economic and constitutional order. Boom-and-bust economic cycles, they explained, were defining features of capitalist markets. True, this depression was looking like an unusually destructive bust, but, ultimately, markets were self-correcting. What was most important – and in the long-term national interest – was to preserve the country's constitutional and institutional structure, which had made the United States the most dynamic, innovative, and prosperous country in the world. The US, the Republicans insisted, should ride out the storm. Politically, however, this was a non-starter: at every level of government, the Republicans had been routed. The Democrats were now in charge. The question was what should they do.

Franklin Roosevelt had long moved in progressive circles: as a New York

State legislator and then governor, he had favored more active, reformist government. But, as he entered the White House, he remained fairly conventional.
He initially hewed to prevailing understandings concerning budget deficits
(bad), and the practical, and liberal constitutional, limits on the powers of
both governments in general, and the national government in particular.
Roosevelt, however, was a consummate political animal – and ambitious to
his core – in a time that cried out for leadership. He proved flexible and pragmatic, insisting on continuous engagement to meet the deluge of national
problems.

Roosevelt demanded immediate action and results. He took risks and tried
new approaches, guided by a supreme self-confidence that made him comfortable with hearing diverse and divergent advice, sometimes vehemently
expressed by members of his "brains trust" of towering egos and intellects.
After listening and considering, he did not hesitate to make firm decisions
and move forward. In a Commencement Speech at Oglethorpe University
in 1932, he lambasted conservatives who advised him to "sit back and do
nothing." "The country needs and . . . the country demands bold, persistent
experimentation," he declared. While members of his administration held
different views on how far to take those experiments, the imperative of new
thinking and quick action was non-negotiable.

To rally the public – a relatively new job definition of the modern presidency pioneered by his progressive predecessors Theodore Roosevelt and
Woodrow Wilson – FDR fixed blame: the American people had been lied to
by the country's smug, self-serving, and selfish (if not self-deluding) corporate and financial buccaneers. They had sold Americans a "dazzling chimera"
about limited government, free markets, and business values. Taking a page
from Wilson, there were moments in which Roosevelt conceded the utility
of businessmen, even when their ethics were dubious. ("The financiers who
pushed the railroads to the Pacific were always ruthless, often wasteful, and
frequently corrupt; but they did build railroads.") But they had exercised
power irresponsibly. The money changers, FDR thundered, must be driven
from the Temple.

It was time to put "the public interest" first. We were living under an
"economic oligarchy." "[E]quality of opportunity as we have known it," FDR,
like his progressive movement progenitors, declared at San Francisco's
Commonwealth Club (1932), "no longer exists." "[T]he small man starts under
a handicap." The answer was a fearless assumption of the responsibility of an
active, public-spirited government – "enlightened administration," with an
eye less myopically focused on the needs of the country's producers, and more
on its consumers, less on its despotic big businessmen, and more on its small,
independent capitalists. The country needed no less than a new "economic
constitutional order," a renegotiation of the "terms of the old social contract."
In his First Inaugural Address (1933), FDR announced that he would assume

"unhesitatingly the leadership of this great army of our people dedicated to a disciplined attack upon our common problems."

Breaking with a precedent first established by George Washington, FDR served in the White House for nearly four full terms. This period in American history – chronicled by the likes of John Steinbeck, Woody Guthrie, Walker Evans, and Dorothea Lange – witnessed an avalanche of new departures in active, purposive government, at the state, local, and federal levels. FDR's slate of programs and policies are typically divided into the more radical and temporary "First" New Deal (including the vaunted "First Hundred Days") (1933–1934), and the stable, and lasting, "Second" New Deal (1935–1936). Following the program he had set out in his First Inaugural Address, FDR took the unprecedented step of ordering the closing of all the country's banks to prevent "runs" (panicked simultaneous withdrawals) that would precipitate their going belly-up. (Banks make money by keeping only a small portion of their deposits on-hand, and investing the rest. The Federal Deposit Insurance Act of 1950 would soon guarantee bank deposits, and end future bank runs.) To inflate the currency – an issue since at least the populists – Roosevelt took the country off the gold standard. To put money in people's pockets and buoy their spirits when the private sector seemed to be saying their services were no longer needed, he created a far-flung archipelago of public works projects and labor corps, many of which became legendary in their spirit and accomplishments: the Tennessee Valley Authority (TVA) and the Rural Electrification Administration (REA) provided electricity to Americans living in formerly isolated and unserved rural areas; the Civilian Conservation Corps (CCC) put teams of young men to work on projects aimed at environmental stewardship, improvement, and sustainability; the Works Progress Administration (WPA) built infrastructure like dams and bridges; the Federal Writers Project (FWP) and Federal Theater Project (FTP) employed out-of-work artists. And there were many others. Roosevelt, moreover, sought to restore order, regularity, and, it was hoped, eventually, prosperity to important economic sectors. He did so by setting up cartels for virtually every major industry (coal, oil, poultry, steel, etc.), fixing wages and prices, and implementing codes of "fair competition."[1] The Agricultural Adjustment Administration (AAA) instituted price supports for farmers. The financial markets were regulated by the new US Securities and Exchange Commission (SEC). The labor regulations that had long been a major goal of the progressive and labor movements – minimum wage, maximum hours, and federal support for unionization and collective bargaining enabling organized labor to act as a counterweight to the power of their employers in negotiations of the terms and conditions of employment – were enacted and institutionalized in the form of the National Labor Relations Act (NLRA, 1935) and The Fair Labor Standards Act (FLSA, 1938). The Social Security Act (SSA, 1935) created a federal pension system to end poverty in old age. To take the edge off, the spirited FDR – who liked a good tipple – supported a successful drive to end Prohibition in 1933.

As a matter of political theory, the New Deal's "workplace constitutionalism" was especially significant. Drawing in part from the British Fabians – including Sidney and Beatrice Webb's *Industrial Democracy* (1897) – progressives like John Commons, John Dewey, Walter Lippmann, Louis Brandeis, and Herbert Croly had long been arguing for (and, in Commons's case in Wisconsin, implementing) the democratization of the American workplace. The purportedly private workplace, these progressives explained, was a key site of governance – of political and economic power. Conventional Lockean liberal understandings of private property rights and the division between the public and private spheres as applied to modern industrial conditions had essentially rendered these spaces autocracies, with the ruler/employer on top, possessed of total power, and the ruled/employee, below, subject to their arbitrary mercy and whim. Progressives had argued for the republican reorganization of workplace governance by instituting what FDR later called "an economic constitutional order" in which workers would be recognized as industrial citizens, with a participatory voice in how the industries in which they worked were run, and in setting their future direction. There had been diverse views among progressives about the structures and mechanisms best suited to implementing this republican, democratic vision. But as FDR and the Democrats swept into power in the 1930s, the moment of decision was at hand.

Drawing on earlier, more delimited experiments in particular industries, the collective bargaining provisions of the NLRA created a government-supervised system that formally brokered the power relations between employer and employees. This new legal structure – still in place today, and supervised by the National Labor Relations Board (NLRB) – set out formal rules and procedures concerning worker representation (through organized labor – unions), bargaining over the terms and conditions of employment, and the resolution of disputes. New Deal liberals celebrated this version of industrial democracy as a long-awaited grand achievement that empowered organized labor, ensured not only its recognition but also its support by the American state, and routinized the exercise of that power as part of the ordinary processes of government. Many became increasingly proud of this achievement as it proved its worth by both creating and anchoring an unprecedentedly prosperous and secure postwar American working and middle class.

Those further to the Left, however, were not nearly as sanguine about these new bureaucratic liberal arrangements. Whatever its origins in earlier calls for republican industrial democracy, the Left argued, the New Deal's workplace constitutionalism not only stopped well short of giving workers an ownership stake in the means of production, but it also effectively vitiated the sort of aggressive conflict in the form of strikes or boycotts that had historically proved essential to wringing any serious concessions from capitalist employers. As they saw it, the NLRB-supervised collective bargaining arrangements instituted by FDR had transformed what was once a site of class struggle and political contestation into an ostensibly apolitical, managerial system of bureaucratic management. Far from supporting organized labor, Roosevelt's New Deal had de-clawed and de-fanged it.

For their part, however, conservatives took these new arrangements – and, for that matter, the rest of the New Deal – as a triumph of leftism incarnate. They condemned what the liberals were calling "workplace constitutionalism" as an illegitimate abandonment of the *actual* Constitution: as they saw it, it had laid waste to the fundamental liberal rights of property and the liberty of business owners and individual workers alike. Had the country at long last succumbed to socialism? Or to a fascist dictatorship, instituted by a charismatic leader, not with a Hitlerian sourness or a Mussolini scowl, but with a confidently upward-jutting chin, an elegant, long-stemmed cigarette, and an insouciant "I-can-do-anything" smile? Although their voices were all but drowned out by the tsunami of New Deal programs unleashed by an earthquake of popular Democratic support, conservatives like Albert Jay Nock, Garet Garrett, Robert A. Taft, Isabel Paterson, Rose Wilder Lane, Westbrook Pegler, and Herbert Hoover were convinced that they were witnessing the triumph of socialism, fascism, or both. After initially taking a strong constitutional stand against Roosevelt's New Deal programs, the Supreme Court – having survived a challenge from the President, who proposed packing it with additional justices not constrained by "horse and buggy" legal understandings – began to systematically uphold FDR's (tweaked and revised) initiatives (1937). One dejected old-guard conservative, Justice James Clark McReynolds, sighed that "the Constitution is gone." Embittered, he later groused that any country that would elect Roosevelt four times wasn't worth saving.

> We must have government that builds stamina into communities and men. That makes men instead of mendicants. We must stop this softening of thrift, self-reliance and self-respect through dependence on government.
> Herbert Hoover (1936)

These charges of radicalism were most on-point when directed at the positions espoused (and, in some cases, written into law) by some of the more radical members of the President's "brains trust" like the Columbia University Professor Rexford Tugwell, who set out a forceful vision for a planned, *dirigiste* economic order, or by Agriculture Secretary (and penultimate FDR Vice-President and 1948 Progressive Party champion) Henry Wallace. Roosevelt himself, however, rejected the socialist (to say nothing of the "fascist") label. He called himself a "liberal." His first concern, he affirmed, was individual liberty. He was committed to making individual liberty a reality under modern conditions. In a departure from some of his progressive progenitors, FDR was fluent and passionate in speaking the language of rights. He called for "an economic declaration of rights" and "a second bill of rights." In one of his most memorialized speeches (1941) defining the country's mission as it entered World War II, he committed the United States to the defense and worldwide promulgation of "the four essential human freedoms": freedom of speech and expression, freedom of every person to worship God in his own way, freedom from want, and freedom from fear. In a departure from so-called "classical" liberalism, however – liberalism as William Graham Sumner and (the later) Herbert Hoover understood it, for instance – Roosevelt made clear that, under modern conditions dictated by the consolidation of private economic power, the realization of these freedoms would require *both* limiting *and* empowering governments, in the interest of both advancing rights and the broader public good. In setting out this "new" or "modern" liberalism, Roosevelt repurposed Sumner's "Forgotten Man," explaining that an active, purposive, and reformist government, far from being the enemy of the "Forgotten Man," was, rather, his fastest friend. In this, Roosevelt insisted, he was neither a socialist nor a classical *laissez-faire* liberal. He was proposing – as the postwar British Labor government was to do across the Atlantic – a bold new "third," or "middle," way. To preserve democracy at a moment in which self-government was confronting its gravest threat worldwide, and save both democracy and economic and political freedom, the role of government, these modern liberals like FDR contended, had to be rethought.

In the 1920s, appealing to what had developed into a symbol of American liberty, Herbert Hoover had described the American pioneers as "the epic expression" of American individualism, of the individual rising to "the challenge of opportunity" offered by a polity brimming over with abundance. The frontier had been pronounced officially closed just before the turn of the century. But Hoover, perhaps pricked by a frisson of unease about what the closing of the frontier portended for the character of successive generations of Americans, declared hopefully that "[t]he days of the pioneer are not over. . . . There will always be a frontier to conquer or to hold as long as men think, plan, and dare." What was essential, he argued, was to preserve the domain of "rugged individualism" by giving everyone a fair chance, and an equal opportunity, to make his way, seek his livelihood and fortune, and make his mark.

FDR had, on the other hand, wondered. To be sure, he explained in a campaign speech at San Francisco's Commonwealth Club (1932), "[i]ndividualism" had long been "made the great watchword of American life." That made sense when, in days that were "long and splendid," "[o]n the Western frontier, land was substantially free." There may have been a boom-and-bust economy. But, since one could always climb into a covered wagon and move west, "starvation and dislocation were practically impossible." The country had changed, however. For government to simply get out of the way now would not enhance freedom and liberate the individual but reinforce the individual's subservience to private power, and limit his opportunities. As he built the memorial to Thomas Jefferson on the Tidal Basin in Washington, Roosevelt was claiming the mantle of his Democratic Party progenitor who had championed limited government and localism, by insisting – in a new way, in new times – that he, too, was forging an "empire of liberty." That, in turn, would involve new departures in domestic government planning and administration, and in outward-looking global American leadership.

The Fate of the Individual in a Mass Polity

By the 1940s, mass entertainment had bloomed through the invention of film, radio, and television. The frontier story and epic – the western – became the country's most popular genre. Many American boys yearned for toy rifles and six-shooters, and played at fighting bandits, outlaws, and the Indians standing in the way of their westward progress. The good-guy versus bad-guy dynamic, and the "High Noon" imperative to stand and fight, was reinforced by the outbreak of the Cold War, in which, in the minds of many Americans, the United States stood for, and was defending, God and freedom, and the Soviet Union represented godlessness and enslavement.

This child's play and these popular narratives, to be sure, were fraught: they were underwritten by powerful ideologies, and dripped with assumptions and implications. One could chart the fate of all of these in postwar American politics across time by, for instance, reading the politics of Hollywood westerns, and even the roles played by the genre's greatest star, John Wayne, in the films of the genre's greatest director, John Ford, from *Stagecoach* (1939) to *The Searchers* (1956), to *The Man Who Shot Liberty Valance* (1962), and onwards to anti-westerns, like Sam Peckinpah's *The Wild Bunch* (1969), made at the height of the Vietnam War. In these later films, coincident with the rise of the "New Hollywood," there was no heroism to be found, just senseless violence of shocking cruelty and brutality.

But in yet another iteration of the paradoxical relationship between individualism and conformity in the United States' egalitarian democracy, "the myth of American individualism" (as the progressive historian Charles Beard described it) was celebrated in the western genre at a time when consumer ideals were displacing – and perhaps subverting – civic ideals: the rugged cowboy individualist was marketed to couch sloths in mass-produced suburban tract housing as a mass consumer product. Patriotism and loyalty, moreover, were not matters left to individual inclination and whim. Nor was belief in God. Both were mandatory. In new departures in "ceremonial deism," the motto "In God We Trust" was added to the currency. A similar reference to the deity was added to the heretofore secular Pledge of Allegiance (written, without the reference to God, in the late nineteenth century by an American socialist).

And one certainly did not have a choice in thinking about which political and economic system was best. America's system of liberal individualism, private property rights, and free markets, rooted in Christian foundations, was plainly superior. "Godless communism" (as the conservative Notre Dame Law

School Dean and right-wing impresario Clarence "Pat" Manion called it) was its antithesis, a repudiation of liberty and democracy in the name of a perverse and corrupt understanding of equality. Socialism, a softer form of communism, informed by Marxist premises, was closer to communism than democratic freedom – it was (the Austrian economist Friedrich von Hayek warned in 1944) paving "the road to serfdom." The United States' Cold War with the Soviet Union entailed a global struggle for spheres of influence fought via espionage, covert subversion, sponsorship of foreign surrogates, dangerous stand-offs and skirmishes (the Berlin Crisis, 1961; the Cuban Missile Crisis, 1962), and hot wars (the Korean War, 1950–1953, and the Vietnam War, 1955–1975, which also involved, mainly or partially, respectively, Communist China). The Cold War had a domestic front, too, however, with putsches against subversives – communists, suspected communists ("reds"), leftists ("pinks") – or civil rights organizations like the NAACP, the Southern Christian Leadership Conference (SCLC), and the Student Nonviolent Coordinating Committee (SNCC), whose political sympathies were alleged to aid the communist cause and undermine free American institutions. The American people were asked by many of their major institutions, including their local, state, and national governments, and their private employers, to formally profess and demonstrate their loyalty to their country – which, in practice, meant publicly professing their faith in God, their Lockean liberal belief in limited constitutional government especially protective of property rights and free markets, and their patriotism. Truly free or "real" Americans would not hesitate to profess and practice this creed, and believe in it. Traitors would demur, or subvert it.

Ironies piled upon ironies, making postwar political thought some of the most intriguing in American history. This cultural celebration of individualism was cresting at a moment of the total triumph of New Deal liberalism, with its promise of a meliorist, interventionist state that would organize society through levers of strong, public-spirited governments directing aggregates of groups and interests. Individualism and free markets were ostensibly being defended by a small "remnant" (as the conservative individualist Albert Jay Nock called it) living under a hostile regime. At the extremes, these included the Russian-Jewish atheist émigré novelist, polemicist, and philosopher Ayn Rand, author of bestselling *The Fountainhead* (1943) and *Atlas Shrugged* (1957), who wrote worshipful Nietzschean allegories of creative individuals swimming in seas of mediocrity and dependence who would flourish if only the United States would institute the "unknown ideal" of *laissez-faire* capitalism. In more balanced presentations, a larger and growing "remnant" would come together, especially under the auspices of William F. Buckley Jr.'s new conservative magazine *National Review* (1955), and the political leadership of Ohio Senator Robert Taft and (after Taft's premature death in 1953) Arizona Senator Barry Goldwater as an insurgency within the Republican Party, to form the modern conservative movement. But, as it happens, businesses themselves were very much a part of the new administered order of large-scale organizations and groups – of bureaucratic, corporate capitalism. Big corporations were hardly consistent opponents of the New Deal state. In many respects, they were part of its clientele and constituency, and welcomed with a place at the table.

These great corporations and conglomerates – headed by businessmen who, as a class, had once been loathed and attacked by Lincoln Steffens, W.E.B. Du Bois, Sinclair Lewis, and others – went from being targeted by progressives to being accepted, if not hailed, by mainstream mid-century liberals as servants and suppliers of the postwar good life, as marketed to an eagerly consuming public by Madison Avenue's elite advertising agencies. We might say the spirit of the 1950s marked a return to the spirit of 1920s, except that something fundamental had changed in the underlying political and economic order: a floor of economic security and assistance had now been established. And the macroeconomy was being professionally managed by economists and public servants schooled in "demand-side" Keynesian economics, pursuing the perpetual expansion of the country's gross national product (GNP) through not only offering incentives to businesses, but also making sure (through legal support for organized labor, the expansion of the civil service payroll, low-interest loans, tax subsidies, unemployment and disability insurance, and the management of interest rates and inflation through informed monetary and fiscal policy) that the consumer – and voter – had money in his or her pocket, and was able to spend. The prosperous middle class exploded, just as FDR had promised.

After a protracted period of pent-up austerity during the Great Depression and World War II, the national mood in the 1950s was one of profound relief. Soldiers were coming home. Thanks to the GI Bill and rafts of other federal policies and benefits, many got college degrees, and started families in a little patch of paradise, in affordable, assembly-line homes in the suburbs. An expansive cohort newly entered what was shaping up to be a broad American middle class. In his "Four Freedoms" speech of 1941, Franklin Roosevelt had promised Americans both "security" and a "constantly rising standard of living." Now that promise seemed on the verge of being realized.

Who Governs? The Liberal Consensus

Progressive and New Deal political thinkers had long campaigned for an active, problem-solving government led by public-spirited civil servants who worked for the "people" over the "interests." They were now in charge, and sought to do just that. They did not understand themselves as governing from the Left, but as governing expertly and dispassionately, solving problems now that the country had at long last transcended ideology.

Liberal intellectuals, like the sociologist Daniel Bell and the theologian Reinhold Niebuhr, suggested that the modern liberal social welfare and administrative state had finally alighted upon the sweet spot between the counterposed claims of individual liberty and community. Modern liberals, they affirmed, valued both individual freedom and the common good. There was no need, as extremists from the Left and Right had argued, to choose one value as supreme and damn the other. Indeed, these ideals were not in tension, but interdependent, and mutually constitutive. The battle between libertarians and collectivists, fought by fanatical dogmatists, had posed a false opposition, Niebuhr explained in *The Children of Light and the Children of Darkness* (1944). "Neither ... did justice to all the requirements of man's social life." This in-between orientation was not a dogma. It set no ironclad rule determining when the claims of the individual or the community should prevail. That had to be determined – as the pioneering sociologist Lester Ward had first argued – by expert policymakers on a case-by-case basis, after due consideration of the available evidence. Sometimes it would be best for the government to assume the burden of imposing regulation or providing aid or assistance. Other problems and spheres were best left to the individual, or the private sphere.

Unlike Ward, Niebuhr, a theologian at New York's Union Theological Seminary, rooted his understandings in both Christian theology and a consonant theory of history. The Doctrine of Original Sin taught that man was a fallen creature – created in the image of God, yes, but subject to all manner of imperfections and sinful tendencies. Man was ignorant, biased, self-regarding, and selfish – skewed by inordinate self-love. He was also, potentially, loving, benevolent, and just. Given his conflicted nature, in his life in a political community, man could aspire to doing justice and advancing the collective public good, enlisting government – or not – in that quest. The decisions he made at any given moment in time were, inevitably, likely to be good, right, and just in some regards, and blind, wrong, and unjust in others. As such, the *status quo* and *status quo* institutions should never be treated as sacrosanct. They needed to be continually questioned, rethought, and re-examined. The task, and responsibility, was perpetual. This was the only way a political society could intelligently move forward and progress, to realize, as best it could, "the potentialities of a higher justice."

An elite no longer rules.   Social scientists, whose status as experts on how society worked
Robert Dahl (1961)   had been raised immeasurably by the new governing order, set
    themselves to studying it from what they held to be an objective, fact-based, and value-free perspective: that is, as scientists akin to chemists and physicists, with no pre-existing ideological bias or position. Behavioralism, which emphasized the "objective," value-free testing of small, rigorously formulated hypotheses concerning the political choices of individual political actors, came to dominate political science. Asking a resolutely empirical

question which transformed political values and world-views themselves into testable hypotheses, the Yale political scientist Robert Dahl described what he observed in the city of New Haven, Connecticut (and beyond), from the New Deal forward, as a progression from Gilded Age oligarchy to modern polyarchy, or pluralism. The country, Dahl confirmed, now subscribed to a set of shared values about the vital center liberalism that underwrote the modern administrative social welfare state. Although, as in any free society, inequalities continued to exist (welfare state liberalism was not communism, or even socialism), political and economic power, Dahl observed, was non-cumulative and widely dispersed. Government was representative and responsive – receptive to public opinion and open to participation. In his landmark study of New Haven, *Who Governs?* (1961) Dahl's pluralist theory argued that American government in this new context was consistent with the theory James Madison had set out in *The Federalist* (particularly Federalists #10 and #51), which held that the polity would be comprised of a sprawling and diverse field of factions (which Dahl conceptualized as the earlier version of the modern "interest groups" that first emerged in the United States in the late nineteenth and early twentieth centuries), and that, far from illegitimately skewing law- and policymaking in the interest of a few, contention between groups would ultimately yield a broader public interest.

Outliers in Franklin Roosevelt's America: The "Radical Right," Marxian Left, and Marginalized African-Americans

While widely shared, Dahl's optimism about the new order was not unanimous. The problem, some believed, lay with an atavistically irrational fringe, which a number of the era's liberal historians like Richard Hofstadter and social scientists like Seymour Martin Lipset set themselves to studying. They observed that there remained a far-right-wing "remnant" of recalcitrant, anti-New Deal conservatives who refused to recognize and adjust to modern conditions, and continued to yearn nostalgically – and perversely – for a vanished world. An especially unhinged obsession of many of these conservatives was communism, which, evincing what Hofstadter described as a pathological "paranoid style," they saw everywhere, and moved aggressively to root out of American institutions – federal and state governments, public schools and universities, the arts (including Hollywood) – through investigations, purges, loyalty oaths, and blacklists, even when the active communists within these institutions were few and far between, and the threat they posed to the country's internal security, if any, had been vastly exaggerated. Liberals were especially concerned with these anticommunist "witch hunts" – Arthur Miller's play *The Crucible* (1953) implicitly analogized them to the delusional mass hysteria of the early seventeenth-century Salem, Massachusetts, witch trials – because efforts to root out alleged communists targeted Americans who had radically questioned and challenged the country's *status quo* political order. For liberals weaned on modern democratic theory founded on the presuppositions of pragmatism, modern science, and Millian liberalism,[2] the willingness of skeptical, critical thinkers to question and challenge prevailing prejudices, practices, and institutions – intellectual and academic freedom – had been foundational to reformist understandings of how people in a democracy should be, and think. Absent the freedom to be unorthodox, to reject the era's prevailing dogmas, and puncture its sanctities, society could simply not progress. It would be mired in the dogmas, myths, stereotypes, and prejudices, in the institutions and the injustices of the past, and paralyzed in its quest to move forward. If people could not say what they thought, and couldn't question society's most cherished beliefs without fear of punishment or reprisal, the pursuit of truth would be thwarted, and democracy at an end. Many of these matters, in diverse guises, were joined in hearings before the House Un-American Activities Committee (HUAC) and the US Supreme Court.

The Harvard political scientist Louis Hartz dove deep into political theory to shine a spotlight on the grand irony of his era's outsized anticommunism. How was it, Hartz asked – as had Alexis de Tocqueville before him – that a people so ostensibly committed to individualism and individual liberty was so manifestly conformist, demanding that everyone be and think alike? The culprit for Hartz was a pervasive and compulsory ideology of Lockean liberalism, which posited an identity of interest among the individuals who comprised it. This left no room for the genuine freedom of political thought and imagination that might otherwise alight upon a more transformative republican vision of enlisting activist government to advance the broader common good. The belief that, in the United States, all were free and equal, and that they all had a chance – regardless of who they were or where they started – to work hard and succeed, was the national myth, the country's civil religion. It was also an idiosyncrasy born of the country's exceptionalist historical trajectory, under which, in contrast to the historical trajectory in Western Europe, the lower orders never had to wage a social revolution to overturn a feudal hierarchy. To not subscribe to the theory – the ideology – of the United States as a country of free and equal individuals with limitless opportunities for those willing to work hard to succeed was, here, akin to being "un-American" – a traitor. And the communists fell clearly into that category. Under the direction of the Soviet Union, they were committed to overthrowing the government of the land of the free, and replacing it with abject slavery. The fanatical anticommunism Hartz saw all around him in the 1950s, to him at least, made perfect sense. And, by promoting the myth of a smoothly functioning, contented, and open post-New Deal society (basically) living by its creed of liberty, equality, and democracy, even moderate, consensus liberals like Robert Dahl – and the mainstream of the Eisenhower era Democratic and Republican parties – far from being part of the solution, were themselves part of the problem: all were wandering blind in a Lockean liberal fog.

Other social scientists at mid-century turned their attention to what they understood as yet another case of mass irrationality: racial and religious bigotry and prejudice. Ascriptive Americanism – an ethno-racial-religious nationalism holding that a white, Anglo-Saxon, Protestant Christian identity was a prerequisite for full civic membership and belonging, for being a "true" or "real" American – had never been stipulated expressly in the country's core civic texts (although the Constitution euphemistically protected slavery, which was racialized). From the nation's inception, however, an ascriptive nationalism had been pervasively expressed in the country's laws, political institutions, practices, and texts. To be sure, there had been challenges to this form of nationalism from the beginning, both in the nation's core texts – such as the Constitution's prohibition on religious tests for public office or, later, in the Civil War Amendments, including the Fourteenth Amendment's provision for birthright citizenship – and by social movement actors and reformers, and a subset of politicians. But the tendency manifestly remained, and, for most, it seemed not to be apprehended as a problem.

World War II helped change that. The Civil War had challenged fundamental parts of the country's racial order. But supporters of the victorious Union had diverse reasons for entering the fight that led to emancipation, including the preservation of the Union and opposition to (at least the spread of) slavery. But even passionate defenders of the Union and opponents of slavery did not necessarily reject ascriptive racial hierarchies. Many of the defeated Confederates, moreover, far from repudiating their belief in racial hierarchy, continued to fight a rearguard action, taking their first opportunity, as Reconstruction waned, to reinstate it. Indeed, part of the extended process of binding up the nation's wounds in the aftermath of the War Between the States involved a decision by political leaders North and South to join in celebrating the commonalities and shared values of (white) soldiers on both sides, and downplaying formerly hot concerns about the treatment and condition of the formerly enslaved peoples and their descendants.

In World War II, by contrast, the racism and religious hostility was at the core of a foreign enemy self-professedly committed to destroying liberal democracy and potentially conquering and ruling the United States. The virulent ascriptive nationalism of the Nazis was also blatantly genocidal in a way that slavery (as opposed to the views of some concerning Native American Indians) was not. As such, this war against the Axis powers – Nazi Germany, Fascist Italy, and Imperial Japan – set a new frame: "the Good War" threw the United States' ascriptive beliefs, practices, and policies into an unprecedentedly stark and negative light. In this new context, many returning black soldiers refused to return to their old subjection. They had registered the same refusal upon returning from fighting World War I – sold by Woodrow Wilson as the war that would "make the world safe for democracy." But this time white Americans were potentially more open to questioning their prejudices and beliefs. If activists could seize the moment of opportunity, following the lead of A. Philip Randolph and Bayard Rustin in their "March on Washington" movement (1941–1946), to argue that racism and religious bigotry were alien and enemy views, inimical to the American values that Gunnar Myrdal, in his influential study of the United States' race problem, *An American Dilemma* (1944), called "the American Creed," change could at long last come.

The outbreak of the Cold War (1947–1991) between the United States and the Soviet Union, much of which involved a global struggle between enemy empires to win the allegiance of the world's non-white and non-Christian "third world" peoples, reinforced an alternative framing of matters of ascriptive racial identity. The American Creed – adopted by the new comic book "superheroes" like Superman (who fought evildoers in the name of "Truth, Justice, and the American Way," 1942) who would absorb the era's postwar "baby-boomers" – assumed the status of a global vision, spread via its inherent appeal, marketing, cooptation, bribery, skullduggery, and often by force, by a country now standing astride the globe like a colossus at the height of its worldwide power and influence. (In 1941, *Time* magazine's Henry Luce proudly proclaimed the twentieth would be "The American Century.") The commitment to the creed was broadly understood as no less than a mission, a responsibility, and a duty, both abroad and at home. Domestic racism now fit uneasily into this self-ennobling and mythologizing broader picture in which America offered itself to the world as a champion of the just, the fair, and the good.

Illegitimate racial and other ascriptive hierarchies were opposed on Christian grounds by African-American – and a small but expanding group of white, progressive, Left-liberal – Christians. Nevertheless, most white Christians (especially in the South, where a legal order was most immediately at stake) were as likely to appeal to their Christian faith to justify and reinforce these ascriptive racial hierarchies as to challenge them. In a sign of cultural shifts in the sources of moral authority, the new social sciences led the way in contesting both the "naturalness" and reasonableness of race discrimination. In undertaking ethnographies of foreign – including ostensibly "primitive" – societies, the new social science of anthropology, pioneered in the early twentieth century by Franz Boas at Columbia University and his students Margaret Mead, Ruth Benedict, Ella Cara Deloria, and Zora Neale Hurston, had implicitly asked Americans to question their own folkways. Social scientific studies of bigotry, prejudice, and bias by the psychologists Gordon Allport (*The Nature of Prejudice*, 1954), Thomas Pettigrew, and others conceptualized the matter as one of individual irrationality or bias, stemming from ignorance and stereotypes. The black psychologists Kenneth and Mamie Clark's "Doll Study" (which was cited by the Supreme Court in its landmark 1954 judgment

Brown v. Board of Education declaring legal racial segregation unconstitutional) illustrated the ways in which, from an early age, African-American children were driven to develop negative self-conceptions – and white American children a sense of their own worth and superiority – by common cultural cues, such as the fact that most of the dolls marketed to children as beautiful and lovable had white skin, a message children of both races, the Clarks showed, clearly got. The answer was education, and exposure, through integration, changing hearts and minds, and promoting "tolerance." This social scientific work, in conjunction with a re-tooled liberal individualist legal frame emphasizing the requirement of equal treatment under law without regard to race, creed, or color, and a re-imagined Americanism consistent with both, set a new postwar liberal frame for what it meant to be a true American.

Rumbling Undercurrents

Much of the allure of the culture and politics of the 1950s arises out of the tension between its sunny public persona showcasing peace, prosperity, and scrubbed-to-a-shine normality and stability (so evident in the sheening photojournalism of the era's mass-circulation magazines, like *Life* and *Look*), and its far darker undercurrents, which much of the country – or, at least, its white middle-class majority – seemed either to not notice, or not acknowledge. Public religiosity assumed new highs at mid-century, as many began to celebrate the "Tri-Faith" consensus of Protestant–Catholic–Jew in a "Judeo-Christian" America, standing proud and tall against what Notre Dame's Clarence "Pat" Manion had dubbed "Godless Communism."[3] Chambers of Commerce, the National Association of Manufacturers, and others publicly championed "free enterprise." Dale Carnegie's *How to Win Friends and Influence People* (1936) – which rose to become one of the bestselling books in American history – provided avuncular but savvy "self-help" advice to the man of the family on how to succeed in large, bureaucratic, white-collar organizations (less sweat-of-the-brow labor, character, and moral virtue; more cultivation of self-image, flattery, and chipper, can-do spirit). Television, radio, movies, and the marketing and advertising of the mass consumer culture celebrated the era's much-vaunted abundance, which made home ownership and labor-saving creature comforts available to a broad swath of the middle class. In his famous "Kitchen Debate" in Moscow with Soviet premier Nikita Khrushchev (1959), Richard Nixon, President Eisenhower's Vice-President from sun-drenched, suburban southern California – where Disneyland had just opened (1955) – boasted that widespread access to the modern suburban lifestyle in the United States, blessed with modern appliances like state-of-the-art refrigerators, toasters, and blenders, stood as clear evidence of the superiority of American capitalism to Soviet communism. Patriotism was *de rigueur*.

A few wondered whether the culture at the time was characterized less by an actual consensus than by an overwrought compulsion to articulate, define, and disseminate one. Many then and later criticized the period's "conformist" atmosphere, with its powerful sense of moral menace, and undercurrent of suspicion of subversion and dissent: the anti-comic books crusade; the obsession with juvenile delinquency; the "lavender scare" targeting gays and lesbians as conniving corrupters of innocent youth and as potentially blackmailable traitors; fevered "McCarthyite" commie hunts – all played a role in setting the tone, and stoking social and political fears. The era was pervaded by fears that the Soviets were behind the addition of fluoride to the country's drinking water; that labor unions and Hollywood had been infiltrated by communist agents; and that the youth were being indoctrinated and corrupted, and the culture polluted, by politically radical, or queer, public school teachers, "sick" humor magazines (like *Mad*, 1952), and books and films that lionized unwholesome freaks and criminals, maladjusted, disrespectful children, and rebellious, spurned, or unseen outsiders: like J.D. Salinger's *The Catcher in the Rye* (1951); Ralph Ellison's *Invisible Man* (1952); Laszlo Benedek and Stanley Kramer's *The Wild One* (1953), starring Marlon Brando; Nicholas Ray's *Rebel Without a Cause* (1955), starring James Dean; Allen Ginsberg's *Howl* (1956); Jack Kerouac's *On the Road* (1957); and Robert Frank's *The Americans* (1959). To make matters worse, purportedly carnal, primitive, and antinomian Negro "race music" (first blues, jazz, then rhythm and blues, and finally rock and roll) was exploding in popularity among white, middle-class youth, portending revolutionary consequences no one could foresee – although, in its author's patented attention-and-controversy-courting idiom, Norman Mailer's essay "The White Negro" (1957) perhaps came closest to the mark. Looming over all of this was the palpable threat of nuclear annihilation, which, in the Cuban Missile Crisis, nearly came to pass.

Even mainstream liberals were uneasy. Among the unusually prescient, at least, the misgivings were of the kind that come after your every wish has been granted. Is this all there is? Why, in the aftermath of triumph, do we feel so dissatisfied and glum? In *The End of Ideology: On the Exhaustion of Political Ideas in the 1950s* (1960), Daniel Bell declared the battles between the contending claims of individualism and collectivism, and socialism and capitalism, to be over. "In the western world ... there is today a rough consensus among intellectuals on the political issues: the acceptance of a Welfare State; the desirability of decentralized power; a system of mixed economy and of political pluralism." Competent and benevolent technocrats were in charge. Questions of politics had been transmogrified into matters of technique. Society was on auto-pilot, and working pretty well. (This was a politics that behavioralist political scientists could measure and model, hypothesizing that it operated, like the laws of physics, according to regular – indeed, eternal – universal scientific laws.)

But where, in all this, Bell wondered, did that leave politics, and the human need for meaning, in the form of political vision and commitment? If ideology was over, what happened to political passion? Where was the hope for – or even the possibility of – fundamental change? What does it mean for the belief in utopias and revolution to be consigned permanently to the past? Bell discerned, "at the end of the fifties, a disconcerting caesura." Where, he wondered, were the malcontents?

Almost in passing, Bell noted, the unreconciled could be found in a small cadre of intellectuals – especially young intellectuals – who had never made their peace with the values of the new, expertly administered technocratic society, or with the business values that it promoted and, supposedly, capably and benevolently superintended. They did not have a clear cause. But, Bell observed, they *yearned*. He found them in the throes of "a restless search for a new intellectual radicalism." "The young intellectual is unhappy because the middle way is for the middle aged, not for him; it is without passion and is deadening."

Later, it would seem remarkable that Bell seemed to hardly notice the enormous passion and commitment of the civil rights movement that, as he wrote, was unfolding under his nose. (The Montgomery Bus Boycott was launched in December 1955, and the Mississippi Freedom Summer [1964] and the Free Speech movement at the University of California at Berkeley [1964] soon followed.) By the end of the 1960s – one of the most politically tumultuous periods in American history, defined, in significant part, by the "Youth Revolt" – the impassioned causes (civil rights, Black Power, antiwar, and others) were crystal clear. "The End of Ideology" – like Francis Fukuyama's later pronouncement of "The End of History" (1989) at the end of the Cold War – seemed like a vanishingly brief interlude, a gauzy and distant memory.

Conclusion

After an extended period of, first, ascendant reformism from the 1890s through the end of World War I (1918) – with the marked exception concerning matters of race – followed by a "Return to Normalcy" in the prosperous 1920s, the "exogenous shocks" of the Great Depression and World War II rocked American, and world, politics. These grand events opened up new opportunities for re-imagining American government and the American nation by the lights of new "progressive" or "[modern, as opposed to 'classical'] liberal," and potentially even radical, terms. The "demand-side" capitalism as expounded by the British economist John Maynard Keynes, in which the government worked actively to grow the country's GNP while maintaining full employment, raising wages, and stimulating both production and consumption, came to inform American (macro)economic policymaking. Pluralism – or, as a later critic, the political scientist Theodore J. Lowi, dubbed it in 1969, "interest group liberalism" – posited that the post-New Deal liberal political order was a basically open and fair political system in which the views of a wide variety of interests and individuals were heard and registered, and ultimately drove politics and public policy. After 1937, Franklin Delano Roosevelt's appointees to the Supreme Court and subsequent modern liberal appointees by both Democrats and Republicans alike put their constitutional seal of approval on more expansive New Deal understandings of the powers of government. Under Presidents Eisenhower and Nixon, the Republican Party, too, had accepted the legitimacy and beneficence of the changes, and helped integrate them into the doctrine and precedent of postwar American constitutional law. In a period of relative peace and prosperity, most Americans understood themselves to be living under a broadly shared consensus, by the lights of an "American Creed."

And yet, for those who looked a little harder, all was not what it seemed on the (relentlessly promoted) surface. Members of a postwar conservative movement had never accepted the so-called "New Deal Settlement." These movement conservatives began to forge a new faction within the Republican Party under the auspices of, first, Senator Robert Taft of Ohio and then Senator Barry Goldwater of Arizona, who set themselves against liberal or moderate Republican leaders like New York Governors Thomas E. Dewey and Nelson A. Rockefeller, President Dwight David Eisenhower, and Senator, then Vice-President, and finally President Richard Nixon.

Anticommunism was a defining issue for movement conservatives, although there was no shortage of liberal anticommunists, including the philosopher John Dewey, Massachusetts Senator John F. Kennedy, and the liberal group Americans for Democratic Action (ADA). A liberal Democratic President Harry S Truman led the United States into the Korean War. The modern liberals Kennedy and Lyndon Baines Johnson played a major role in escalating the conflict in Vietnam, both specifically aimed at containing communist power. The twilight struggle of the Cold War hung ominously over the era, portending subversion, if not nuclear annihilation. The purported consensus itself was questioned even by its proponents, who wondered what was to become of the quest for meaning once all the fundamental conflicts of politics had – except in the deranged and diseased minds of fringe crackpots, racists, and kooks – been effectively settled. Few prominent political thinkers took note of the emergent civil rights movement as portending anything different for the overarching liberal settlement. Yet rumblings began to be heard from a motley assortment of outsiders for whom the achievement of the American Dream began to look rather like a nightmare. As America entered the 1960s, these undercurrents would soon become a driving force in American politics and in American political thought. Looked at in the rearview mirror, what many at the time took to be the polity's final destination would later be described by a prominent historian as "The Great Exception."[4]

Questions

1. Is it best to think of Franklin Roosevelt's New Deal as a much-needed and necessary updating of American government in light of modern conditions? Or was it an over-reaction to a crisis that would ultimately have been self-correcting?

2. Scholars continue to debate whether the New Deal was a radical "socialistic" program, ostensibly discontinuous with earlier traditions of American political thought and practice, or, rather, a (disappointingly) conservative moment, a "missed opportunity" that left the American liberal capitalist system not only intact, but on even firmer footing, and ultimately more entrenched than ever before. What do you think?

3. Did the postwar consensus liberal consumer society under a managed capitalist economy inaugurate new understandings of what it meant to be a virtuous citizen or a "successful" person? Did it invite new understandings of the yardstick of "success" for, or the "health" of, the polity as a whole? If so, were these advances or regressions?

4. Was postwar anticommunism a phenomenon fueled by paranoia and fearful over-reaction? Or did it arise out of a clear-eyed understanding of a genuinely grave societal and civilizational threat?

5. Many mid-century liberals understood political disagreement and contention, at least on many of this era's major issues like race, to be a consequence of irrationality. How useful is the concept of irrationality as an entry point for thinking about political disagreement and contention?

6. How much do the predominant approaches to the study of politics (e.g. among college- and university-based political scientists), whatever their pretensions to objectivity, reflect – if not reinforce – the underlying substantive political visions and understanding of their era? Is the academic study of politics inherently political?

7. Is it in any sense meaningful, or useful, to talk – in this or any other period – of an "American Consensus"?

8. What is the relationship between the regnant genres of popular culture – in this era, western or science fiction films or rock music; in our own, zombie, fantasy, and superhero films and hip-hop – and an era's political ideology and thought? Should we consider the study of popular culture a legitimate, or useful, part of the study of political ideas?

9. Is the study of fringe political movements of any value? How? Why?

10. How seriously should we take prognostications about the future by political thinkers?

7

Radical Stirrings, Civil Rights, the Contentious 1960s, and the Rise of Modern Conservatism

Franklin Roosevelt's New Deal transformed American government, and the baseline understandings of what it could, and should, do. By the time of Roosevelt's death during his fourth term (1945), the country had emerged from the greatest economic crisis in its history as the triumphant leader of a globe-spanning alliance that had defeated fascism and vindicated liberal democracy. Millions of demobilized troops returned home. With support from the federal government under the GI Bill, veterans enrolled at colleges and universities – often the first in their families to do so. After years of austerity, most looked to relax and live a little – to make money in a clean, secure, and stable job, marry, buy homes, start families (launching the "baby boom"), and enjoy consumer luxuries: a suburban home with trees and a patch of grass, peace and quiet, and modern appliances (refrigerators, gas and electric stoves and ranges, toasters, televisions). It seemed to many at the time, and perhaps even more in hazy memory, that the immediate postwar period was a golden age of peace and prosperity.

At the same time, it was impossible not to sense, sometimes barely consciously, disturbing undertones. No one could ignore the dawn of the nuclear age and the onset of the Cold War (1947) between the United States and its erstwhile ally the Soviet Union. By dropping the atomic bomb – developed secretly during World War II by a team of government scientists assigned to the Manhattan Project in Los Alamos, New Mexico (in conjunction with teams at Oak Ridge, Tennessee and Hanford, Washington) – on Hiroshima and Nagasaki forcing an immediate Japanese surrender, the United States had led the world into the fearsome age of nuclear war. Through great leaps in science and technology, advances heretofore largely perceived as unalloyed boons, it was suddenly possible for human beings to destroy all life on the planet with, it was said – in an eerie parallel to the age of mass consumer convenience – "the push of a button."

The stakes were raised exponentially year by year. The development of vastly more powerful thermonuclear weapons, chiefly the hydrogen (or "H-") bomb, and galloping advances in rocket and missile technology promising major improvements in warhead range, accuracy, and reliability, only heightened the sense of a crescendoing madness. The Communist Party, moreover, was ascendant in France and Italy and (with Soviet backing) had seized power in

Czechoslovakia (1948). It was in this context that "the Marshall Plan" (1948) providing massive economic aid to Western Europe was launched and the North American Treaty Organization (NATO) (1949) was founded. Almost immediately, the Soviets, perhaps through the ministrations of well-placed communist spies in the United States, Great Britain, and Canada, shocked the world by exploding their own atomic bomb (August 1949).

The world divided into antagonistic, belligerent camps. With the stakes raised by the wave of postwar decolonization in Asia and Africa following the collapse of the prewar European empires, non-aligned and neutral nations were taken by the United States and the Soviet Union (and their allies and surrogates) to be in play in a worldwide, and perhaps ultimately apocalyptic, life-or-death competition and struggle between "the free world" and abject slavery. The Korean War began when communist North Korea – backed by communist China – invaded western-aligned South Korea, which, in collaboration with the Soviet Union, the United States had occupied and created following the Allied victory over Imperial Japan (1945), which had been ruling the Korean peninsula as a colonial power since 1910. (The Soviets were given authority over the land north of the 38th parallel, and created North Korea.) Acting under United Nations auspices, the United States came to the defense of the South, at the cost of tens of thousands of American lives.

The issue was framed by American "cold warriors" as an existential struggle between the forces of freedom and collectivism, between a politics stemming from a belief in God and one from an atheistic faith in humanity – between good and evil. A Cold War politics unfurled, fed by often far-flung events, incidents, and stand-offs, and localized "hot" wars, open and covert alike. Fears and suspicions multiplied, were confirmed (the Cuban Missile Crisis), and ran wild. These dynamics suffused much of the era's foreign and domestic political thought. Often, the line between one and the other was vague.

Postwar America's admixture of placidity, optimism, and menace could be disorienting. On the one hand, for mainstream liberals and reformers, the future seemed almost unimaginably bright. The prosperous, middle-class "consumer republic" seemed to portend a new age of previously unimagined "space age" leisure and convenience.[1] On the other hand, however, some Americans spied something rotten. They objected to the period's often strident anticommunism as extreme and excessive. It seemed to them as bad as or even worse than the disease – a betrayal of the very creedal liberal commitment to individual liberty and free thought that anticommunists purported to defend. These matters radiated outward from the targeting of the miniscule number of former or actual communists. Because of their ostensible susceptibility to blackmail, gender non-conforming gays and lesbians were deemed national security risks (and criminals), and purged from government positions. Civil rights advocates, gays and lesbians, atheists, and militant labor union activists were also deemed threats to the nation's security for criticizing American society and its institutions at a moment of existential vulnerability, ostensibly undermining the country's unity and force in the global fight. By the lights of the Cold War version of American providentialism, if the United States was God's chosen country, to criticize American views was to lend aid and comfort to God's enemies. Civil libertarians stood against these challenges to the right to think and speak even the most unpopular views. But, especially during the most heightened moments of Cold War tensions, they faced an uphill fight.

Anticommunist excesses were far from the only problem discerned by a rising cohort of postwar political dissenters and critics. Some economists and sociologists found flies in the ointment of even the vaunted postwar prosperity. The Harvard economist John Kenneth Galbraith's *The Affluent Society* (1958) opened by conceding that "Wealth is not without its advantages." But Galbraith put a critical spin on post-New Deal government policy promoting an ever-upward trajectory of material production, promising perpetually rising wages and increased consumption (a foundation of the new Keynesian economics). Surveying this scene, Galbraith found a society that, while generating unprecedented private wealth, was condemnably stingy in its public sphere initiatives to advance the collective public good. Affluent consumers were being manipulated by advertisers to purchase goods that, in many cases, they neither needed nor wanted. Galbraith wondered whether corporate interests – with the assistance of their hired guns on Madison Avenue – were funneling Americans onto a treadmill of dissatisfaction: they could never have enough. (As the poet E.E. Cummings put it: "ever/ybody/wants more/(& more &/still More) what the/hell are we all morticians?")[2] Just as political elites in a mass democracy were undertaking what Walter Lippmann called the "manufacture of consent,"[3] individual economic choices were being surreptitiously manipulated from above for private gain. The ecological implications of such a lifestyle, moreover, were troubling. To counteract these dynamics, the affluent society needed a new economics. Galbraith recommended raising sales taxes and using the revenue to invest in an ambitious program of public goods and services.

Mass Conformity: The Diagnosis and the Rebels

A series of landmark works by sociologists across the 1950s also trained a critical lens on affluent society triumphalism. While loudly trumpeting the liberal individual freedoms enjoyed by its members after victory in "the Good War" and at the high point of "the American Century" in the new mass society, the Harvard sociologist David Riesman (et al.) observed in *The Lonely Crowd* (1950) that the supposed free American individual was not actually the author of his or her own choices. Rather than the "inner-directed" autonomous, self-determining agent celebrated by proponents of liberal individualism, modern

Americans, the study showed, were increasing "other-directed": they decided what they wanted by looking outward to what others around them wanted, or had. They were always trying to 'keep up with the Joneses – to simultaneously distinguish themselves and fit in. In the process, the supposedly self-determining liberal individual had, in fact, become alienated from him- or herself.

William H. Whyte (*The Organization Man*, 1956) and Vance Packard (*The Hidden Persuaders*, 1957; *The Status Seekers*, 1959) found other-directedness – conformity – pervading the affluent society's white-collar corporate offices. Given the unprecedented expansion of the white-collar workforce – the foundation for the burgeoning postwar American middle class – Whyte wondered about the continuing relevance of our perception of the businessman as an exemplar of the "industrial virtues" praised by William Graham Sumner or of Herbert Hoover's "rugged individualism." In her own strident idiom, Ayn Rand's hectoring, didactic – and bestselling – novels raised the same objections to what she took to be the new bureaucratized and domesticated American male, whom she depicted as a castrated hulk, a slave to mediocrity, drained of any generative will or ambition. What would become of rugged individualism and masculinity – and, others might have asked, republican citizenship, and even political self-determination (democracy) – in the age of the conformist, other-directed, company man, relentlessly bombarded with Madison Avenue advertising hawking mandatory purchases and lifestyles, ensconced within the collectivist corporation, or the rule-hemmed, paper-pushing government bureaucracy?[4]

The Texas-born radical Columbia University sociologist C. Wright Mills offered a similar diagnosis in *The Power Elite* (1956). But Mills went further in positing new associated structures of governing power. In mass society, he observed, ordinary people "feel that they live in a time of big decisions ... [but] they know that they are not making any." The gap between the rulers and ruled had become a chasm. Political power had been consolidated by an "interlocking directorate" of interdependent government, corporate, and military elites who now administered the country's major institutions. This new "power elite" had emerged from a middle class "whose members know one another, see one another socially and at business, [and think alike] and ... in making decisions, take one another into account." They constituted, Mills argued, a distinct, and separate, governing class. The implications for democracy, he warned, were ominous.

Mills himself, fond of motorcycle-riding and clad in blue jeans and a black leather jacket, bridged what was then a divide in formality and respectability between the buttoned-down, tweedy academic critics like John Kenneth Galbraith and David Riesman and the younger, free-ranging social rebels now busting out in biker films, hip to jazz, or gyrating to rock and roll. Perhaps the most intellectually significant of these rebels were a fledging group of bohemian writers and poets arising out of Columbia University on the east coast and the North Beach area of San Francisco in the West soon dubbed "the Beat Generation." Allen Ginsberg, William S. Burroughs, Jack Kerouac, Lucian Carr, Gary Snyder, Michael McClure, Philip Whalen, Diane di Prima, and others began to paint a portrait of America using a very different palette than had been adopted by the prevailing public culture. In who they were, what they valued, and what they saw, the Beats – short for "beatnik" – stripped bare the ostensibly successful and respected pillars of the community, and beatified the country's outsiders. In so doing, they described the ugliness and horror of what lurked below the surface sheen, bore witness to (as the social-ist economist Michael Harrington soon would describe the affluent society's invisible poor) an "other America,"[5] and, with echoes of Langston Hughes ("Let America Be America Again," 1935), beginning with Allen Ginsberg's *Howl* (1956), Jack Kerouac's *On the Road* (1957) and *The Dharma Bums* (1958), and William S. Burroughs's *Naked Lunch* (1959), imagined an alternative America, submerged and smothered, unrealized and inchoate, yearning to be liberated . . . or invented.

> I saw the best minds of my generation destroyed by madness, starving hysterical naked/ . . . angelheaded hipsters burning for the ancient heavenly connection to the starry dynamo in the machinery of night . . . .
> Allen Ginsberg, *Howl* (1956)

Ginsberg's *Howl* brimmed with shockingly explicit deviant sexu-ality, blasphemy, drug use, and criminality, which, in his own way, Ginsberg celebrated as portals to subversive and generative social and political ideas.

His publisher, the poet and bookstore owner Lawrence Ferlinghetti's City Lights Books in San Francisco, was prosecuted for obscenity. But Ginsberg's poem was far from nihilistic. It was a visionary and prophetic religious text. Its beatific hipster angels dwelled and traveled among society's dismissed, despised, execrated, and abominated – its blacks, homosexuals, thieves, drug users, and mental patients, all of whom, Ginsberg and other Beats suggested, had been driven to madness by the abominations and terrors of straight, square, and (according to exiled Frankfurt School critical theorists like Theodore Adorno and Herbert Marcuse) "totalitarian" United States, with its anti- and inhuman capitalism, materialism, racism, militarism, puritanical, sex-abominating heteronormativity, intolerance, conformism, and violence.

What the mainstream took as madness, Ginsberg intimated, was instead an ecstatically expressive resistance – a grand spiritual refusal and last stand by free individuals against a society, if one looked behind the branding and veneer, in all-out war with the human soul. In a world on the precipice of nuclear annihilation, who could truly say that society's ill-adjusted deviants and delinquents were the crazy ones? The truth might, in fact, be exactly the other way around. (A new species of Hollywood films – such as Samuel Fuller's *Shock Corridor* [1963] and Stanley Kubrick's *Dr. Strangelove* [1964] – was soon expressing similar themes.) True insanity was to be found in the CEO's suite at General Motors, in the Joint Chiefs of Staff headquarters at the Pentagon, in the halls of Congress, in the Oval Office, or speaking with false authority from an endowed chair at Columbia or Harvard universities. The Manhattan Project and the pledge to an ever-expanding GNP were genuinely insane. For those dehumanized by modern America, insanity was only rational response.

Truth was found at the margins. Art and lives at the edges – and over them – were mad dashes for emancipation from "the free world's" totalitarian order ruled by the iron fist of mechanized time, efficiency, productivity, and profit, and its pulverizing landslide of arbitrary, oppressive rules and systems. The irrational, disordered, deformed, and deranged, free verse, jazz, narcotics and hallucinogenic drugs, eastern spirituality, impulsivity, play, joy, ecstasy, wherever it could be found, was personal, social, sexual, spiritual, and, ultimately, political liberation. Kerouac put his spontaneous, bop-happy heroes Sal Paradise and Dean Moriarty in a car, heading west, in the American way, to freedom, without a plan, timetable, or goal, just seeing and being, utterly liberated, and tuned to the vitality of the now. Tutored by the ancient religions of the east, Kerouac's Dharma bums synchronized their clocks to eternity.

The music and argot were supplied by African-Americans, as the country's original despised and excluded, who, as both W.E.B. Du Bois and James Baldwin had observed, saw the country without illusions, with a fullness and clarity denied to those who so readily and obliviously fit in. Younger white artists like the Beats, Norman Mailer, and Robert Frank looked to "the problem of the color line" as a portal to the real America, beyond its myths and marketing, and its depths, disfigurement, tragedy . . . and beauty.

Postwar Conservatism's Political Rise

Some of the most relentless opposition to the triumph of postwar liberalism came from the other end of the ideological spectrum. Even in (Lockean/ Hartzian) liberal America, conservatism itself was not new. Animadverting against "consolidation" and "regimentation," the "Old Right" had fought vehemently but futilely against FDR's New Deal and the establishment of the modern administrative and social welfare state. The Old Right, moreover, called for an isolationist foreign policy. It rejected the notion that the United States should take on the world's problems, insisting (before Pearl Harbor) that the country put "America First" by opposing US entry into World War II. Former President Herbert Hoover, once something of a master planner and administrator, and even, in his own restrained way, a progressive, moved increasingly rightward, becoming an outspoken voice for what the idiosyncratic right-wing libertarian-anarchist Albert Jay Nock (author of *Our Enemy the State*, 1935) had called "the remnant": conservatives who, despite being outnumbered, written off, and even despised in a radically modernized world, had kept the traditionalist flame alive.

By the 1950s, even the label "conservative" – which smacked of Old World "Throne and Altar" medievalism – was in near-total disrepute; the term "Americanism" was preferred. But that reticence was changing. Ohio Senator Robert A. Taft might have been a better-known transitional figure had he not died young in 1953. The unapologetic Taft had boldly mounted an unsuccessful challenge from the Right to the liberal Republican New York Governor Thomas E. Dewey for control of the Republican Party. Afterward, the Republican President Dwight David Eisenhower (1953–1961) had followed Dewey's program in making peace with the active, purposive, problem-solving modern state. By mid-century, the country's two major political parties were on the same page on the core issues – a placid consensus so pervasive and apparently entrenched that even the liberal American Political Science Association issued a report calling for stronger, more ideologically polarized political parties that would offer voters a genuine choice.[6]

Crucial steps in conservatism's crusade against "me-tooism" were taken in the world of ideas. A blast against creeping socialism in (soon to be) postwar Europe issued from the pen of the free market Austrian economist Friedrich Hayek in *The Road to Serfdom* (1944), which was serialized in the United States in the mass-market *Reader's Digest* and published by the University of Chicago (where Hayek would soon move to teach). Russell Kirk, "the Sage of Mecosta" (Michigan), published *The Conservative Mind: From Burke to Eliot* (1953), distilling and claiming a hoary tradition of sophisticated right-wing political thought with which, he insisted, American conservatives should proudly identify. And in 1955, still basking in the glow of the *succès de scandale* of *God and Man at Yale* (1951), which had denounced his *alma mater* for its abandonment of its commitment to teaching the principles of limited government, the Christian faith, and individualism for statism, secularism, and collectivism, William F. Buckley Jr. founded what would become the movement's pre-eminent mass-circulation magazine, *National Review* (1955). *National Review* aspired to ecumenicalism, welcoming the incipient conservative movement's diverse strands, running the gamut from libertarianism to moral traditionalism, while, it was said, weeding out the kooks – conspiracy theorists like the over-the-top anticommunist John Birch Society and anti-semites. (Although the magazine was tepidly critical of racist violence, it supported segregationists throughout the civil rights movement.) Buckley helped establish the pre-eminent conservative youth group Young Americans for Freedom (YAF), whose founding manifesto the Sharon Statement (1960) articulated a clear vision for a new American Right. Ayn Rand published *Atlas Shrugged* and other works celebrating *laissez-faire* capitalism, and calling for unshackling society's generative genius visionaries. She then promulgated an "objectivist" philosophy holding selfishness to be man's highest ethical ideal.

It was not long before thoughts turned to enlisting this spray of ideas in a new political mobilization. Through the ministrations of University of Notre

Dame Law School Dean Clarence "Pat" Manion, the Right recruited Arizona Senator Barry Goldwater to sign his name to a clarion manifesto of conservative principles (ghostwritten by William F. Buckley Jr.'s brother-in-law L. Brent Bozell Jr.) entitled *The Conscience of a Conservative* (1960), and then to run as an insurgent candidate for President within the establishment liberal/moderate Republican Party. In a stunning turn, Goldwater prevailed in the party primaries. Following an introduction at the Republican National Convention at San Francisco's Cow Palace by the up-and-coming future California governor, Ronald Reagan – a former B-list Hollywood actor and corporate spokesman – Goldwater was nominated as the party's candidate for President. He was then resoundingly drubbed by the liberal Democrat Lyndon Baines Johnson, who, as Vice-President, had assumed the presidency in the aftermath of President John F. Kennedy's assassination in Dallas, Texas. Johnson soon launched a visionary turn leftward in US domestic policy by announcing a "War on Poverty" and a concerted push for building the "Great Society." But, in one of the most tragic turns of any American presidency, Johnson's grand liberal ambitions crashed and burned as he expanded the Vietnam War, the counterculture bloomed, and students revolted. As a wave of riots and assassinations rocked the country and the civil rights movement veered toward a militant black nationalism, and as students began to hoist the flags of the Viet Cong and communist China, and lionized third-world revolutionaries Mao, Ho Chi Minh, and Che Guevera, the conservative alternative became increasingly attractive. While Goldwater's run for the White House from the unapologetic Right may have seemed quixotic just a few years earlier, it now seemed to more and more like a harbinger of a conservative American future.

Conservative Political Thought

Conservatism in the United States has always belied facile stabs at classification and taxonomy. Many of diverse political persuasions had long since concluded that the US lacked a genuine conservative tradition. Purists held that true "conservatism" stood in resolute opposition to modernity or liberalism: it was the corpus of political thought that liberal modernity had formed in opposition to, and against. The United States was said to be "exceptional" because it was the first truly modern nation – founded on Lockean liberal political principles. The sense of a fixed, hierarchical social and political order ordained from above, and not created by those subject to its superintending rule and rules, was, it was said, wholly alien to American political experience. Unlike its European peers, the United States was born free instead of having to become so.

While the broad outlines of this story make a certain sense, it nevertheless does not jibe with the reality that, notwithstanding, there have always been conservative forces in American politics striving for political power, shaping public discourse, and setting public policies. To locate and identify postwar US conservatism, it is perhaps better to disaggregate – to think less in terms of a movement or party and more in terms of key strands or currents of conservative political thought that have been braided together (or not) in diverse ways over the course of American history.

At a time when a group of political thinkers, politicians, and activists stood ready to proudly claim the name and seek political power under its aegis, seminal postwar movement thinkers like Russell Kirk, Frank Meyer, and (later) the intellectual historian George Nash described the conservative political disposition, if not philosophy. Kirk, a Burkean traditionalist, offered a compendium of conservatives external (e.g. Edmund Burke, Sir Walter Scott, Samuel Taylor Coleridge, Benjamin Disraeli, Cardinal John Henry Newman) and internal (e.g. John Adams, Fisher Ames, John Randolph, John C. Calhoun, James Fenimore Cooper, Henry Adams) to the United States, and argued that, intellectually, philosophically, and spiritually, they were cut from the same cloth. As such, Kirk presented conservative political thought in America as part of a broader tradition of conservative political thought that had set the foundations for western civilization. Frank Meyer, by contrast, understood American conservatism as a coalition. It was constituted by a political union forged between libertarians and traditionalists who shared a belief in a transcendent moral order that provided the foundations for a political system committed to limited constitutional government and pledged to the protection and preservation of a set of morally grounded individual rights. (Mayer called this union "fusionism.") In *The Conservative Intellectual Movement in America since 1945* (1976), George H. Nash offered a concrete demonstration of the broader fusionist thesis by depicting the parameters of postwar movement thought as it had actually developed and the ever higher profile that it was assuming in American life. These new departures in the study of American conservative political thought pushed back hard against the idea that there was no conservatism in liberal America that constituted anything more than "irritable mental gestures" (as the Columbia University panjandrum Lionel Trilling sneered), irrational paranoia (as Trilling's colleague in Columbia's history department, Richard Hofstadter, described it), or status anxiety. Kirk, Mayer, Nash, and others insisted that American conservatives were possessed of a stable of sophisticated ideas that constituted an identifiable political philosophy or set of philosophies.

Conservative thought in modern America was comprised of different strains and camps. Traditionalists emphasized the claims of a transcendent – and, most believed, a divinely ordained – organic moral order, which man, as God created him, was made to live in harmony with, and obedience to. When he did so, both individuals and societies could live well, and flourish. When he did not, bad – and, sometimes, the very worst – things could happen, and did.

The best forms of government recognized and honored this superintending moral framework. They designed their institutions in ways that were consistent with it and cultivated and promoted it. Traditionalists are unbowed and unembarrassed believers in categories, classifications, and hierarchies. These, after all – true and false, right and wrong, good and evil – derive from the transcendent, divinely ordained moral order. Traditionalists reject moral relativism, historicism, legal positivism, secularism, secular humanism, and a host of modern ideologies that they hold to be derived from them (like progressivism, Freudianism, and feminism), which, as they see it, have taken up arms against the natural order, and human nature itself.

Libertarianism, by contrast, valued individual liberty above all. While allowing that government is necessary to provide for national defense, preserve peace and good order, and neutrally adjudicate disputes over private rights – property, contract, civil injury (torts) – libertarians also believe, at the same time, that government poses the greatest threat to freedom. As such, libertarian political theory is preoccupied with the task of both minimally empowering and aggressively limiting government. Many libertarians start from Lockean liberal premises. They posit a state of nature in which a slate of unalienable natural rights are recognized but whose protection, practically speaking, is uncertain. To secure those rights, individuals voluntarily come together to formulate a social contract creating a government that is powerful enough to protect the rights, but limited in all ways not authorized by the initial contract, to provide the widest practical scope for individual freedom. While they differ in their orienting touchstones (whether Locke; neo-classical, public choice, or Austrian economics; "objectivism"; "the Founders' Constitution," etc.) and at times about the policy implications of their underlying principles, libertarians tend to construe the powers of government authorized by the initial social (or constitutional) contract – and especially those of the US national government – strictly: they react strongly against any claims by governments to move beyond their clearly authorized powers. These, as they see it, are threats to foundational liberal and (commercial) republican commitments to the rule of law, and the promise of individual liberty.

Business conservatism might be its own category. Here, the distinctiveness is less in the originality of the ideas than the points of emphasis. Business conservatives in the postwar United States often emphasized the special contributions that capitalists and capitalism have made to the success of liberal democratic political orders. They evangelized for capitalism at a time when they took it to be under threat from proto-socialists at home and communist subversives abroad. They bristled at the shaming of businessmen and business values both by populist, progressive, and liberal reformers from the late nineteenth century through the New Deal – those whose attitudes, many of them believed, had a malign influence in shaping the structures and policies of the modern American administrative and social welfare state – and liberals (especially) in the contemporary Democratic Party. Business conservatives extolled the virtues of those who used the liberties afforded by a free society productively to accomplish things in the world – to innovate, invent, and build – reaping the financial rewards, to be sure, but also giving people what they wanted. Along the way, businesses employed scores of others, providing livelihoods that allowed free individuals to pursue happiness as they liked, and dreamed. As such, businessmen were seers, doers . . . and public servants.

Succeeding in business, moreover, required a set of virtues estimable in their own right: sobriety, probity, punctuality, responsibility, industriousness, and self-discipline, to say nothing of creativity and imagination. Business conservatives differed over the legitimacy and utility of the modern administrative and social welfare state. In the postwar United States, few were anti-New Deal libertarians. Many believed that FDR's reforms had appropriately sanded down the shaper edges of "tooth and claw" *laissez-faire* capitalism. This was the only rightful and moral thing to do, especially in a prosperous society that could afford it. Under extreme conditions, as some more communitarian and statist conservatives had always argued, providing a basic welfarist floor below which no member of the political community would be allowed to fall, far from undermining capitalism, would actually help stabilize and reinforce it. That said, they nevertheless argued that the country's new activist government must work in partnership with business to cultivate a climate supportive of individual and corporate enterprise: what was good for business was good for America, and vice versa. The country's CEOs were, as such, to be afforded a special place at the table.

Although relatively few in number, neoconservatives – mostly elite social scientists and public policy experts and intellectuals – wielded a disproportionate influence within the modern conservative movement, in part because, rather than starting from philosophical principles, they delved into the details of the modern American regulatory and social welfare state's contemporary public policies, offering trenchant critique, and proposing concrete, but resolutely pragmatic, reforms. Unlike moral traditionalism or libertarianism, *neo*conservatism was new. This cohort of policy intellectuals, many of whom, initially or perpetually, spurned their classification as "conservatives," were disillusioned liberals who, as Great Society liberalism reached the apotheosis of its ambitions and a New Left formed in the mid-1960s, grew increasingly uneasy with the direction the modern American state and, indeed, the country, was taking. They were drawn from the class of experts in whose hands the promise of a scientifically informed activist government advancing the common good had been placed. In contrast to other conservatives, they shared the preoccupations of their class and profession: poverty, urban and education policy, fiscal and monetary policy, diverse modern regulatory regimes (securities, communications, transportation, and labor regulation), civil rights and civil liberties, and other areas in which modern governments sought to alleviate or solve social problems. As supporters of the New Deal and the civil rights movement (circa the Civil Rights Act of 1964 and the Voting Rights Act of 1965), neoconservatives affirmed the legitimacy, and inevitability, of the modern administrative and social welfare state. As its programs developed, especially across the mid-1960s, however, they objected not that the programs were unauthorized or illegitimate but that hard empirical/social scientific evidence showed that they were either ineffective or counterproductive (although, over time, moral arguments loomed increasingly larger in the movement).

Neoconservatives often alighted upon a set of dynamics endemic to the modern liberal administrative and the social welfarist mindset – its "ideology" – as the source of the failures and problems of the contemporary state. They challenged the conceit that the modern state was being staffed by neutral, a-political experts. Heedless of human nature, many of these experts were overly ambitious about what could be accomplished by social policy. The admittedly good intentions behind much of this raft of programs and policies, they insisted, had to be separated from their actual effects. Many social problems like poverty or unemployment were less likely to be "solved" than ameliorated or mitigated. Well-intentioned policies were rife with unintended consequences that spilled over into areas that were outside the focus, and competence, of those who were formulating them. As such, many of the ambitious new policies of Great Society liberalism – such as busing to remedy racial segregation, which purportedly exacerbated white flight; or rent control laws or stringent health and safety regulations, which drove up prices for the poor and middle-class renters and potential buyers of apartments or automobiles – might actually make things worse. Policies, moreover, might create perverse incentives ("moral hazard") that undermined the social capital and values (such as individual initiative and responsibility) that underwrote the freedoms made possible by a lightly governed society. In time, many neoconservatives, most prominently Norman Podhoretz and Irving Kristol, became more comfortable being classed as part of the Republican conservative coalition than as insider critics of liberalism. Others, like Nathan Glazer and Daniel Bell, however, continued to understand themselves as liberals.

A subset of neoconservatives focused on foreign policy. These, too, began as – and, many would continue to insist, even while holding key positions in the Reagan administration, remained – liberals. Once comfortable in the pre-Vietnam War, anticommunist, Cold War *realpolitik* liberal Democratic Party that had been unapologetic about the aggressive promotion of American economic and military interests, however, they became known as "neoconservative" by simply sticking to these convictions across the late 1960s. Doing so distinguished them sharply from a rising cohort of New Left thinkers increasingly influential among younger Democrats like William Appleman Williams, Walter LaFeber, and Noam Chomsky, who launched a raft of attacks against American militarism and imperialism, and assumed a critical stance toward the United States, its relentless anticommunism, and its aggressive global pursuit of its military and economic interests. The neoconservatives of mid-century liberal Truman–Kennedy–Hubert Humphrey–Henry "Scoop" Jackson vintage apprehended this ascendant New Left and, in time, liberal foreign policy vision as naïve, pro-communist, and un- and anti-American.

Until the ascension of the Trump administration in 2016, "populist" conservatism (or what Nancy Fraser and other Left critics have called "reactionary populism") was rarely represented in anthologies of American political thought. Historically, "populism" had been most closely identified with the agrarian Left: the Farmers' Alliance, the People's Party, and William Jennings Bryan. These late nineteenth-century populists reacted against the depredations wrought by concentrated corporate capitalist power in ways that undermined democratic and egalitarian values, and demanded strong, countervailing government action. But that earlier populism had been, all the same, constituted by a rural, patriotic, evangelical Christian, agricultural base anchored in the periphery's deeply rooted moral communities. Its at times ascriptive nativist hostility to outsiders making claims to status and resources they held to be properly the possession of the (white, native-born, evangelical Christian) common people, to elites and elite rule, and to powerful and distant government – at least when its powers were exercised in ways that were bureaucratized and held to be out of touch with local needs, interests, and concerns – was patent. In a later context, such touchstones certainly had the ring of "conservatism."

The plain-folk political style of the demotically unmannered United States was perhaps most effectively expressed in one of the chief forms of conservative expression during the ascendancy of the modern Right: country music. Many country songs – such as Roy Acuff's "Stuck Up Blues" (1941), Merle Haggard's "Okie from Muskogee" (1968), and Hank Williams Jr.'s "A Country Boy Can Survive" (1981), "If Heaven Ain't a Lot Like Dixie" (1987), and "If the South Woulda Won" (1988) – celebrated rural values, and distinguished them from the lifestyles of the distant, decadent, effete and effeminate, snooty, and condescending urban elites. Manly patriotism and loyalty were perpetual themes, as was the nostalgia-tinged sense of decline, and call for a renewed love of country, traditional morality, and foundational political (and personal) virtues and principles. Many of these country songs extolled the liberal producerist ethic of hard work and individual independence, as defined against the shiftlessness and dependence promoted by the policies of the modern liberal welfare state (see Haggard's "Working Man Blues," 1969, and, more wistfully, "Big City," 1981). The heroic republican courage, patriotism, and sacrifice of America's soldiers were a regular theme of albums like the Louvin Brothers' *Weapon of Prayer* (1962) (covering the World War II vintage "There's a Star Spangled Banner Waving Somewhere"), Staff Sergeant Barry Sadler's

Vietnam era "The Ballad of the Green Berets" (1966), and Lee Greenwood's Reaganite "God Bless the USA" (1984).

Civil Rights Resistance

Many conservatives, especially in the South, were fervently committed to the maintenance of ascriptive racial hierarchy and a segregationist "Jim Crow" white supremacist regime. This regime was challenged in "the Second Reconstruction" launched in the mid-1950s by the modern civil rights movement. Although she was following in the footsteps of a long line of less heralded predecessors, Rosa Parks's orchestrated refusal to yield a seat in the "whites only" front section of a Montgomery, Alabama, city bus sparked a game-changing bus boycott led by the Reverend Martin Luther King Jr. The Montgomery Bus Boycott was designed to at last bring the issue to a head following decades of organizing and direct action. By the mid-1950s, the context had changed, occasioning a new sense of possibility. After the Great Migration northward, American blacks now lived where they could vote. President Harry Truman had desegregated the US military and had issued the report *To Secure These Rights* (1947) supporting civil rights. At long last, the decades-long, stepwise litigation campaign of the NAACP's Legal Defense and Education Fund (LDF) to have the Supreme Court overrule *Plessy v. Ferguson* (1896) had yielded fruit with the US Supreme Court's landmark ruling declaring *de jure* segregation in public schools unconstitutional (*Brown v. Board of Education*, 1954). Nevertheless, Martin Luther King Jr.'s direct action set itself against a virulently revanchist, last-ditch southern rally for "Massive Resistance" to civil rights. An epic battle was at hand.

One of the major controversies at the time, among African-Americans and beyond, was the decision by key movement leaders like King – in association with the Southern Christian Leadership Conference (SCLC), Bayard Rustin, the Congress of Racial Equality (CORE), the Student Nonviolent Coordination Committee (SNCC), and other allied individuals and groups – to adopt peaceful civil disobedience as their major political strategy. In this, King, Rustin, and others – like their anticolonial Indian compatriot Mahatma Gandhi – had been heavily influenced by Henry David Thoreau. King's *Letter from a Birmingham City Jail* (1963) would became a renowned statement of the duty to resist and defy unjust laws. A Southern Baptist minister, King advanced his case by drawing from Christian (St. Thomas Aquinas, St. Augustine) and secular philosophical ideas and sources.

> History is the long and tragic story of the fact that privileged groups seldom give up their privileges voluntarily.
> Martin Luther King Jr. (1963)

Many were put off. Thurgood Marshall – the lead LDF attorney on *Brown* and, later, the first African-American appointed to the Supreme Court – had spent decades working within the legal system to establish the legal precedents that culminated in the landmark 1954 desegregation decision. The LDF's strategy had been to appeal to the majesty of the Constitution's formal guarantees of the equal protection of the laws, and to demand that those laws be obeyed and enforced. As these civil rights lawyers saw it, King's decision to openly defy the law reinforced the legitimacy of the white supremacist southerners who were mounting lawless massive resistance. Others, whether segregationists, moderate conservatives like Herbert Storing, or the moderate pro-civil rights liberals to whom King's *Letter from a Birmingham City Jail* was addressed, worried both about the potentially baneful effects, both for the movement itself, and, generally, of lending moral sanction to an apparent disrespect for the law. Others – conservatives especially – condemned the civil rights protestors for making the United States look bad at a time when it was facing an existential threat from its totalitarian communist enemies, undercutting it in its globe-spanning Cold War fight for the world's hearts and minds. At the extremes – including within Director J. Edgar Hoover's FBI – it was alleged that King was a foreign agent, a communist, and that the civil rights movement was a communist plot. By the mid-1960s, from the other end of the spectrum of black politics, came the charge that the movement's insistence on non-violence evinced a weak and undignified refusal to engage in self-defense. This challenge gained its most prominent champions in the followers of the Nation of Islam leader Malcolm X and in the militant self-defense organization the Black Panthers.

Black Nationalism

Black nationalism reached new heights from the mid-to-late 1960s into the 1970s. With roots dating from Martin Delany and Marcus Garvey's Back to Africa movement, the black nationalist vision premised on black self-reliance, self-discipline, self-defense, and political and economic self-determination was not new. But a succession of searing and signal events – the violent resistance of the white South to the civil rights movement, the Vietnam War, a series of devastating assassinations, including that of Martin Luther King Jr. by a white supremacist in Memphis, Tennessee (April 4, 1968) – drove a cohort of black activists to more radical insights and action. Inspired by dark-skinned third-world revolutionaries in the post-World War II wave of decolonization in Algeria, Latin America (Fidel Castro, Ernesto "Che" Guevera), and Vietnam (the Viet Cong, led by Ho Chi Minh), and the radical critiques of ascriptive racist colonialism by Frantz Fanon (*Black Skin, White Masks*, 1952; *The Wretched of the Earth*, 1961), the Nation of Islam minister and spokesman Malcolm X and the increasingly radical civil rights movement foot-soldier Stokely Carmichael – who soon adopted the African name Kwame Ture – elevated "Black Power" (Carmichael's phrase) as a major force in late 1960s American politics. In this way, postcolonialism and third-world nationalisms were joined with a radical, and even revolutionary, politics at home. Black nationalism, Black Power, and Black Pride found creative expression in music, through groups like the Last Poets, in the flowering of the Black Arts movement, and in the era's mass-market popular music (including James Brown's "Say it Loud – I'm Black & I'm Proud," 1968, and Nina Simone's "To Be Young, Gifted and Black," 1969, later covered by Aretha Franklin).

Many of these more radical figures questioned the Christian faith that ran so deeply in black America, a faith whose ministers and churches were sheet anchors of the civil rights movement, and of the thought of leaders like King, whose universalist vision of the "beloved community," and soaring pulpit rhetoric, was suffused by it. In *The Fire Next Time* (1963), James Baldwin turned a cold eye to his upbringing as a Harlem minister's son in the bosom of the Black Church, and his time as fervent, desperate, believer, and a charismatic boy preacher in a storefront church. When it came to race, Baldwin had long since concluded, few hypocrisies were as brazen as those of America's smugly pious Christians, black and white alike. In a text shot through, he acknowledged, with biblical and Christian imagery, rhetoric, and allusions – including its title – Baldwin indicted the very foundations of the Christian faith for the profound disfigurement and damage it had wrought across the ages to the human psyche and soul. Christianity's first principles "were Blindness, Loneliness, and Terror, the first principle necessarily and actively cultivated in order to deny the two others." Christians professed universalism and love, but their foundational premises were hostility to strangers and outsiders. The precepts of their faith reinforced human beings' worst inclinations to pride, a sense of superiority, and hate. It seemed obvious to Baldwin that America's white Christians had been taught from the moment they were baptized that God was white. As such, their faith had played a powerful role in sanctifying society's *status quo* power relations. This had weaponized the Christian faith into a brutal instrument for the institution and maintenance of hierarchy, exclusion, domination, subordination, falsehood, and oppression.

Baldwin then turned to an alternative to Christianity newly on offer in the black community, the Black Muslim movement. In *The Fire Next Time*, he recounted a visit to the home of the Honorable Elijah Muhammad, the leader of the rising Chicago-based Nation of Islam movement. (Malcolm X was the Nation's spokesman; the boxer Muhammad Ali – formerly Cassius Clay – was one of Elijah Muhammad's most prominent disciples.) The turn to Allah was offered to African-Americans as a reclamation of the ancestral African faith that had been stolen from them when they renounced it after being forced to kneel at the foot of the Cross by Christian slaveholders – godly men with names like "Baldwin" or "Little." (Little was Malcolm's last name before he replaced it with an "X" to signify his lost ancestral African name.) Baldwin observed that the Nation of Islam's theology had neatly inverted America's racial order. The

Honorable Elijah Muhammad came bearing the truth that God was black, and blacks were His chosen people. Satan, by contrast, was white, and white people were his wicked devils. White people, moreover, had deliberately, and satanically, concealed this truth, and reversed it, with the aim of illegitimately and malevolently ruling the world's dark-skinned peoples. Baldwin appreciated that, under the circumstances, this was an immensely powerful and attractive vision for many black people. By this point, however, he was too disillusioned with the wiles and workings of religious faith of any kind to find it a plausible hope or alternative.

Malcolm X, though, was a fervent adherent, and enlisted Islam as a foundation for his broader black nationalist vision. With his declaration that "now we have the type of black man on the scene in America today . . . who just doesn't intend to turn the other cheek any longer," Malcolm announced a post-Christian militantism, in direct opposition to Martin Luther King's Christian pacifism. Malcolm's militantism arose out of a cold assessment of the forces black Americans were up against: all the powers of white people, their governments, and, indeed, their culture were – and always had been – arrayed against them. Uncle Sam's hands, Malcolm insisted, were soaked with blood. The consequences for African-Americans had been devastating: poverty, crime, alcoholism, drug abuse, sexual promiscuity, and rampant self-loathing and self-hatred. Gone were the days of appealing to the benevolence and conscience of whites and to their professed ideals. (King had cited American heroes like Jefferson and Lincoln and the country's revered founding documents, like the Constitution and the Declaration of Independence.) It was time for blacks to come together as a unified community, without regard to white support or alliances – that is, on their knees as supplicants to a white world and white power. It was time for them to come together as an independent nation, and do what nations do: take immediate sovereign control of their destinies, and responsibility for their security and self-defense. Nations do not renounce violence. They form armies, and defend themselves. Militant blacks, Malcolm stipulated, would not strike first, or pick unnecessary fights. But they would defend themselves by force of arms. "I'm nonviolent with those who are nonviolent with me," Malcolm rejoined against King. "Any time you demonstrate against segregation, and a man has the audacity to put a police dog on you, kill that dog, kill him. I'm telling you, kill that dog."

Like Stokely Carmichael, who had made his way from SNCC to the Black Panther Party and, finally, back to Africa, Malcolm rejected the very paradigm of the racial integrationist vision and hope, declaring it profoundly pernicious. No one, Malcolm observed, calls an all-white school or neighborhood "segregated." This is because all-white neighborhoods or schools are governed by those who work, study, and live inside them: they possess the powers of self-determination and self-government. All-black schools or neighborhoods are called "segregated" because the people who work, study, and live in them are ruled by those outside their community – by absent white people. To be "segregated" is to live subject to a (hostile or indifferent) outsider's power and control. Carmichael described the situation as a species of colonialism, and black nationalism as a domestic anticolonial and anti-imperialist movement – hence its close identification with the revolutionary anticolonial movements of the third world/global south. All were confronting the same problem, and bravely stepping up to the same high political responsibility.

The civil rights movement's campaign for racial integration – the darling of often distant liberal whites who were not personally affected by it – was, at best, a distraction. It came cap in hand, begging white people to do black folk a good turn by reconsidering their attitudes toward and treatment of them. As such, no one should be surprised that its great accomplishment to date had been to grant a small subset of black people – those adjudged by whites to be the "best," "most qualified," or best-behaved – "passports" ("a couple of university degrees") to white middle-class American life, "siphon[ing] off" the "'acceptable' Negroes." Carmichael acidly observed that the integrationist program envisaged "the final solution to the Negro problem." It was racial and cultural genocide – the path by which black America, should it go down that road, would "abolish itself."

Carmichael's demand for "Black Power" and "Black Liberation" called for the revival of a suppressed and stolen native culture that would assume its rightful position at the heart of a black nation. "The racial and cultural personality of the black community must be preserved," Carmichael insisted, "and the community must win its freedom while preserving its cultural integrity." "This," he explained, "is the essential difference between integration as it is currently practiced and the concept of black power." Only after "the Negro community is able to control local office, and negotiate with other groups from a position of organized strength" would it be possible to establish "meaningful political alliances" to achieve concrete political ends.

Other black leaders believed that, following the passage of the landmark Civil Rights Act of 1964 and Voting Rights Act of 1965, that point had already been reached. In the mid-1960s, the federal government was on its way to building a strong "civil rights state," morally and legally committed to fighting race (and sex) discrimination in voting, employment, organized labor, housing, and education. Bayard Rustin, who earlier had been a proponent of (peaceful) disruption and mass protest, and the chief organizer of the 1963 March on Washington, insisted that the time had now come to call down the curtain on the politics of disruption, and re-orient the pursuit of civil rights toward the hard work of building alliances and seeking influence through the main channels of electoral, interest-group pluralist, and partisan politics – to work within the system. This, the gay pacifist/socialist labor organizer Rustin insisted, did not entail a lowering of expectations, but signing on to the high social and economic justice ambitions of President Lyndon B. Johnson's "Great

Society" and "War on Poverty" – the high tide of postwar American liberalism that Rustin believed to be both good for African-Americans and good for America.

Questions of the most appropriate stance and strategy had long been central to African-American political thought. But the period between the mid-1960s and the mid-1970s – marked by deeply disturbing bloodshed and a cascade of mass political mobilizations – proved uniquely combustible and contentious. Both Malcolm X and Martin Luther King Jr. were assassinated. The Vietnam War escalated. Smoke was rising from America's inner cities. Radicals called for a war on law enforcement, and the violent overthrow of the American government. At the end of the 1960s, the besieged Lyndon Johnson refused to seek a second full term in office. Into the void stepped conservative Richard M. Nixon, who had cut his teeth as a red-baiting anticommunist US Senator from southern California in the 1950s. Nixon positioned himself as a spokesman for the country's "silent majority." In 1968, he was elected President of the United States.

The center of gravity of black politics became highly unstable. Some, like Rustin and the National Urban League under Whitney Young Jr., positioned themselves at the pragmatic middle. After a black nationalist turn under Roy Innis and Floyd McKissick, CORE and the National Urban League moved rightward. (By 1972, CORE was supporting President Nixon.) The Black Panther Party, a militant, revolutionary, black nationalist, self-defense organization, was founded (1966) and fronted by charismatic radicals like Bobby Seale, Huey Newton, David Hilliard, Eldridge Cleaver, Kathleen Cleaver, Stokely Carmichael, Ericka Huggins, and Elaine Brown. Marching as an army under strict discipline in uniforms capped by Cuban revolutionary berets, with rifles slung over their shoulders, and spouting wisdom from Chinese communist revolutionary premier Mao Zedong's *Little Red Book* (1964) ("A revolution is not a dinner party"), the Panthers stepped up – most visibly in their home base of Oakland, California – to transform the militant black nationalist vision into a boots-on-the-ground reality.

It was a time of leftist schisms and off-shoots. The Black Liberation Army (BLA) split off from the Black Panthers as the latter spiraled downward, both in the wake of internal (at times violent) power struggles, and under the weight of (at times violent) government repression, including the US government's execution of Chicago Panther leader Fred Hampton (1969). Led by Assata Shakur (Joanne Chesimard) and Eldridge Cleaver, the BLA attacked their erstwhile comrades for (they said) abandoning revolution for reform. The BLA declared themselves at war with the racist, sexist, capitalist, and imperialist American government, and launched a campaign of bank robberies, bombings of government buildings, executions of police officers (whom they treated as enemy soldiers in time of war), and prison breaks – meeting what they held to be relentless systemic and structural violence with a disciplined and committed violent resistance. As late as 1981, in alliance with the May 19 Communist Organization, itself a spin-off of the violent revolutionary leftist (and largely white, student radical-led) Weather Underground (in turn an offshoot of Students for a Democratic Society, SDS), the BLA perpetrated a daring robbery of a Brink's armored car just north of New York City, to liberate money to bankroll the overthrow of the American government. In the process, they killed two police officers – one black. The perpetrators were captured and jailed. This appeared to be the last gasp of the revolutionary American Left in which Black Power and black nationalism had played a critical part. The conservative Republican Ronald Reagan – who had been governor of California when the Black Panther Party had formed, and supported more stringent National Rifle Association (NRA)-backed gun control laws aimed at controlling them – was in the White House, and would be elected for a second term as President of the United States.

The New Left

C. Wright Mills dubbed the "New Left" formed by university students in the early 1960s "new" to distinguish it from what was once known as "the Left," but which Mills now called the "Old Left," tossing it into the dustbin of history. Following Marx, the late nineteenth- and early twentieth-century (Old) Left understood the workers as the revolutionary vanguard, and their antagonism to capitalism and the capitalist class to be the engine of history. The Old Left had been comprised of and led by the labor movement. Its constellation of constituent organizations had been the communist and socialist parties, the Knights of Labor, the Congress of Industrial Organizations, the United Mine Workers of America, the International Ladies' Garment Workers' Union, the United Autoworkers, the United Steelworkers, the Brotherhood of Sleeping Car Porters, and other working-class and labor organizations. The Old Left's leaders were "Big Bill" Haywood, Eugene V. Debs, Lucy Parsons, John L. Lewis, Mary Harris "Mother" Jones, Ella Reeve "Mother" Bloor, Samuel Gompers, A. Philip Randolph, Harry Haywood, David Dubinsky, Harry Bridges, and Walter Reuther. Whether in its more radical industrial or (confrontational) reformist trade-unionist form, the earlier Left had been focused on the problems of the capitalist mode of production, and on the relations of the antagonistic capitalist and laboring classes. It was a materialist movement of the industrial working class pursuing revolutionary or reformist objectives: the overthrow of capitalism, or higher pay, better hours, safer and healthier working conditions, restful weekends, paid vacations, injury compensation, and retirement pensions. Segments of America's emerging "New Left" adopted the stories of the Old (Labor) Left in the folk music revival of their generational compatriots (like

Judy Collins's "Coal Tattoo," 1964, or Joan Baez's "I Dreamed I Saw Joe Hill Last Night," 1970/1936). Woody Guthrie served as a touchstone, and bridge figures like Pete Seeger underlined the continuities between the Old and New Left. But the younger New Left activists placed a renewed emphasis on the most immediate problems of their times: racism, militarism, colonialism, consumerism, business values, automation, bureaucratization, and "[a]n unreasoning anti-communism." They called for a new commitment to civil rights, civil liberties, racial "diversity," ecological stewardship, global justice, the end of poverty, "relevant" education, boldly ideological parties offering voters clear alternatives, "participatory democracy," and the host of "post-materialist values" that came to define the era's "new social movements" – in short, they called for a "new politics."[7]

In "Letter to the New Left" (1960), C. Wright Mills congratulated the rising generation of activist youth for stepping up. The historic agent of deep societal – structural – change under exploitative capitalism, Mills explained, had long been the working class. But by the 1950s, American workers had become self-satisfied and complacent. Mills chided the graying remnants of the Old Left for their reflexive resort to "a labour metaphysic . . . a legacy from Victorian Marxism that is now quite unrealistic." While insisting he was not writing off the working class, Mills urged them to shed their sclerotic outlook and to take a fresh look at the world around them. "[W]ho is it that is getting fed up . . . [g]etting disgusted with what Marx called 'all the old crap'? Who is it that is thinking and acting in radical ways? . . . [I]t is the young intelligentsia." If there was a new revolutionary vanguard, Mills suggested, it would be found on the country's university campuses. In the same year, in *The End of Ideology* (1960), Mills's fellow sociologist Daniel Bell similarly observed, albeit in a different spirit, that the grand ideological causes that had underwritten the great struggles of labor and capital seemed to have ended. "[T]he workers, whose grievances were once the driving energy for social change, are more satisfied with the society than the intellectuals." Without a grand cause, however, Bell found those young intellectuals bereft: they were "yearning," restlessly searching "for a new intellectual radicalism." Bell did not anticipate, however, that they were on the verge of finding it.

The Port Huron Statement (1962), the founding statement of the premier New Left organization Students for a Democratic Society (SDS), was written (mostly) by the University of Michigan undergraduate Tom Hayden as a direct counter to the Sharon Statement (1960) of the conservative Young Americans for Freedom. While acknowledging their privileged status as the children of the affluent society, the students proclaimed their profound discomfort with "the world we inherit." American democracy was broken and stalemated, rent by apathy, complacency, and self-seeking minority rule. It was shallow and hypocritical. "The decline of utopia and hope is . . . one of the defining features of social life today," the students lamented. They declared themselves for authenticity, group solidarity, the empowerment of majorities, and revolutionary action.

Much of the students' ire was aimed at universities themselves, and their remote and complicit liberal faculty and administrators, whom they accused of squelching students' passion for learning, and crushing their souls, with the aim of pulverizing the students into inert and virtually identical mass-produced products, fit to be slotted into quiescent servitude to the country's amoral business, military, and governmental institutions. Where many had conceived of the "ivory tower" as a blessedly a-political refuge and place apart, where scientists and humanists could pursue knowledge and pass on western civilization's great traditions, at a time when the GI Bill had opened American higher education to a broader cross-section of the population, SDS demanded a "relevant" education. "[U]niversities are an overlooked seat of influence," the Port Huron Statement pointed out. It called upon students and allied faculty to "make the university a ... base [for and agent of] a movement of social change." The new ideal valorized activist students and politically engaged scholars.

> We are people of this generation, bred in at least modest comfort, housed now in universities, looking uncomfortably to the world we inherit.
> Students for a Democratic Society (1962)

New Left critiques were echoed in new intellectual paradigms and departures in political science and history. A slate of prominent political scientists – including Elmer Schattsneider, Grant McConnell, Theodore J. Lowi, and Peter Bachrach and Morton Baratz – assailed the sunny pluralist models of postwar American politics, brashly pointing out (as Schattschneider had put it) that "the unheavenly chorus sings with an upper-class accent." New Left historians like James Weinstein and Martin J. Sklar limned the outlines and processes of what Weinstein called the "corporate liberal" state. The political theorist Sheldon Wolin lambasted the assumption that the United States was in any meaningful sense a democracy, and, after critique, formulated his own affirmative democratic vision. In the context of the Cold War – which, for young Americans, was turning dangerously hot in Vietnam – the historian William Appleman Williams traced the implications of New Left understandings of the American state, and the systems of power upon which it was premised, to American militarism, expansionism, and imperialism.

Deciding to at long last shunt aside their southern segregationist base in the moment of opportunity opened up by the Kennedy assassination and a booming economy, the Texan New Dealer Lyndon Baines Johnson, joined by his "Happy Warrior" liberal Vice-President Hubert Humphrey, committed themselves fully to the fight for civil rights. The Johnson administration took ownership of the campaign for the enactment of the landmark Civil Rights Act of 1964 and the Voting Rights Act of 1965. Under Attorneys General Robert F. Kennedy, Nicholas Katzenbach, and Ramsay Clark, it sought to aggressively enforce both. At the same time, the Democratic administration launched an ambitious series of domestic programs – (the "Great Society"): a flotilla of community-based anti-poverty initiatives; an expansion of the food stamps program; money for urban renewal; increased aid to public schools, colleges, and universities; and expanded student loan programs. The Great Society programs offered funds for early childhood education for poor children that would give them a "head start" in life. They provided support for bilingual education for English as a Second Language (ESL) students, expanded the New Deal Social Security program, and launched major new initiatives providing government medical care for the poor and aged (Medicaid and Medicare). The Johnson administration enacted bold new regulations aimed at environmental and consumer protection. Moreover, it created a new set of government institutions manifesting a bold national commitment to arts and culture: the National Endowment for the Arts, the National Endowment for the Humanities, and the Public Broadcasting Service. In its commitment to civil rights, environmental and consumer protections, the War on Poverty, and its broad support for education, the arts, and culture, the Johnson administration seemed to be on track to fulfilling many of the shared public policy ambitions of mainstream liberals and the rising New Left alike.

The Full Flowering: The Late 1960s Counterculture

Although it burst onto the American scene seemingly all at once, with an éclat of Day-Glo effulgence, the late 1960s counterculture[8] had been presaged by an array of earlier subcultures, movements, and social critiques dating back to at least the mid-nineteenth century, and most immediately to the 1950s Beats. Most accounts, however, list its date and place of birth as the January 1967 "Be-In" (a play on the civil rights movement "Sit-In") held in San Francisco's Golden Gate Park (billed as a "Gathering of Tribes," with music by local bands the Jefferson Airplane, Blue Cheer, Big Brother and the Holding Company, Quicksilver Messenger Service, and the Grateful Dead), and the "Summer of Love" spectacle that took place a few months later across the street in the city's Haight-Ashbury neighborhood. While some have said the "hippie" movement among American youth that was the face of the countercultural revolt of the late 1960s was all about the hair (long, scraggly), the clothes (cheap, home-made or recycled, rootsy, improvised, funky, and unwashed), and the drugs (pot, acid), the hippie lifestyle entailed a broad-ranging rejection of a wide tranche of mainstream cultural, social, and political values, and a seeking, groovy quest for better ones. Hippies held matters of daily life and personal style to be "political" in the broadest and deepest sense. The hippies mounted a full-scale rebellion against the social, economic, and political expectations in which most of its denizens had been raised as relatively privileged white, middle-class, suburban children in the prosperous post-World War II 1950s. The counterculture's first premise (shared with feminism) was that the personal is the political. From this perspective, politics is not only about such things as voting, elections, political parties, the institutions of government, and lawmaking, but also about how, on a day-to-day basis, one lived one's life.

In *Howl*, Allen Ginsberg, both Beat and hippie, had imagined 1950s American society as a biblical Moloch, devouring its own children. Ginsberg discerned intimations of salvation in the country's beatific scorned, cast-out, and despised. Moving beyond the horrific vision of Moloch devouring its own, the hippies were soon imagining beautiful hopes: "How many tomorrows can you see?" asked the Strawberry Alarm Clock ("Sit With the Guru," 1968). The clothes, the hair, the sex, and the drugs were all deliberate bids by the young to defect from the values of their purported class and kind, and proudly write themselves into the book of America's outcasts, with the hope that, before long, thanks to their generation's rebellion, society's traditional outsiders, fortified by legions of the country's defecting youth, would soon be calling America's tune.

The counterculture took the prevailing rules and mainstream "middle-class" expectations of how they should live as disciplinary (in the Foucauldian sense).[9] It spelled "Amerika" with a "k," an allusion to a submerged authoritarian, if not "totalitarian," order lurking behind the smokescreen of the ordinary spelling. Taking its lead from the émigré political philosopher Hannah Arendt's description of the genocidal German Nazi order as premised less on some devouring monster (the Bible's and Ginsberg's Moloch) than on unquestioning obedience by ordinary bureaucratic functionaries focused only on their job within this system,[10] countercultural voices in the movement's alternative newspapers – *Ramparts*, *The Berkeley Barb*, *The Village Voice*, *The East Village Other* – and a coast-to-coast archipelago of alternative press outlets referred to mainstream governing officials, including businessmen and law enforcement officers ("pigs"), as "little Eichmanns."[11] The culture was slotting these passive, unquestioning middle-class kids into careers as respectably compliant and conformist, scrubbed and sanitized, self-sublimating, nuclear family-dwelling, mass consumers and corporate drones. Those who participated in the late 1960s counterculture decided *en masse* to defy these ostensibly mandatory expectations. Where middle-class capitalist society said to dress neatly, keep your hair short, and your body clean and deodorized (to fit easily into your job at IBM or Lockheed-Martin, and please your boss), hippies let their hair grow long, wore weird, tattered clothes, spurned antiperspirant, and washed their hair and bodies only when they felt like it. Expected to start at the bottom of the corporate hierarchy and work their way up via the ruthlessly competitive "rat race," hippies thumbed their noses at corporate America, taking jobs paying just enough to get by for now – all one could ever count on – and allowing the maximum amount of free time to hang out, get high, listen to music, delight in nature, seek a higher consciousness, and just "be." Enjoined to use respectful language, they swore freely, and gleefully adopted a playful, wonder-struck movement argot ("Groovy," "Far Out!"). Rejecting the nuclear family and the worship of private property, some lived in group houses, or even communes. The movement esteemed unmediated naturalness, including unprocessed natural foods and organic farming. They went "back to the land," as celebrated in songs like Canned Heat's "Going Up the Country" (1968) and Joni Mitchell's "Woodstock" (1970). The prevailing ways of thinking and, indeed, the consciousness itself of "the Establishment," deformed by its binaries, dualities, hierarchies, violence, materialism, commercialism, consumerism, competitive gospel of success, and hyper-rationality, were to be altered, with the aid of drugs like pot, "shrooms," and acid, blowing up disciplinary outlooks, and opening up "the doors of perception" (Aldous Huxley's memorable phrasing, adopted by the LA rock group the Doors).

One way to break out of the dualities, hierarchies, and hang-ups of western capitalist culture was to turn away from the West and look East. Interest in eastern religions (Hinduism, Buddhism – including Zen) exploded. The turn to the East pervaded the counterculture's music. After the Beatles went to India to study Transcendental Meditation with the Maharishi Mahesh Yogi, and incorporated Indian stylings and instruments into their songs, they were joined by the era's emerging psychedelic music scene headlined by groups like Austin, Texas's the 13th Floor Elevators, LA's Love and the Strawberry Alarm Clock, and San Francisco's Moby Grape and the Jefferson Airplane. The Grateful Dead followed, making music enhanced by a drug-induced altered consciousness and eastern musical instruments, keys, scales, modes, sights (liquid light shows), smells (incense and patchouli), philosophy, and mysticism melded with traditional African-American blues and jazz. (Excluded, oppressed, and alienated, American blacks, key counterculture figures insisted, had forged their own alternative culture from the beginning.)[12]

In contradistinction to the stations on the AM dial, where much of the once seemingly rebellious rock and roll was packaged in the standardized form of a two and a half minute Brill Building product, FM radio provided a forum for the new musical ethos. FM played songs of unstandardized length, compiled as part of "artistic" long-playing (vinyl) albums ("LP's"), and extended, free-form jams. At the Golden Gate Park Be-In, the hippies smoked up, dropped tabs, danced freely, loved openly ("make love, not war"), and embraced the natural world's gorgeous evanescence ("Flower Power"). Society's "squares" – often their parents – were appalled. For hippies, the experience presaged a new dawn, and a descending liberation and enlightenment, a sense captured by hit songs of the time like Scott McKenzie's "San Francisco (Be Sure to Wear Flowers in Your Hair)" (1967), the Youngbloods' "Get Together" (1967), and the Fifth Dimension's "Age of Aquarius" (1969).

"Yippies" like Jerry Rubin and Abbie Hoffman, who lived the hippie lifestyle but spoke and acted in more recognizably "political" ways, mocked the era's organized movement politics of meetings, marches, banners, picket signs, and demands – to say nothing of (square and pointless) voting and elections. In *Revolution for the Hell of It* (1968), Hoffman denounced bureaucracy and sexual "puritanism." He looked with admiration to the third-world revolutionaries Fidel, Che, and Ho. In *Steal This Book* (1971), billed as "a manual of survival in the prison that is Amerika" preaching "jailbreak," Hoffman offered guidance on how to live outside the prevailing economic, political, and social system by getting stuff for free (e.g. hitchhiking, stealing furniture from building lobbies and ketchup, mustard, and toilet paper from restaurants), along with instructions for assembling easily tossable homemade bombs ("Molotov Cocktails"). In *Do It: Scenarios of the Revolution* (1970), Hoffman's Yippie compatriot Jerry Rubin spurned the gospel of "Respectability and Success" of "capitalist Amerika," "the separation between work and play, school and fun, property and freedom," and denounced the Eisenhower era's stultifying sexual repression. Rubin called for a politics infused by the liberating spirit of rock and roll, born, like "a predestined pissed-off child, from Elvis's gyrating pelvis." The Yippies heralded a "new consciousness," "a politics of ecstasy." "Politics to me," Hoffman said, "is the way someone lives his life," adding, in a characteristically playful paradox, that "Political irrelevance is more effective than political relevance."

Mind-altering drugs were central to the counterculture, not as short-cuts to escapism or bodily pleasure (as moonshine and whiskey were for "rednecks" and "hillbillies," and gin and tonics and scotch and sodas were for stockbrokers and insurance company executives), but as enlightened pathways to alternative ways of being. Materialist capitalism had enslaved the human body and colonized the human mind. One of its chief instruments was time itself, which capitalism had remade to serve its ends. The insight was not new. In his film *Modern Times* (1936), the comedian Charlie Chaplin played a hapless worker charged with mechanically repeating a single, simple, task all day long: turn a screw one twist with a wrench as indistinguishable metal widgets whizzed by on an assembly line, the very picture of the efficient division of labor under capitalism advocated by the scientific management pioneer Frederick Winslow Taylor. Chaplin, an ordinary man who can't keep up, is repeatedly upbraided by the line foreman to no effect, until he is finally devoured whole by the machine as he tumbles onto the conveyor belt joining the endless line of widgets. Down the chute he goes, into the gears of the spinning, industrial engine. When the others realize what has happened, the machine is reversed, and the prostrate line worker is spat back out. The belt is restarted: Chaplin is back to work on the line, trying desperately but hopelessly to keep up. He simply doesn't have enough time: he never can, or will. Even earlier, in a 1907 essay in *Mother Earth*, Emma Goldman had condemned an economic system in which "in machine subserviency, our slavery is more complete than was our bondage to the King," and fixed the "clock-like mechanical atmosphere" of industrial capitalism, whose "highest attainment is the reduction of mankind to clockwork."

The counterculture imagined a world freed from the colonialism of standardized time. A fringe cohort of researchers in the psychology and religion departments at Harvard and MIT, including Timothy Leary, Andrew Weil, Richard Alpert (Ram Dass), and Huston Smith, suggested that the acid trip might provide a chemically synthesized short-cut to the most profound and elusive religious experience involving apprehensions of eternity and the oneness of creation. Leary, the group's most wacked evangelist, was soon fired for dosing Harvard students with acid. But this, for him, was not the end but the beginning. Freedom in America has a direction – West: keep going, all the way to California, until there is nothing but surf, sea, and sky. California is where, in the American imagination, West becomes East, the end augers a beginning, and the sunset promises a new dawn.[13] Leary headed to San Francisco, where he became the Pied Piper evangelizing America's youth *en masse* to "Turn On, Tune In, and Drop Out." Psychedelic drugs – LSD, magic mushrooms, and others – enhanced by music that broke from western music's strictures of time, tempo, and scale (like the Indian classical music performed by Ravi Shankar), were soon broadly touted as a means of lifting trippers out of time's confines, to glimpse the Aquarian promise of "the mind's true liberation."

Conclusion

While the circus-like counterculture grabbed headlines and set the tone for many young people, by the late 1960s, the country's two-party electoral politics had begun to unravel. Their domestic liberalism notwithstanding, the Johnson administration's elite bureaucrats and public servants – "the Best and the Brightest" – remained rooted in the Cold War liberal anticommunism of what to the young increasingly seemed to be another, darker time and era. The Cold War liberal framework underwrote the administration's escalation of the war in Vietnam in support of the anticommunist South Vietnam's resistance to conquest by communist-led (and Maoist Chinese-allied) North Vietnam, led by Ho Chi Minh. The White House insisted that it would not abandon a friend and ally desperately fending off an invading totalitarian enemy, portending, via "the domino effect," the "loss" of all of Southeast Asia, in which the United States' credibility was at stake. Many on the New Left and beyond, including in the civil rights movement, and many young people who were eligible for the military draft, saw something else entirely: the rearing up, in perhaps its ugliest form to date, not only of an exaggerated, "fearful," and "McCarthyite" anticommunism, but also of the malignant pathologies of American militarism, imperialism, colonialism, and racism. These dissenters took Ho's Viet Cong North to be engaging in a longstanding nationalist, anticolonialist resistance – a resistance by dark-skinned peoples against an invading white, capitalist, military colossus (first, the French colonialists, and then the Americans who had replaced them). The tension between the domestic and foreign policy programs was soon tearing the administration – and, in short order, the Democratic Party and the country – apart. A widespread antiwar movement developed, with Johnson as its chief target. When Johnson stunned the country by announcing in 1967 that he would neither seek nor accept the Democratic Party's nomination for a second (full) term as President, his loyal Vice-President, Hubert Humphrey, who followed Johnson in supporting the Vietnam War, stepped up in his place to beat back an antiwar insurgency led by Eugene McCarthy and then Robert F. Kennedy (who was assassinated while campaigning for the nomination in California). At the party's 1968 Convention in Chicago, violent and bloody conflict (truncheons, teargas, beatings) erupted in the streets between antiwar and New Left forces and white, ethnic, blue-collar, and staunchly patriotic and pro-US military Chicago police loyal to their Democratic Mayor Richard J. Daley (a cohort that had until then been solidly allied with the working-class Democratic Party since Franklin Roosevelt's New Deal). The party was in shambles; Humphrey's candidacy, already weakened by the entry of the third-party candidacy of the racist demagogue Alabama Governor George Wallace, was doomed. Into the breach stepped the Republican nominee, Richard Nixon, who promised a return to "law and order," and to speak for the country's "silent majority."

The context leading up to President Nixon's election, and its aftermath, heightened the feeling of moral and political chaos. Martin Luther King and Robert F. Kennedy had been assassinated and, in the riots that followed King's death, America's inner cities were set aflame from coast to coast. The 1968 Democratic Convention had sparked pitched battles in the streets of Chicago. Jimi Hendrix, Janis Joplin, and Jim Morrison were felled by drug overdoses. And that is to say nothing about the grotesque, cult "hippie" Manson (Tate–La Bianca) murders, the shootings by the National Guard of unarmed student antiwar demonstrators at Jackson State (Mississippi), Orangeburg (South Carolina), and Kent State (Ohio), the Hell's Angels stabbing at the Altamont Music Festival (1969), and the surprise Tet Offensive (1968), which portended an American defeat in Vietnam. While the counterculture had promised a new dawn, chaos, and even moral anarchy, was descending – captured by Joan Didion's "new journalism" reporting in *Slouching Toward Bethlehem* (1968) and *The White Album* (with essays from 1968 to 1978); by Jimi Hendrix's dark and soaring rendition of "The Star Spangled Banner" to a sparse crowd during his early Monday morning set at the Woodstock Music Festival (1969); by the violent, spent climax of Dennis Hopper's longhairs-versus-rednecks road film *Easy Rider* (1969); and by the Doors' incantatory nightmare "The End" (1967). New fault lines, fragments, and fissures opened up across American culture and politics that have shaped the country to the present.

Questions

1. Do the powerless and marginalized see and understand US culture more clearly than those born to and living with privilege?
2. Is American political culture individualistic or conformist?
3. Is the United States in its own way a "totalitarian" or even "fascistic" society?
4. Was there anything new in the political understandings advanced by mid-twentieth-century conservatives? Or was their political thought an effort to return the country to the political understandings and foundations that had been shunted aside by late nineteenth- and early twentieth-century leftists and progressive and New Deal liberal reformers?
5. Is conservative political thought irrational? Is it fundamentally committed to the reinforcement of hierarchies, whether ascriptive, economic, or otherwise? If so, is that a problem?
6. Is modern liberal political thought irrational? Is it fundamentally committed to a radical, and radically levelling, egalitarianism? If so, is that a problem?
7. Did the Democratic Party, American leftists, or American liberals ever regain their political footing after the violence and chaos of 1968? If so, how? If not, how might they do so?
8. How effective is non-violent resistance as an engine of significant social change? Is it a legitimate tactic?
9. Was/is black nationalism a viable political vision?
10. Has Christianity been a boon to proponents of racial justice in America, or a distraction from, if not an enemy of, the cause?
11. Did the movement from an Old Left to a (post-materialist) New Left doom radical politics in America? Or was it a useful, and perhaps even inevitable, advance?
12. Did the counterculture offer a significant and viable political vision? Or was it a circus, or a sideshow?
13. How new was the counterculture in the annals of American political thought?
14. Does non-western thought and religion suggest alternative ways of being, individual and collective, that offer a healthy escape from the pathologies of American political culture and thought?

8

The Identity and Post-Materialist Left, the New Right, and Third Way Liberalism

The political violence and chaos that ended the 1960s lingered into the 1970s, a time of disorder and decay. The antiwar movement fought against the Nixon administration's escalation of the war. Radical fringe organizations – the Weather Underground, the Symbionese Liberation Army, and the Fuerzas Armadas de Liberación Nacional (FALN – which continued the armed struggle for Puerto Rican Independence that had murdered members of Congress and attempted to assassinate President Truman in the early 1950s) – undertook bank robberies, kidnappings, prison breaks, airplane hijackings, and bombing campaigns. A crime wave swept the country, and the nation's poor and densely populated inner cities grew especially dangerous. President Nixon's besieged administration was felled by the Watergate scandal, in which the President was caught hiring burglars to break into the headquarters of the Democratic National Committee and other offices in search of damaging personal information on his political opponents, and then tried to illegally cover up evidence of the crimes. Intervening against supporters of Israel in the (October 1973) Yom Kippur War, the Arab-dominated Organization of Petroleum Exporting Countries (OPEC) unleashed an embargo against the United States that led to major shortages of gasoline and an economy-shredding spike in oil prices, and, after the embargo ended, inaugurated a period of OPEC production cuts aimed at increasing prices. These oil supply cuts, in turn, sparked a new phenomenon that mainstream economic theory had heretofore held impossible: a simultaneous rise in both unemployment and inflation ("stagflation"). In 1979, Islamic revolutionaries in Iran overthrew the US-installed Shah of Iran and held the staff of the American embassy captive for 444 days. (Along the way, humiliatingly, a military rescue mission launched by President Jimmy Carter, literally crashed and burned in the Iranian desert.)

At the same time, in a sharp turn away from the 1960s politicization, mainlines of the popular culture turned inward. Politically radical folk music morphed into the age of the singer-songwriter, of the lone introspective individual, with a guitar or piano – Joni Mitchell, Carole King, Neil Young, James Taylor, Janis Ian, Jim Croce – baring their souls, confronting love, loss, aging, and alienation in a deeply and sometimes painfully personal tenor, although sometimes the music soared in joy toward the discovery and realization of the true self.

The turn inward of the 1970s "Me Decade" represented a retreat from politics arising out of disillusionment, cynicism, or simply exhaustion. But in important precincts, the turn inward augured a new form of politics arising out of that old friend of the American soul: the sovereign self, newly illuminated by the rebellions and social upheavals of the 1950s and 1960s. Feminists had long insisted that the personal was political. In the 1970s, it became clearer to perhaps more people than at any previous time in American history that in starting from abstract assumptions about presumably fungible individuals – which were steeply ascendant, and on their way to becoming hegemonic in economics and political science – and in building out formal models of governmental power and authority, political thinkers had neglected to delve into questions of individual identity and the relationship between those identities and the structures of social, economic, and governmental power. Politics was about much more than materialist concerns about who gets what and the relative powers of the executive, legislative, and judicial branches. And it was about more than government. It was also about the way that pervasive structures of power, formal and informal, made, and perhaps disfigured – did violence to – the true self, whose autonomous agency has supposedly assented to the legitimacy and authority of those structures.

Sex and Gender

Many have described feminism as a series of "waves," with the first in the second half of the nineteenth century, and the second emerging in the late 1960s and into the 1970s.[1] The wave schematic suggests a cyclical dynamic in which periods of relative quiescence alternate with crests of new political thought and mobilization. We can question whether this is an accurate or helpful way of conceptualizing the trajectory of American feminism.

That said, something was definitely happening across the 1960s and into the 1970s, a time of intense and, in some cases, (would-be) revolutionary mobilization on the American Left. In the movement society of the 1960s/1970s, women's voices became increasingly assertive in ways that reflected the times' broader political currents and imperatives. Soon after the end of World War II, the French existentialist philosopher Simone de Beauvoir's *The Second Sex* (1949) ("One is not born but becomes a woman") began to be widely read in the United States, opening up a host of new inquiries about, and insights into, the status of women in a male-dominated world. In *The Feminine Mystique* (1963), Betty Friedan – a student of one of the era's leading psychologists of personal identity and its relations to the broader society, Erik Erikson, and a reader of de Beauvoir (and Marx) – paused to notice a disturbing psychological undercurrent in American women's lives during a time in which they were repeatedly told that, luxuriating in the relative ease of their prosperous suburban lives as wives and mothers ("housewives"), they were living in a golden age. Friedan provocatively observed that an unusually high number of these ostensibly privileged women were suffering from a "yearning," an emptiness, dissatisfaction, and desperation. Although they had not yet found the words to express their inchoate feelings, Friedan argued that they were essentially asking "Is this all?" She called the condition "the problem that has no name." And she diagnosed its cause. It was not attributable to an individualized failure on the part of these women to adjust in a psychologically healthy way to an objectively good life that they should find satisfying, rewarding, and fulfilling. It was attributable, rather, to a system that foisted upon these women a belief in the "mystique of feminine fulfillment," which told them that a woman's greatest satisfactions in life should come from her naturally ordained role as a wife and mother. Borrowing from Erikson, Friedan argued that these deeply unhappy women were suffering from an "identity crisis." Their roads to genuine fulfillment through the discovery of their true natures and selves – the path "to becom[ing] fully human," to flourishing – had been sharply circumscribed by societal understandings and expectations about women and their purportedly "natural" needs and roles. These understandings and expectations were limiting their horizons and crushing their spirits. Women needed to reclaim their lives, and their agency, from the prison of the feminine mystique.

It was not long before the experiences of women active in the progressive movements of the 1960s set a match to this smoldering new thinking, igniting second-wave feminism as a full-blown social movement. Jo Freeman, Robin Morgan, Nancy Hawley, Rita Mae Brown, Susan Brownmiller, and other women involved in the New Left, civil rights, antiwar, and Yippie movements of the 1960s were increasingly put off by the sexism they experienced there. They responded by launching their own mobilization for "women's liberation." The writings flowed out in a deluge: Robin Morgan's pioneering collection *Sisterhood is Powerful: An Anthology of Writings from the Women's Liberation Movement* (1970) showcased varieties of the new thinking. Additional analyses followed: Kate Millett's *Sexual Politics* (1970), Germaine Greer's *The Female Eunuch* (1970), Shulamith Firestone's *The Dialectic of Sex: The Case for Feminist Revolution* (1970), and others. A succession of radical activist and "consciousness-raising" groups formed, fiercely committed to awakening women to their reality and plight: the Redstockings (Ellen Willis, Shulamith Firestone), WITCH (Women's International Terrorist Conspiracy from Hell), and New York Radical Women. In the spirit of the times, these organizations unleashed a succession of radical demands, statements, and declarations: the SCUM (Society for Cutting Up Men) Manifesto (1967); the Redstockings Manifesto (1969); and the BITCH Manifesto (1969).

Given the defining insights of feminism concerning the pervading politics of the private sphere, it would be somewhat inaccurate to draw too sharp a distinction between liberal and radical versions of feminist thought, as we did with the earlier labor, civil rights, and student/antiwar movements. It is nevertheless useful to distinguish liberal from more radical varieties of second-wave feminism, in a way that, given the earlier intra-movement tensions arising out of the initial introduction of the proposed Equal Rights Amendment (ERA) in the 1920s by Alice Paul's National Women's Party (NWP), movement participants themselves would have recognized. In a reflection of the core paradigm of liberal political thought, liberal feminists placed their primary emphasis on the natural rights of individuals. The underlying framework was there in John Locke, and in the Declaration of Independence, which had been so stirringly invoked in the Seneca Falls Declaration of Sentiments (1848) ("We hold these truths to be self-evident, that all men and women are created equal"), and had served as a touchstone for the abolitionist Frederick Douglass. It posited that all persons are born free and equal, and, as such, are possessed of a set of God-given natural rights. This entailed a universal right of free individuals to equal treatment under law. Full civic membership was underwritten by laws that were neutrally applied, without distinction on the basis of irrelevant characteristics, such as race or sex. Laws that discriminated against people on the basis of these characteristics – on the basis of bigotry or prejudice – whether on their face or as applied, were a denial of the fundamental rights whose protection was at the heart of liberal theories of the origins of a legitimate political order.

Liberal feminism had been the central paradigm behind both the Seneca Falls Convention and much of first-wave feminism. It had underwritten the early twentieth-century suffragist campaign that, via the adoption of the Nineteenth Amendment, had secured women's constitutional right to vote. The liberal framework also underwrote the prohibition on sex discrimination in the landmark Civil Rights Act of 1964. It was the central paradigm that informed the founding in 1967 (by Betty Friedan, Pauli Murray, and others) of the peak advocacy organization the National Organization for Women (NOW), which fought for women's equality under law. The NOW *Bill of Rights* (1967) called anew for the adoption of an Equal Rights Amendment to the Constitution; the enforcement of non-discrimination laws in support of women in the workplace and education; paid maternity leave; public support for women with children (e.g. day care); and recognizing women's control over their own reproductive lives and choices via the repeal (or judicial voiding) of laws restricting access to contraception and banning abortion. Adopting the tactics of liberal civil rights organizations like the NAACP, NOW aggressively pursued its agenda through both legislation and litigation, backed by mass mobilizations and participation in electoral politics. NOW's campaign succeeded on a number of fronts, including the passage of new laws, new legal doctrine concerning sex discrimination, and new interpretations of the Fourteenth Amendment's Equal Protection Clause holding discrimination on

the basis of sex to be a "suspect classification" entailing strict judicial supervision of laws and government action.

While it seemed well on the way to ratification in the late 1970s, the proposed
ERA was defeated in significant part by an antifeminist countermobilization
– some called it a "backlash" – spearheaded by the conservative midwestern
Catholic Phyllis Schlafly, who had cut her teeth as a Barry Goldwater champion and was now assuming a prominent role in the rising anti-abortion and
anti-gay rights movements, and as a prominent "New Right" supporter of
Ronald Reagan. Many of the benefits that would have been brought by the
ratification of the ERA were nevertheless enshrined in law through interpretations of the Constitution by the (liberal/moderate Nixon-Republican) Supreme
Court.

Some of the most prominent and provocative second-wave feminists, however, spurned the liberal paradigm. Radical feminists – like labor, civil rights,
and other radicals before them – rejected it as profoundly misguided. As they
saw it, that paradigm ultimately served to reinforce the underlying power
relations that were the root cause of the political problem and predicament.
The gravamen of the radicals' rejection of liberalism is that its vaunted freely
choosing moral agent, the "individual," does not exist: "the individual" me
is a fiction. Or, more precisely, the individual does not exist except as constituted by power. What's worse, to act as if "the individual" exists as a free,
self-determining agent whose understandings and choices are not constituted
by the power relations of the society of which that person is a part serves to
both enforce and reinscribe those pre-existing power relations – systems of
domination and subordination. Since the liberal political thought rulebook
holds that all rightful political authority derives from the free, uncoerced
choices made by autonomous, self-directing individuals consenting (whether
expressly or tacitly) to the social contract, the liberal paradigm presumes the
"consent" of the liberal subject to his or her own domination and subordination by the prevailing societal structures of power, implicitly legitimating
an unjust and oppressive political order. A woman, for instance, might say
– and even believe – that what she wants most in life is to marry a man and
devote her life to serving as his helpmeet, supporting his career, and raising
his children. In response, a liberal might explain that we should honor and
respect this woman's individual choices as to what she wants and values
most. But are those choices really the product of an autonomous self, freely
reflecting upon what she truly wants or needs to be happy and to flourish? Or
are they the product of a lifetime of roles, scripts, and expectations of those
holding power in society, who have designed the society's institutions in a
way that indoctrinates its subjects, and imposes norms, understandings, and
rules on women to serve the interests of those in a position of power – like
men? Radical feminist critics of liberalism press us to ask how we might come
to know what women really want – or would want, if they were possessed of

the genuine freedom to reflect uncoerced on their true situation, needs, and wants.

People, radical political theorists often emphasize, lack even the language to imagine a world in which their wants and needs would be genuinely available and met.[2] This is why the commitment to "consciousness-raising" suffused second-wave feminism: liberal feminists considered it a prerequisite for a more just and legitimate liberal order. Radical feminists, however – like other radical leftists focused on the overarching systems and structures of power ordained by capitalism or racism – committed themselves to unmasking the deep structures of systems of domination and subordination that, as they elucidated at length, were inherent in the very concepts, categories, and language in common use everywhere, at every level, including by governments and government officials (in saying, for example, that "the race problem" was one of "bigotry" or "prejudice" [individual], rather than "white supremacy" [structural/systemic]). By these lights, far from offering a pathway out of oppressions, liberalism was implicated and complicit in what would more accurately be called "the racism problem." (This is what the radical black lesbian feminist Audre Lorde meant in 1979 when she said that "the master's tools will never dismantle the master's house.")

> [O]ur society, like all other historical civilizations, is a patriarchy.
> Kate Millett (1970)

The political theorist Kate Millett's *Sexual Politics* offered a sustained exposition of the predicament of woman as ruled object, as opposed to self-directing subject. Millett's account of the ruling patriarchal order traced its genealogy to the very creation myths of western civilization – to stories like the Greek myth of Pandora's Box (the "box" being a woman's vagina), or the Genesis story of Adam and Eve (where Eve, tempted by the serpent, destroys paradise and sinks all of humanity into the fallen world constituted by the "original sin" of [woman's] disobedience). As such, the "interior colonization" of the hearts and minds of women and men alike was deeply embedded in western culture: virtually all of its institutions, power structures, and beliefs – the root of a pervading "false consciousness" that underwrote systemic injustice – needed to be fought, and overcome.

This is why, moreover, radical feminists – but also, in their own way, even liberal feminists – largely rejected the categorical distinction that liberals since Locke had tended to draw between the public and private spheres. Women had long been consigned to – indeed, confined to – roles within civil society's private sphere (homes, families), where they were enlisted to serve, support, and reproduce. "Politics" for feminists involved any sphere or space where the prevailing system of domination and subordination – the patriarchy, as Millett would have it – operated, and was reinforced, reinscribed, and perpetuated.

The radical feminism of this time took many dramatic forms that shocked the mainstream culture. But the second wave's radicalism, from the rumored "bra burnings" that titillated the evening news, to the feminist-separatist events, including womyn-only gatherings such as the Michigan Womyn's Music Festival (MWMF, 1976–2015), which welcomed and celebrated womyn of any self-understanding and variety, including lesbians and the gender-non-conforming, self-consciously cultivating new forms of consciousness and solidarity (in time the MWMF evolved toward a lesbian separatist movement), nevertheless reflected these extensively theorized concerns. In these new departures, radical feminists challenged sex and gender essentialism, which attributed a set of characteristics, like "woman's innate maternal instinct" (Phyllis Schlafly), or the traits associated with "femininity," to nature, God, or "nature, as God created it," rather than to social/cultural/political institutions and imperatives. Second-wave feminists would come to argue, for instance, that femininity was socially and historically constructed to serve the requirements of a political system of domination and subordination in which women, constructed as an alien "other," were defined primarily in relation to, and as less than, men.

Much of this transformative thinking and activism had real-world effects, including landmark works of reclamation like the Boston Women's Health Book Collective's *Our Bodies, Ourselves* (1970), in which politically conscious women taught their sisters about their own bodies (and especially sexuality) in ways that empowered them to transform themselves from passive, ruled objects to agency-wielding subjects. Women organized to confront endemic violence and abuse that had long been denied, ignored, or suppressed by men and male-dominated institutions. The first battered-women's shelters were founded. Susan Brownmiller's *Against Our Will: Men, Women, and Rape* (1975) and Diana Russell's *The Politics of Rape: The Victim's Perspective* (1975) launched early salvos in the critique of "rape culture," in which the threat of rape operates an instrument of systematic male domination and subordination. Catharine MacKinnon published *Sexual Harassment of Working Women: A Case of Sex Discrimination* (1979), which argued that sexual harassment in the workplace was a form of illegal sex discrimination. As the polity entered the more conservative 1980s, Andrea Dworkin joined with MacKinnon to have pornography legally classed a form of sex discrimination.

As these developments unfolded, radical and liberal feminists often clashed in ways that both echoed and remade earlier intra-movement debates. The liberal feminist psychologist Carol Gilligan's *In a Different Voice* (1982) smacked to many leftist feminists of "essentialism" in positing that men and women were possessed of different moral psychologies, with men more likely to be attuned to a more abstract ethic of justice, and women to a more organic "ethic of care." (Gilligan became associated with what became known as "difference feminism," which led to heated debates between leading proponents and critics of that paradigm.)[3]

The Intervention of Feminist Women of Color

The most widely disseminated forms of second-wave feminism were preoccupied with the particular set of grievances and critiques of those who comprised the movement's core membership: middle-class, relatively educated and affluent white women. The deadening and repressive consequences of exclusion from the workplace, as exemplified by the suburban housewife at the center of Betty Friedan's *The Feminine Mystique*, did not apply to many, if not most, African-American women, and to other women who had long worked outside the home – and indeed, had no choice, economically, but to do otherwise. While these women had their own grievances and problems, some of which they shared with middle-class white suburban women, they were clearly not suffering from "housewives' syndrome." Many of these women felt that their voices were marginalized in the emerging second-wave feminist movement.

This sense of voicelessness, exclusion, and absence of "comradery between black and white women" was noted in some prominent places, including in an article in *The New York Times Magazine* by the editor and novelist Toni Morrison entitled "What the Black Woman Thinks About Women's Lib" (1971). "Distrust," she answered, quoting Nikki Giovanni, who had expressed the view in *Essence* that "The Woman's Liberation Movement is basically a family quarrel between white women and white men," before going on to explicate the predicament and problems of black women in particular, including those that had proved endemic to their problems with black men. Similar matters were taken up in a series of essays and speeches by Audre Lorde from the mid-1970s through the early 1980s and beyond, including in a colloquy with James Baldwin (*Essence*, 1984) in which Baldwin pushed back with sympathy for the perpetually emasculated black male, and Lorde forcefully returned the volley.

Lorde's writings and speeches explored the dynamics of what later came to be known as "intersectionality." Lorde often articulated her views by first announcing her standpoint. She expressly stipulated that she was speaking "as a" black, lesbian, feminist, woman. Lorde noted the ways that the broader culture's assumptions and frameworks – starting from a "mythical norm" ("white, thin, male, young, heterosexual, Christian, and financially secure") – to say nothing of the frameworks of even the most radical of white feminists (like Mary Daly), silenced and erased the individual experiences of women like her. "Black feminism is not white feminism in blackface," Lorde challenged. "Black women have particular and legitimate issues which affect our lives as Black women, and," of necessity, speaking not only to white women but also to black men, "addressing those issues does not make us any less Black." Lorde chastised white feminists for "ignor[ing] differences of race, sexual preference, class, and age," of basking in "their built-in privilege of whiteness." She condemned the systemic "depersonalization" wrought by the interlocking operation of racism, sexism, heterosexism, and homophobia. "[T]here are so many silences to be broken," she urged, lamenting the culture's "inability to recognize the notion of difference as a dynamic human force, one which is enriching rather than threatening to the defined self, when there are shared goals." That vision of difference – diversity – as a "dynamic human force" that might seed the ultimate arrival of a truly just political order loomed as a hope, and possibility.[4]

"Gay Liberation" and the Politics of LGBTQ + Identity

The postwar period marked new departures in vanguard political thinking concerning sexuality, first by the "homophile" movement of the 1950s, and then, in the late 1960s and 1970s, in the name of "gay liberation." A widely noted first shot was fired by the controversial Kinsey Reports (*Sexual Behavior in the Human Male*, 1948; *Sexual Behavior in the Human Female*, 1953), the work of pioneering sexologists at Indiana University. The Kinsey Reports offered scientific evidence demonstrating that, in their actual lives, Americans engaged in more varied and fluid sexual behaviors than the ambient culture seemed to recognize and normatively and legally endorse, privilege, encode, and enforce. Not long after, at Washington University in St. Louis, the psychologists William Masters and Virginia Johnson launched their own series of strikingly frank, sex-positive studies of the full range of human sexualities and sexual practices. Both of these scholarly initiatives were suffused with the vaulting scientific optimism and ambitions of the postwar "space age."

Strictly speaking, the celebration of alternative and experimental sexualities and lifestyles was not a new phenomenon in American culture and thought. From the (evangelical Christian) "Free Love" experiments of John Humphrey Noyes's utopian Oneida Community in upstate New York (1848–1881), to the LDS/Mormon practice of plural marriage, to Walt Whitman's homoerotic Calamus poems (1860), to early twentieth-century Greenwich Village (New York City) sex radicalism, the boldest expressions of it nevertheless tended to issue from radical religious and fringe utopian experiments, and from boundary-flouting urban bohemia. What was so shocking – or liberating – to so many about the Kinsey Reports was the argument that, despite what we preached and purported to value and practice, the sex lives of Americans were a lot more venturesome then we were allowed to publicly imagine or acknowledge, a reality that was reflected in the slogan later adopted by the gay rights movement: "We are everywhere!"

The postwar United States' small "homophile" movement, spearheaded by groups like the Mattachine Society (1950; Harry Hay) and the Daughters of Bilitis (1955; Del Martin, Phyllis Lyon), spoke the language of liberal equality. It organized to protest and advocate on behalf of gay and lesbian civil rights.

At about the same time as the Kinsey Reports, Edward Sagarin's *The Homosexual in America: A Subjective Approach* (1951) – written, as Sagarin felt essential for his safety at the time, under a pseudonym, Donald Webster Cory – offered the dispassionate testimony of the homosexual, not as a disgusting, dangerous, deviant and pervert, but as an ordinary person, with what happened to be a different sexual and affectional orientation. For his part, although typically classed as a harbinger of the 1960s counterculture, the Beat writer Allen Ginsberg, like his hero Walt Whitman, also wrote openly and passionately about same-sex desire and love (for which he faced criminal obscenity charges). Unlike Sagarin/Cory, however, and the early gay rights groups advancing the first prominent public claims for gay and lesbian civic equality and civil rights, all of whom made the case for homosexuals as being (as the gay conservative Andrew Sullivan later argued) "virtually normal," Ginsberg offered a prophetic vision which proudly inscribed the sexually aberrant and non-conforming into the book of American society's outcasts, deviants, and perverts, whom he held to constitute the culture's visionary vanguard of seers and seekers. "Virtually normal" was not, for Ginsberg, anything that any fully realized, actualized, and emancipated human being should ever want to be.[5]

When, after years of contentious resistance against police raids on a succession of New York City gay bars, the multi-racial, ethnic, and gendered queers at Greenwich Village's Stonewall Inn (1969) stood up and said "no more," attracting increasingly sympathetic attention, what we take as the modern "gay liberation" or "gay rights" movement began. Given its arrival in the late 1960s, the fault line between the liberal reformist model calling for full civic inclusion in a regime of universal, equal, individual rights, and more radical claims to particularist identity liberated from the society's disciplinary structures of power, were baked into the gay rights movement from its inception. These intra-movement tensions – often bitter and deep – issued from rivalrous political understandings and frameworks implicating fundamental political questions about the respective claims of liberal reformism and inclusion, and radical and revolutionary aspirations and imaginaries.

Whether the Stonewall Riots represented the first step in the fight for liberal political equality of gays and lesbians, or a major salvo in the struggle for the revolutionary overthrow of oppressive norms of gender and gender identity, has remained a bone of contention in the movement ever since, as reflected in anxieties about the very name of the cause itself, which began by dropping the clinical "homosexual" in favor of the proud and defiant "gay," but soon was compelled to identify itself as "gay and lesbian," then "lesbian, gay, and bisexual," and then "lesbian, gay, bisexual, and trans" – with an added "Q" (Questioning/Queer) and then a "+" (basically, an etcetera). Many took to calling themselves simply "queer." Some scholars have flagged a recent trend toward bio-essentialism within the movement ("Born This Way"), while others have either resisted or abandoned the search for (limiting and reifying) boundaries and definitions, celebrating instead the perpetual fluidity and autonomy of "just me" – the sovereign self.

In the late 1960s and early 1970s, lesbians like Adrienne Rich (*Of Women Born: Motherhood as Experience and Institution*, 1976; "Compulsory Heterosexuality and Lesbian Existence," 1980) and Rita Mae Brown and Charlotte Bunch of Washington DC's Furies Collective (1971) more systematically applied and extended second-wave feminist theories of patriarchy that had been elaborated earlier by Simone de Beauvoir and Kate Millett to assail "hetero-normativity" or "compulsory heterosexuality," as underwritten by heterosexuality's presumptive "naturalness." A raft of gay rights organizations (the Gay Liberation Front, 1969; the Gay Activists Alliance, 1969; the National Gay Task Force, 1973) and publications (*The [Los Angeles] Advocate*, 1967/1970; *Come Out*, 1969, and many contemporary successors) were founded which, to various degrees, presented views and positions across the liberal-universalist/radical-revolutionary spectrum.

The AIDS crisis that devastated the gay (male) community across the 1980s pushed the movement's political thought in both directions. AIDS effectively "outed" Americans from places and families across America, killing without regard to race, creed, color, geography, or politics, forcing homosexuality into the universal mainstream of American culture. Major works of art – high, mainstream, and folk – confronting AIDS (Larry Kramer's play *The Normal Heart*, 1985; David Wojnarowicz's lacerating pieces, including the photographic record of his friend Peter Hujar's devastation by the disease; the AIDS Memorial Quilt, 1987; and Tony Kushner's *Angels in America*, 1991) brought gay life and politics to broad public attention. At the same time, the public policy squeamishness about gay love and sex, and an inclination by leading figures on the ascendant Christian Right to attribute death from the disease to a sick and perverted lifestyle, provoked a radicalized backlash in core sectors of the gay community. New mobilizations, like the establishment of the Gay Men's Health Crisis (1982) – in its way, an enlistment of the model of the earlier Boston Women's Health Book Collective – and, in turn, the more brashly confrontational movement politics of Larry Kramer's ACT-UP (AIDS Coalition to Unleash Power; 1987), underlined the conviction that, in the broadest, and now most literal, sense, in the words of the multiculturalist gay anthem by Holly Near, a "gentle, angry people" were "singing for [their] lives."[6]

Racial and Ethnic Identity and Pride: the Chicano and American Indian Movements, and Beyond

While its far-ranging implications were downplayed by its advocates, who focused instead on the questions of legal justice and equality that had been contemporaneously raised by the mid-century civil rights movement, the

Immigration and Nationality Act of 1965 put an end to the strict "national origins" quotas that had kept the majority of America "white" by law since the draconian Immigration Act of 1924.[7] The transformational 1965 Act set the stage for a significantly more ethnically, racially, and religiously diverse American populace. The demographics of that new post-1965 populace would come to test the credibility of the country's professed creedal nationalism: that is, of its oft-reiterated insistence that in the United States civic membership was defined not ascriptively by race, national origins, ethnicity, or religion, but instead by a universalistic commitment to the principles of liberty, equality, and democracy. For most of the nation's history, many of those on American soil who were not white Protestant Christians had questioned the nation's fidelity to its self-professed creed, feeling themselves – with plenty of evidence – to be a domestic "other," denied the fruits of the full and equal civil membership that had been so routinely assumed by the country's racial and religious majority. In times when their numbers swelled, or when incidents or events sparked inter-racial, inter-ethnic, or inter-religious tensions, strong nativist and anti-immigrant movements had arisen. The Immigration Act of 1924 was just one in a long line of efforts by white Protestant nativists to nip the problem in the bud by stopping what they took to be disturbing demographic transitions dead in their tracks.

From another perspective, of course, the understanding of "America" as white Protestant Christian had long been a fantasy. It was a willful denial of the on-the-ground reality of the territory that became the geographic United States. Two national, ethno-cultural, racial, and religious groups that did not fit the country's white Protestant ethno-cultural imaginary were resident on the land prior to the Atlantic coastal European settlement: the indigenous Native Americans, from coast to coast, and, subsequently, Mexicans, whose land, as the United States expanded westward, the European settlers would seize and claim the right to rule. In the late 1960s and across the 1970s especially, inspired in significant part by the Black Power and Black Pride movements, these two groups launched their own sometimes militant movements, the Chicano Movement and the American Indian Movement (AIM).

The Chicano Movement, sometimes referred to as La Raza or El Movimiento, while eventually national in scope, was nevertheless centered in California, which, like much of the US Southwest before the Mexican–American War (1846–1848), had been part of Mexico. (That war is known in Mexico as the Intervención Estadounidense en México – the United States intervention in Mexico.) It was a movement for Mexican-American empowerment encompassing a wide range of concerns, issues, and causes. Some involved civil liberties and civil rights claims that appealed to universal principles of liberal equality and full civic membership, such as voting rights and immigrant rights, while the movement also called for an end to racial and ethnic discrimination and police abuse and brutality (most prominently by the LAPD). Some took up causes of special concern to Mexican-Americans, like the fight to improve the schools in El Barrio, and the farmworkers' rights movement spearheaded by Cesar Chavez and Dolores Huerta's founding of the United Farm Workers, which launched a succession of strikes and boycotts to improve the working conditions of agricultural laborers. The Chicano Movement made common cause with others on the Left in mounting a vigorous opposition to the Vietnam War.

Much of the political thought of the Chicano Movement, however, followed the contemporaneous Black Nationalist, Black Power, and Black Pride movements in emphasizing issues of culture and identity. The aim was the recovery of a lost – or, more precisely, a coercively stolen and erased – Chicano self firmly rooted in a Mesoamerican history and heritage. The Chicanismo outlook called for the reclamation of Chicano identity through consciousness-raising education in authentic Mesoamerican history and culture, a project boldly imagined in Rodolfo "Corky" Gonzales's poem *Yo Soy Joaquin/I am Joaquin* (1969). "Brown Beret" protestors adopted their own version of the militant uniform of the Black Panther Party – which itself had been adopted from anti-colonial third-world resistance movements. Recognizing the complex legacies of the Spanish conquistadors from whom many of these mestizo peoples were also descended, proponents of Chicanismo boldly reclaimed the legacies of both the ancient Aztec and Mayan civilizations, and of Pancho Villa and Emiliano Zapata, in their own bid for a self-determining Chicano nationalism, free of the taints of an externally imposed, inscribed, and performed identity. Like other liberal/Left movements of the era, the Chicano Movement of the late 1960s and 1970s comprised groups, wings, and offshoots across the spectrum of thought and militance. Some emphasized separatism and difference. Others advocated a liberal universalism that looked toward alliances, whether with others committed to liberal universalism, or with and as socialists, in solidarity with a broad coalition of the anti-capitalist working class. There were criticisms from within the movement that it was neglecting or silencing its Chicanas, who grappled with questions of intersectional identity. Other Spanish-speaking peoples in the United States, like Puerto Ricans in Chicago and New York City, were becoming politicized at the same time along similar lines, with groups like the Young Lords fighting for justice within their own neighborhoods in Lincoln Park, Brooklyn, and Spanish Harlem.

The contemporaneous American Indian Movement, founded by Dennis Banks, Clyde Bellecourt, Vernon Bellecourt, and Russell Means, followed a similar trajectory. Across the late 1960s and 1970s, a rising cohort of movement leaders were adamant in pointing out that North America's indigenous peoples – the Iroquois of the Northeast, the Cherokee and the Seminole of the Southeast, the Navajo and Comanche of the Southwest, the Lakota of the Great Plains, and the Ojibwe and Cree of the upper Midwest (and what is now Canada), and many others – had existed for 500 years, and resisted, before being described as a "movement." But riding the crest of the Black and Brown Power movements, the country's indigenous peoples now began to organize more systematically and anew for "Red Power." What began as a protest and resistance movement in Minneapolis (1968) against police brutality and poverty affecting "urban Indians" (a growing cohort of Native peoples pushed off their rural tribal lands and into the country's cities by the latest round of assimilationist "termination policies" in the 1950s) grew into a broad and sustained campaign with a range of political goals. While AIM certainly fought for the civil rights and individual rights of native peoples, it was the one ethno-nationalist movement of its time that had the strongest claim to having been comprised of actual, extant, independent, self-governing, and self-determining polities ("first nations") on the territory subsequently conquered and colonized by the European settlement that led to the founding and geographic expansion of the United States. Grasping for an appropriate legal and political category for America's indigenous Indian tribes, a set of early Supreme Court opinions written by Chief Justice John Marshall had described them, oxymoronically, as "domestic dependent nation[s]."[8] Relations between the United States and these tribes were conducted as if the latter were independent countries – via treaties, the chief instrument under international law for formal agreements between sovereign states. But, from the beginning, the United States' settler colonialists – its celebrated "pioneers" on its legendary "frontier" – acted, when they wanted or needed to, as if they were not bound by those agreements: over the course of US history, they violated every one of them, often egregiously, when it suited their interests. AIM's pre-eminent demand was for the restoration of tribal sovereignty, and the reclamation and enforcement of treaty rights. A significant part of the movement involved matters of identity in which sustained efforts were undertaken to reclaim the native histories and cultures lost to what Indian activists did not hesitate to call a cultural – and literal – genocide. The *Trail of Broken Treaties 20-Point Position Paper: An Indian Manifesto – Restitution, Reparations, Restoration of Lands for a Reconstruction of an Indian Future in America* (1972) set out the indigenous peoples' grievances, demands, and political and cultural visions.

AIM took direct action to advance the Indian cause, holding conferences, councils, and pow-wows, staging marches, takeovers, and occupations, and initiating youth and health services and jobs programs, while moving to strengthen community institutions like schools. Some of AIM's actions were politically prominent and dramatic. These included the movement's nineteen-month occupation of Alcatraz Island in San Francisco Bay (1969–1971), and its occupation of Wounded Knee on South Dakota's Pine Ridge Reservation (1973). The "Trail of Broken Treaties" march on Washington (1972) and the "Longest Walk" across America drew national attention to recent legislation negatively affecting Indian peoples.

AIM also helped spark a revival of interest in native spirituality, native history, and native culture among Indians and non-Indians alike. The publication of books like Vine Deloria Jr.'s *Custer Died for Your Sins: An Indian Manifesto* (1969) and Dee Brown's *Bury My Heart at Wounded Knee: An Indian History of the American West* (1970), along with renewed interest in the recovered *Black Elk Speaks* (1961/1932) by John G. Niehardt, fed the hunger for more richly informed understandings and selves.

Ecology and Environment

Perhaps the most prominent post-materialist "new social movement" of the 1970s was the "ecology" or environmental movement. "Eco," from the Greek *oikos*, signaled a concern and care for the human home, the earth's natural environment. Among the specific concerns in the 1970s were overpopulation, natural resource depletion, and the pollution of the air and water of what the inventor and futurist R. Buckminster Fuller, announcing a new planetary imaginary, called "Spaceship Earth."

Modern environmentalism was not *sui generis*. In the mid-nineteenth century, as white settlement was giving rise to an increasingly tilled, populous, and industrialized Northeast, romantic and nostalgic Hudson River School landscape painters like Thomas Cole, Frederic Church, Asher Durand, and Albert Bierstadt soon took to celebrating unsubdued nature's sublime, arresting, and sometimes fearsome majesty. (Bierstadt turned his pictorial gaze to the – purportedly – unpopulated and unspoiled American West.) At about the same time, in an eastern mystical spirit, the New England Transcendentalists Ralph Waldo Emerson (*Nature*, 1836) and Henry David Thoreau (*Walden*, 1854), looked to nature as the embodiment of the soul of the universe. In the Berkshire mountains of western Massachusetts, more traditional Christians like the Williams College "natural philosopher" Mark Hopkins – writing in the age of von Humboldt, Darwin, and Agassiz – studied it as the fullest manifestation of God's creation. The naturalist John Muir, a reader of Emerson and founder of the Sierra Club (1892), began as a boy by reveling in the rich natural world of the North Sea coast of his native Scotland and his family's adopted home of Wisconsin before lighting out for northern California's Yosemite and High Sierras, whose dramatic landscapes he portrayed in enraptured writings that brought him national fame. By the 1890s, Muir was already chronicling the damage and destruction wrought by local ranchers. He was instrumental in lobbying for the creation of the United States' first national park at Yosemite, and others that followed, including Grand Canyon National Park. Muir's *Our National Parks* (1901) seized the attention of President Theodore Roosevelt. Soon the two were collaborating on a conservationist vision and philosophy that advanced a new understanding of the relationship between humans and the natural world rooted in a national commitment to conservation, preservation, and stewardship. Starting from transcendental and spiritual premises, Muir was a strong proponent of maintaining a sanctified, untrammeled, and pristine wildness. Gifford Pinchot, however, the first head of the US Forest Service and Theodore Roosevelt's Secretary of the Interior, initiated new departures in public policy that reflected a somewhat different vision committed to "conservation" through utilitarian management of the nation's natural resources directed toward sustainable human use. In a similar spirit that both esteemed the beauty of nature and provided for abundant human access and enjoyment, the new field of landscape architecture pioneered by Frederick Law Olmsted led to the design of accessible urban oases, including the Boston Fenway's "Emerald Necklace," Brooklyn's Prospect Park, and Manhattan's Central Park. In the 1930s, during the Great Depression, Theodore Roosevelt's cousin, President Franklin Delano Roosevelt, melded demand-side (Keynesian) economics, a Lockean liberal (and Christian calling) commitment to wholesome, productive labor, republican service, and esteem for conservation and stewardship of the natural world by hiring legions of unemployed young men to work in a Civilian Conservation Corps (CCC) devoted to the maintenance and improvement of the nation's great public lands and parks.

At the same time, the radicals Helen and Scott Nearing began modeling a new way of life that counseled a return to the land by committed individuals who would live by their own wits independently, naturally, and ethically, in harmony with nature, unsullied by the moral compromises, abominations, and tragedies of industrial capitalist modernity. In the depths of the Great Depression, declaring themselves "against the accumulation of profit and unearned income by non-producers," and "want[ing] to make our living with our own hands," and committed to pacifism, vegetarianism, organic farming, and autarkic, localist collectivism, the Nearings fled New York City and headed north to the Green Mountains of Vermont, where they began their "personal search for a simple, satisfying life on the land, to be devoted to mutual aid and harmlessness, with an ample margin for leisure in which to do personally constructive and creative work." Rejecting "the yoke of a competitive, acquisitive, predatory culture," with its "hectic mad rush of busyness," the Nearings sought "a quiet pace, with time to wonder, ponder and observe," a life in which "worry, fear and hate" were replaced with "serenity, purpose, and at-one-ness." [9]

Aldo Leopold, a professor at the University of Wisconsin and the father of contemporary environmental philosophy and ethics, got his start in Gifford Pinchot's National Forest Service. In the posthumously published essay collection *A Sand County Almanac* (1949), which melded science, principles of public policy and management, and moral investigation, Leopold posited a "land ethic" entailing an ethical relationship between human beings and the environment. In its seminal theoretical essay, Leopold argued on behalf of a duty of care for nature as a moral obligation. Just as human beings stood in moral relation to each other, Leopold insisted, they stood in community with the natural world. This meant that human beings had a moral obligation to engage with that world – soil, water, air, plants, and animals – according to dictates of right and wrong. This duty of care included a moral responsibility of all of us to engage with and live in relationship to the natural world by venturing into nature and exploring it. "A thing is right," Leopold held, "when it tends to preserve the integrity, stability, and beauty of the biotic community. It is wrong when it tends otherwise." Beginning from these premises, he supported public policies that promoted wilderness preservation and restoration, and game and wildlife management.[10]

No book drew more mass public attention to environmentalism than Rachel Carson's *Silent Spring* (1962). While the Nearings had warned about the threats that modern chemicals (including DDT) posed to the ecosystem and the human food supply in their small-press, back-to-the-land memoir and manual, the marine biologist Carson published the articles that would be assembled into her signature work in the influential *The New Yorker*. Written in an absorbing personal and poetic voice that marveled at the beauty of the natural world, while buttressing its arguments with a thicket of footnotes to scientific journals, *Silent Spring* opened with an epigraph from Albert Schweitzer ("Man has lost the capacity to foresee and to forestall. He will end by destroying the earth") and "A Fable for Tomorrow," recounting a day not long in the future when human beings will wake up to a world denuded of birdsong. "No witchcraft, no enemy action had silenced the new life of this stricken world," Carson plaintively explained; "The people had done it themselves." "A grim specter has crept upon us almost unnoticed, and this imagined tragedy may easily become a reality we all shall know." In the pages that followed, Carson anatomized "the contamination of air, earth, rivers, and sea with dangerous and even lethal materials." Human beings had heedlessly upset the ecosystem's hard-won balance. While specialists took to solving particular human problems – often by recourse to the wonder of modern chemicals – no one was looking out for the cumulative effects of this "progress" on the system as a whole. Carson's book – which accumulated back-cover endorsements from William O. Douglas, Margaret Mead, and Richard M. Nixon (who went on as President to create the Environmental Protection Agency, 1970) – was a call to action that, like Harriet Beecher Stowe's *Uncle Tom's Cabin* (1852) and Ralph Nader's *Unsafe at Any Speed: The Designed-In Dangers of the American Automobile* (1965), would spark real-world political and policy action.[11]

Soon, the back-to-the-land ethos of the Nearings, the reverence for nature of Leopold, and the moral and ethical imperatives formulated by the Nearings, Leopold, and Carson were championed in their own distinctive idiom by the 1960s counterculture. Its ecological sensibilities were sustained, refined, and developed across the 1970s to the present, where they have become mainstays of public policy and mainstream electoral politics. In 1968, Stewart Brand launched *The Whole Earth Catalog*, a compendium of tools for sale to free-spirited, self-sufficient, ecologically attuned, off-the-grid, and anti-institutional countercultural pioneers. The Catalog's inaugural cover featured what at the time was a remarkable first: a view from space of the whole of the planet earth. The message was clear. In this tiny unlikely planet in an infinite universe, our fates were inevitably joined: we were all in this together, and would live (or die) as one human community. (This sense was wondrously reinforced one year later, on July 20, 1969, when, declaring "One small step for man; One giant leap for mankind," the astronauts of Apollo 11 walked on the moon.)

For their part, utopian theorists imagined an ecologically saner future. In Ernest Callenbach's *Ecotopia* (1975), the fictional *Times-Post* sends correspondent William Weston to a new country, comprised of the former states of Washington, Oregon, and Northern California, which had seceded from the United States and were now strictly policing all entrance and exit. The Ecotopians, Weston found, had committed themselves to using only all-natural, biodegradable materials (no plastics), renewable energy (solar, wind, and, in some cases, nuclear and hydroelectric power), recycling, and organic food, and to eliminating both the light pollution that had obscured the stars and the overwork that hindered their freedom to enjoy them and the other bounties of nature. They had, moreover, adopted holistically integrated cradle-to-grave health care, participatory (as opposed to fan-based, spectator) sports, and food co-ops, and had banned individual automobiles and instituted electric buses and taxis and public bicycle shares and bike lanes. All of the public policies of Ecotopia took strict account of the externalities caused by any public or private initiatives, including population growth, soft drinks, and sugary snacks. The Ecotopians spurned both economic growth and global capitalism (trade), while fiercely debating the wisdom of "Ecology in One Country." Autarky, health, and sustainability were their watchwords.

Utopian visions inspired real-world initiatives and experiments. The Jimmy Carter administration (1976–1979) promoted a host of renewable energy initiatives. In *Gaia: A New Look at Life on Earth* (1979), the Englishman James Lovelock set out his Gaia hypothesis, which conceived of the earth as an ecosystem in balance in which the planet's living and non-living parts functioned as a single organism. The Gaia hypothesis in turn led a group of American scientists in the late 1980s and early 1990s to initiate the Biosphere II project – a sealed and (ostensibly) self-sustaining biodome in Oracle, Arizona. This visionary endeavor could be understood as the latest in a line of American utopian experiments dating back as far as the Shakers, Brook Farm, Bronson Alcott's Fruitlands, Robert Owen's New Harmony, and John Humphrey Noyes's Oneida. But its proponents preferred to see it as part of a forward-looking data collection project linked to the possible establishment of human colonies in space – an end that, given the damage we were wreaking on the planet, Neil Young had warned with crushing sadness in his song "After the Gold

Rush" (1970), might be less voluntary aspiration than a dire, last-ditch human necessity.

These hopes and concerns, reflected in the announcement of the first "Earth Day" (April 22, 1970), eventually gave rise to the concept of the "Anthropocene," the controversial name given to the current geological age – the "human epoch" – in which human activity has been the predominant influence upon the earth's climate and environment. For many contemporary environmental thinkers and activists, including those confronting the effects of perhaps cataclysmic climate change, and related questions of de-forestation, biodiversity, and sustainability, although it remains contested by scholars and activists alike, the concept of the Anthropocene continues to structure much contemporary ecological and environmental thought, politics, and policy.

The New Right

The postwar conservative movement might have seemed to its most impassioned adherents, at least, poised to assume political power with Barry Goldwater's triumphant seizure of the Republican nomination for President in 1964. More sober analysts – including William F. Buckley Jr. – knew better. The Cow Palace catharsis was thrilling, but it was much too soon. The Democratic incumbent Lyndon B. Johnson was re-elected in a landslide in which Goldwater was portrayed as a dangerous – and perhaps psychologically unhinged – lunatic whose election, among a parade of other horribles, might very well propel the world into a nuclear holocaust.

Johnson's re-election ushered in one of the most liberal, reformist eras in American history, spearheaded by his Great Society and War on Poverty programs, and the passage of transformational civil rights legislation. But the Democratic Party was soon undone by an internal civil war, ignited by Johnson's escalation of hostilities in Vietnam. The party's Cold War liberal establishment base found itself under siege from a rising New Left and antiwar movement, an effulgent counterculture, militant demands for Black Power, and a violent revolutionary Left. New York Senator Robert F. Kennedy belatedly but dramatically entered the Democratic race to succeed Johnson as an antiwar candidate, bidding to bridge the divides between the party's establishment liberals, white working-class ethnics, people of color, and its ascendant antiwar and student movement New Left. But when Kennedy was assassinated in Los Angeles hours after winning California's Democratic primary – thus ensuring that pro-war Johnson Vice-President Hubert Humphrey would be the party's nominee – Republican Richard Nixon pounced on the rift with an appeal to the country's "silent majority" of hard-working, patriotic Americans committed to law and order and traditional values. Nixon won. By the end of the 1960s, the Republicans were in charge.

Nixon's relation to the broader conservative movement was nevertheless ambiguous. As he was a once prominent member of the House Un-American Activities Committee, it would have been hard initially to question at least his anticommunist *bona fides*. But Nixon had been the moderate Dwight David Eisenhower's Vice-President, and had selected the decidedly liberal Republican New York Governor Nelson Rockefeller as his running mate. Where, to the delight of movement conservatives, Goldwater had called for an intransigent roll-back of Soviet power, Nixon was soon pursing "détente" – a plan for arms control and peaceful co-existence – with the Soviet Union. Even more shocking to many on the Cold War Right, Nixon was soon taking steps to establish diplomatic relations with Mao's communist China. Like Eisenhower, moreover, Nixon did not seem interested in assailing the legitimacy of the modern New Deal administrative, regulatory, and social welfare state. What's more, he took notable steps to expand it by launching new regulatory initiatives (on, among other things, environmental protection and a guaranteed minimum income). Nixon, to be sure, swung to the Right when it came to crime control and some other policy arenas, as well as – contrary to his campaign promises – in escalating the Vietnam War. This heartened some conservatives, at least until the Watergate scandal. But it also provoked an increasingly inflamed antiwar resistance. When faced with his likely impeachment and removal from office for commissioning criminal skullduggery against his liberal political "enemies," Nixon was forced to resign. Once he had stepped down, the future of the Republicans was uncertain.

Events on the ground across the 1970s – rising crime rates, high inflation, high taxes, high unemployment (and, contrary to standard economic theory, a simultaneous rise in both: "stagflation"), the "urban crisis," and the "energy crisis" – sparked a renaissance of new conservative economic and political thought, fueled by a sense of genuine political opportunity. Since the 1930s, there had been a broad consensus among policymakers in both parties around the "demand-side" macroeconomics formulated by the British economist John Maynard Keynes. Classical economic thought understood markets as ultimately self-correcting: in time, without government intervention, drops in production and rises in unemployment (recessions, depressions) would resolve themselves as prices fell. Famously quipping that "In the long run we are all dead," Keynes argued, on the contrary, that the immense damage wrought by economic downturns would not be resolved within any reasonable period of time by declining prices. Government "counter-cyclical" fiscal stimulus policies, including deficit spending, however, would do the trick by stimulating aggregate demand for goods and services in a way that promised both full employment and renewed economic growth.

In the context of stagflation, which flummoxed the era's Keynesians, conservative economic thinkers proposed alternatives to Keynesianism which were skeptical about, if not dismissive of, interventionist, demand-side economics. Sophisticated monetarist macroeconomic theory (pioneered by Milton Friedman and Anna Schwartz) argued that government should focus less on the fiscal side and more on carefully calibrated, restrictive, and consistent management of the nation's money supply to achieve healthy economic growth with low unemployment and inflation.

Monetarism became widely accepted (including by Keynesians), but the "supply-side economics" advanced by the era's conservative economists has, ever since, proved as controversial as it has been influential. While formulated by academic economists like Arthur Laffer and Robert Mundell, large swaths of supply-side theory – which, as its name suggests, rejected Keynes *in toto* – were promulgated and proselytized for by business-oriented journalists (especially at the *Wall Street Journal*) like Jude Wanniski, Robert Bartley, Bruce Bartlett, and George Gilder, and by cheerleader politicians like New York State congressman (and ex-pro-football player) Jack Kemp. The supply of goods and services, these supply-side evangelists claimed, would create its own demand. And the way to encourage supply is not through deficit government spending to fuel aggregate demand, but through tax cuts (income, capital gains, and inheritance/estate), free trade, and the deregulation of business, which would generate the profits that would, in turn, be plowed back into investment that would stimulate production, lower prices, and ultimately yield unprecedented economic growth. (Along these lines, the supply-side economist Arthur Laffer's famous "Laffer Curve" – first drawn on a napkin over dinner in 1974 to illustrate the point to Wanniski, Dick Cheney, and Donald Rumsfeld – suggested that, if properly set, moreover, lower taxes would actually increase government revenues.) When Ronald Reagan was elected President and adopted supply-side economics as his administration's official economic philosophy, this alternative to Keynesianism acquired an additional name: Reaganomics.

> In this present crisis, government is not the solution to our problem; government is the problem.
> Ronald Reagan (1981)

Neoconservative policy intellectuals, who had begun to rethink the particulars of the modern administrative and social welfare state in seminal journals like *The Public Interest* (founded in 1965 by Irving Kristol and Daniel Bell), addressed particular areas of public policy like crime, welfare, housing, education, and diverse areas of government regulation. In *Losing Ground* (1984), the political scientist Charles Murray argued that, by providing perverse incentives to their purported beneficiaries and reinforcing negative mindsets and behaviors, social welfare entitlement programs encouraged dependence, perpetuated poverty, and harmed the very people they had been designed to help. While this led Murray to call for the end of those entitlements, others like Lawrence Mead, in *Beyond Entitlement* (1986) and *The New Politics of Poverty* (1993), argued instead that social welfare programs should be restructured with new requirements and incentives for work.

Influential work by the neoconservative Harvard political scientists Edward Banfield and James Q. Wilson turned a skeptical empirical eye on government, and, in particular, on its expert bureaucrats and bureaucracies. Although not rejecting the modern state out of hand, Banfield and Wilson went against the grain of longstanding progressive and other reformist thought by unleashing two cheers for the much-maligned old-school politicians, parties, and political machines. In their own less systematized and roundabout ways, the two politi-cal scientists argued, the heavily contextualized, on-the-ground horse-trading and deal-making methods of these politicians did a much better job than was commonly understood at resolving social problems (to the extent that was possible) and advancing the broader public good.

While not condemning social welfare programs on principle, Banfield and Wilson emphasized, variously (depending on the particular program and issue), certain problematic dynamics that bedeviled many such programs and administrative and regulatory regimes in the modern United States: the assumption that good intentions and higher funding will necessarily lead to better outcomes; an obliviousness to the spillover effects and the unin-tended consequences that might be unleashed by blinkered actions focused on a single problem, often by narrowly trained or focused experts; a refusal of policymakers to accept that some social problems might be either intractable or caused by deep issues of class and culture not easily amenable to govern-ment intervention; and, relatedly, a systematic aversion to acknowledging the degree to which a frank attentiveness to the encouragement of morals and morality was essential to promoting both good outcomes and socially desirable behavior. When Ronald Reagan moved into the White House in the early 1980s, ushering in what many consider to be a new conservative era in American politics, arguments like these – including Wilson's emphasis on swift, predictable criminal punishment and imprisonment and "broken windows" policing to fight the era's spiking crime rates – became enormously influential during Republican administrations, but also during the admin-istrations of the "Third Way" liberals like Bill Clinton (discussed below) who were elected and governed within this new – and, in many respects, ongoing – context.[12]

The ascendant New Right of the late 1970s and 1980s that swept Reagan into office was additionally fueled by yet another cohort of conservatives, the "Religious Right," largely comprised of white evangelical and fundamentalist Christians. This cohort had long understood the United States as a foundation-ally "Christian nation." At first widely distributed across both of the nation's political parties, during the 1960s and 1970s, conservative evangelicals and fundamentalists came to understand themselves to be under threat – if not direct attack – by the forces unleashed by the "the 1960s" (which many believed had taken over the Democratic Party: "We didn't leave them; they left us") and the 1970s "Me Decade" "culture of narcissism," self-centeredness, rising secularism, and anti-Christian animus. These developments portended the abandonment by God's chosen nation of its Christian foundations, which had, as they saw it, underwritten its exceptional constitutional and political freedoms. Others observed that the self-anointed "moral majority" looked suspiciously like the racist southern white Christian segregationists and white supremacists who, not coincidentally, had suffered one defeat after another with *Brown v. Board of Education* and the enactment of the Civil Rights Act of 1964 and the Voting Rights Act of 1965, and who were now supplementing their longstanding animus toward African-Americans with animus toward perceived enemies of traditional understandings of sex, marriage, and the family like feminists and gays and lesbians.

The modern conservative movement had long trained its sights on the liberal Warren Court (1953–1969) as a driving force behind the advance of an illegitimate, anti-constitutional secular liberalism. But two rulings by the Supreme Court were taken by the proto-Christian Right as especially ominous: *Engel v. Vitale* (1962) and *Abington v. Schempp* (1963), which declared voluntary teacher-led prayers and devotional readings of Bible verses in public schools, respectively, to be violations of the First Amendment's Establishment Clause.[13] In time, though, the Reagan era Christian Right found its rallying-cry: the succession of the Court's earlier rulings that carved out an increasingly expansive realm of constitutionally protected sexual freedom and autonomy culminating in its holding in *Roe v. Wade* (1973) that a woman had a constitutionally protected right, under most conditions, to choose to terminate her pregnancy. To the Reverend Francis Schaeffer and others who would forge the "Pro-Life Movement," this was the final straw that definitively proved that the country had abandoned its Christian foundations, and was on the road to eternal damnation. In conjunction with a sub-set of political active Catholics – whose Church, in contrast to even the most conservative evangelical churches up to that point, had long held that abortion was infanticide (murder) – the Pro-Life Movement led the way in forging a united inter-religious and inter-denominational Christian Right. As a candidate for the White House, Ronald Reagan pronounced himself a believer in and agent of their cause.

> Why has our society changed? The answer is clear: the consensus of our society no longer rests on a Judeo-Christian base. . . . It puts man rather than God at the center of all things. . . . Of all the subjects relating to the erosion of the sanctity of human life, abortion is the keystone.
>
> C. Everett Koop and Francis Schaeffer (1979)

Under the leadership of Reagan's close advisor and Attorney General Edwin Meese, moreover, the modern Right committed itself to a creedal constitutional faith (dubbed "originalism") that would unite the diverse elements of the modern conservative movement, whether business, free market libertarian, or Burkean or religious traditionalist, under the umbrella cause of fighting to preserve "the founders' constitution" – which, as it happened, aligned with the principles, politics, and policy commitments of the modern conservative movement. Assisted by Meese, the Yale Law Professor Robert Bork, and the University of Chicago Law Professor Antonin Scalia, conservative law students founded the Federalist Society as a gathering place and promoter of originalism. Ever since, the organization has served as a lynchpin for the staffing of Republican administrations, and the promotion of "originalist" conservatives to federal judgeships, including on the US Supreme Court. One of their defining objectives from the outset has been to secure the Supreme Court votes necessary to overturn *Roe v. Wade*.

Third Way (Neo)Liberalism

Both the pitched battles of the 1968 Democratic Convention, which reflected deep divides within the party, and the subsequent election of Richard Nixon pushed the Democrats to pause and rethink their path forward. Structure and process were of as much concern as substance. Indeed, increasingly, the two were understood as intertwined. Clubby bosses, party operatives, and machine pols at the state and local level had a stranglehold on the national party. One thing 1968 made clear to many was that the old ways of doing things were now untenable. The structural and procedural exclusions had built a party in which grassroots sentiment in general, and young people, women, African-Americans, Latinos, and gays and lesbians in particular, had little voice in proportion to their numbers. All this was in a time when American politics was teeming with mass social movements speaking to critical social and political issues.

Moving into the 1972 presidential election, the forces associated with South Dakota Senator George McGovern, the party's eventual nominee, instituted systematic reforms aimed at creating a more representative and inclusive Democratic Party. This meant a diminished role not only for machine politicians but also for the labor union bosses who had been cut into the governing power structure by the version of industrial democracy instituted under the collective bargaining arrangements of the 1930s New Deal. It meant a larger role for social movement activists and those focused on issues of particular concern to the newly democratized Democratic Party membership.

McGovern's landslide loss to Nixon in 1972 – in which the rural, western, Christian World War II combat veteran was tarred by the Right as the candidate of "Acid, Amnesty,[14] and Abortion" – prompted yet another round of churning within the party about its direction and future. The Democrats' new openness paved the way in 1976 for a surprise insurgency presidential nominee and victor: Jimmy Carter, an evangelical Christian peanut farmer, Navy veteran, and former Georgia governor, whose positions on the liberal–conservative spectrum were eclectic. A series of economic and political shocks (including the Iran Hostage Crisis) and administration missteps, however, made for an unusually tumultuous one-term presidency. When the Republicans nominated the longtime conservative movement stalwart, former California Governor Ronald Reagan, to challenge Carter, the time was at long last ripe for the postwar American Right: buoyed by both the old guard and the ascendant

New Right, Reagan won in a landslide. Four years later, with a forty-nine-state victory, Reagan drubbed the Democratic nominee Walter Mondale. Reagan's highly consequential two-term presidency ushered in a conservative era of American government that, in many respects, is still with us today.

Yet again, at the height of the Reagan triumph, some Democrats stopped to rethink their party's philosophy and direction. In 1985, Al From and Bruce Reed founded the Democratic Leadership Council (DLC), which was highly critical of the direction the party had taken since the McGovern reforms. These "New Democrats" argued that, in 1972, the party had redistributed power into the hands of a fractious alliance of often antagonistic identity and interest groups, each of which put their particular causes first, and chafed at subsuming their demands to any much-needed unifying political vision. Driven by an "elitist, interest group liberalism," moreover, DLC members argued, the party had moved to the Left of the American people, all but sealing its fate as a perpetual loser in national politics, and permanently ceding power to the Reagan Republicans.

The DLC's charter members – often westerners like Gary Hart and Bruce Babbitt, midwesterners like Dick Gephardt and Rahm Emanuel, and southerners like Chuck Robb, Sam Nunn, Al Gore, and Bill Clinton – proposed a new "Third Way" for the party that would be more business-, growth-, and market-friendly (free trade; charter schools; health care reform preserving private insurance), more skeptical about big government, and more cognizant of legal and regulatory incentive structures (the earned income tax credit; educational standards and testing; measured deregulation; welfare reform; more aggressive community policing; harsher criminal sentencing and renewed support for the death penalty; various programs aimed at "reinventing government" through data-driven analysis), more committed to the muscular promotion of American interests abroad, and more concerned with the cultivation of moral and virtuous and citizenship (national service; more faith-friendly government programs). This new direction for the party, it was argued, would more effectively advance its core liberal and republican commitments to providing equality of opportunity and advancing the broader common good – and, not incidentally, help it to once again win elections.

The party's Left-liberals, however, chafed. Vermont Governor Howard Dean called the DLC "the Republican wing of the Democratic Party." But the New Democrats succeeded in putting two popular two-term Democratic administrations in power, first Bill Clinton and then Barack Obama. The Republicans, of course, tried to tar the New Democrats as 1960s radicals in disguise, as unregenerate statists and socialists. The left wing of the Democratic Party, on the other hand, which gained a new voice after the 2008 financial meltdown and the subsequent Occupy Wall Street movement, fixed another label on the New Democrat agenda: neoliberalism.

While too new to the political scene to have been directly involved with this party history, Barack Obama, who was elected as the country's historic first black President in 2008, staffed his administration with some of its leading lights – including his primary opponent Hillary Rodham Clinton. Drawing deeply from the well of Third Way ideas, Obama ran the country as a centrist. Notably, however, in an increasingly polarized country rent by mounting economic inequality, widening geographic polarization, and an increasingly inflamed anti-government, free-market, and white Christian nationalist Right, a resurgent Left, key elements of which were professedly socialist (Bernie Sanders, Rashida Tlaib, and Alexandria Ocasio-Cortez), began to emerge within the party. Some black thinkers like Cornel West, moreover, were highly critical of what they took to be Obama's moderate, centrist positions on race.

> The forgotten men and women of our country will be forgotten no longer. . . . This American carnage stops right here and stops right now. . . From this moment on, it's going to be America First. . . . The time for empty talk is over. Now arrives the hour of action.
>   Donald J. Trump (2017)

As the country's first black President with an unfamiliar (and, to many, foreign-sounding) name, however, the partisan politics surrounding Obama went well beyond issues of political philosophy and public policy. Many were of the view that Obama's historic election augured, at long last, a "post-racial" America. These hopes did not last long. The Right "othered" Obama from the beginning. Legions of conservative white evangelical Christian nationalists – the shock troops of the New Right, and the perfervid base of what became Donald Trump's Republican Party – insisted, against all evidence, that Obama, whose father was Kenyan, was not a Christian, but a Muslim. In the long wake of the September 11, 2001, terrorist attacks on New York and Washington, DC, by Islamic fundamentalist radicals (Al-Qaeda), this suggested that Obama was an enemy of, if not a traitor to, his country – and perhaps a foreign plant. Touting wild conspiracy theories that Obama's presidency was illegitimate because he had not been born in the United States (as the Constitution requires), and lambasting immigrants, abortion rights, and (neoliberal) free trade policies, the demagogic political neophyte, real estate developer, and reality television star Donald Trump, notwithstanding occasional griping about his personal morals, attracted loyal legions of the Christian Right, and eventually won the rock-solid support of the movement-conservative Republican Party. As candidate and President, the pugnacious Trump manifested a pugilistic commitment to defending (white, right-wing) people of faith and the Christian nation that, as they saw it, had been stolen from them by 1960s radicals, secular coastal elites, "deep state" conspiracists, socialists, progressives, Blacks, Mexicans, Asians, and Muslims (amongst others).

The rise of a nativist, nationalist, and "populist" Right has brought to the fore foundational questions concerning American identity – civic membership – the role and limits of government, and the stark ideological polarization of the country's two major political parties. A blatant ascriptive hostility to racial and religious minorities and immigrants, and a renewed commitment to tax cuts and an aggressively anti-regulatory agenda (with the important exception of free trade), became hallmarks of Donald Trump's oft-reiterated commitment to stop the "carnage," "Make America Great Again," and "Put America First."

Conclusion

Prior to the late 1960s and 1970s, materialist understandings and values stood at the core of the political thought of both the American and global Left and the reformist liberalism with which, in sometimes fractious coalition, it has often made common cause. On the Left, the materialist thought was that of the radical, revolutionary Marx, who had argued that class interests and antagonisms – the conflict between labor and capital – set the driving engine of history, economy, politics, and ideas. For liberals, claims of immediate material interest counseled a pragmatic, meliorist, and reformist modern liberalism, which looked to powerful, but appropriately limited, public-spirited governments to serve as a balance wheel that would level the playing field and equalize power relations between increasingly concentrated and unduly powerful private interests and ordinary workers, who, it was acknowledged, would benefit (under appropriately supervised and managed conditions) from the prevailing capitalist economic order. As such, the materialist liberals, as exemplified by Samuel Gompers's AFL, emphasized government protection and promotion of organized labor, improved working conditions, and government-provided old age, disability, and unemployment insurance. The hope was that these programs would shore up a prosperous and stable working and middle class, within a regulated, and appropriately redistributionist, liberal capitalist political-economic order.

In the late 1960s and 1970s, however, the reformist materialist base of the Democratic Party in particular was aggressively challenged from within, in ways that transformed American domestic politics, and sparked new directions in American political thought. A new cohort of activists who included racial and ethnic minorities, gays and lesbians, feminists, and environmentalists emphasized questions of identity, and put non-materialist causes at the forefront of their agendas. In the process, they displaced organized labor – especially blue-collar organized labor – as the party's core constituency. These ascendant post-materialist forces had spent decades on the margins of the country's political life, where they took up what may have seemed like radical or fringe projects aimed at reconstituting and reconstructing more authentic, rooted, and liberated selves. They were adamant that only such reconstituted political subjects could enter the public sphere, at long last, as genuinely self-determining democratic agents. It was at this point that they would be prepared to exercise their rightful – and long-overdue – republican claims to full civic membership, and bid to rule, setting the course, first, of the Democratic Party, and then of the nation.

And yet, even today, these matters are far from settled, even among the Democrats. Disturbed by the ascent and eventual consolidation of conservative Republican rule, and policies that sought to eviscerate the modern liberal regulatory and social welfare state and the power of organized labor, prominent liberals like the historian Arthur Schlesinger Jr., the sociologist (and former New Left [SDS] leader) Todd Gitlin, the political philosopher Richard Rorty, and the journalist-scholar Mark Lilla expressed deep concern that, by foregrounding anti-universalist claims arising out of "identity" politics and pleading on behalf of a coalition of special interests reluctant to make liberal universalist claims positing a shared conception of the public good, and consigning issues of economics and class to the back-burner, the Democrats were underwriting the expansion of the conservative coalition, while abandoning their proud legacy and longstanding commitments. Third Way liberals sought to restore some balance in this regard. But some significant achievements notwithstanding, they continued to find themselves on the defensive within their own party, both from an identitarian Left and, in time, from a renewed socialist movement, spearheaded by figures like the old-line materialist Vermont Senator Bernie Sanders and New York City Representative Alexandria Ocasio-Cortez, who positioned herself ambiguously somewhere between the traditional socialist focus on the working class and the new politics of identity.

For its part, the Republican Party began preaching its own brand of identity politics. The Republicans increasingly foregrounded the claims of white, native-born (and nativist), evangelical, conservative Catholic, and fundamentalist Christians, while fostering alliances between their own identitarians and those more materialistically focused on business values, free markets, and economic growth. It was this New Right Alliance that had first elected Ronald Reagan, and has maintained its control of the Republican Party through the presidencies of the two Bushes and, most recently, Donald Trump.

Questions

1. Is a politics grounded in identity – the self – inherently selfish and self-defeating? Or does it offer the possibility of founding a truly democratic politics, where, perhaps for the first time, individuals would enter the public sphere as genuinely free and equal, self-determining democratic subjects and agents, possessed of full civic membership?

2. Do you find the Left or the liberal versions of 1960s and 1970s second-wave feminism, gay liberation, or Chicano and Native American nationalisms more compelling?

3. Is rule by the Left (as opposed to modern liberal, Third Way, or neoliberal rule) ever a genuine possibility in the United States? Or is it an occasional side-show that will perpetually be co-opted by, or succumb to, a hopelessly entrenched Lockean/Hartzian liberalism? Does this time period provide evidence, one way or the other, that helps us answer this question?

4. Was 1970s environmentalism new? Is it best understood as late-stage extension of the 1960s counterculture? Or was it as old as the country itself?

5. Many have argued that in the 1970s and 1980s, both of the United States' major political parties broke sharply with their traditional political bases and thought traditions. The Democrats, for their part, adopted a McGovernite framework that emphasized a coalition of identity and other particularist interests. The Republicans reoriented themselves around an ascendant Christian Right. Is this true? If you think there was a notable shift, was it, in each case, for the good?

9

Conclusion

How should we approach the study, and phenomenon, of "American political thought"? To ask this question is the very beginning of the task. We can question and interrogate almost every possible point of entry and avenue of investigation. From the initial presumption that "American political thought" is meaningfully distinguishable from political thought more generally, to decisions concerning what counts as serious or significant enough to warrant our attention, a critical orientation toward the subject is often the most illuminating.

That said, many teachers, scholars, and political thinkers have fairly clear views on these matters. They presume American exceptionalism while at the same time positing the universalism of the American experiment. For these teachers, scholars, and thinkers, American political thought has a distinctive essence. It has been defined catechistically by the country's commitment to an "American Creed" of presumptively noble and universally applicable principles: individual liberty, equality, and democracy (or popular sovereignty). And it has been studied by an examination, reflection upon, and enlistment of these principles by Americans across the length and breadth of their national history – especially, perhaps, by those who have reflected most profoundly on each. This entails a creedal and often celebratory orientation toward the subject.

Others, by contrast, approach the subject empirically. For these teachers, scholars, and thinkers, American political thought is what Americans have thought and said about politics across their history – period. Plainly, much of that has involved considerations of the nature and application of principles of liberty, equality, and democracy. But these empiricists are open to the possibility that there might be other veins of American political thought that might not map so easily onto these coordinates. It might even spurn some or all of them, whether on principle, or as applied to particular people or institutions. It hardly seems idiosyncratic to observe, for instance, that, over the country's long history, there were significant thinkers who thought democracy was more important than liberty (or vice versa), or thinkers who held to the ascriptive conviction that some races and ethnicities were in no meaningful sense "equal" to others.

There can be little doubt, at least, that much of the political thought of

Americans has involved disagreement about the core questions concerning liberty, equality, democracy, and a host of associated questions concerning legitimate sources of political authority – of who appropriately gets to tell you what to do – of the role of the state, the place of God in public life, and of the terms of civic membership. There can be little doubt, moreover, that, in many ways, Americans have approached these questions in ways that are, for the most part, characteristic of western nations. We would be remiss to not observe that these are questions that confront all human societies engaged in the distinctively *political* task of ordering the lives of individuals within communities.

My own view is that American political thought is distinctive in the emphasis it has tended to place on particular questions, in the framing of those questions, and in the answers it has tended, tentatively, to arrive at, if not necessarily permanently, then for sustained periods of time – eras and epochs, even. This distinctive political culture – and I believe that *all* societies in some sense have their own distinctive political cultures – is, in some ways, as old as the nation itself. While sometimes genuinely new ideas have been introduced, the same frames/patterns/ideologies have appeared again and again. But this political culture is also mutable. It has been continually reworked and remade. Its characteristic views, perspectives, frameworks – such as Lockean liberalism, civic republicanism, ascriptive Americanism, and Christian nationalism – have been actively recombined and reconfigured across time by office-seeking politicians and parties, social movement actors, and intellectuals/scholars in response to events and the perceived problems of their time.

As the revolutionary crisis unfolded, for example, soon-to-be Americans sought to make sense of their grievances by recurring both to the Lockean liberal natural rights philosophy of the origin of legitimate political authority and civic republican understandings of societal decline through corruption by distant elites. As the war began, republican theories of virtue, sacrifice, and service came to the fore. Those same theories, however, were largely mistrusted by the framers of the Constitution as a reliable foundation for free governments – though they were valued quite highly by the Constitution's Antifederalist opponents. Liberal natural rights arguments were enlisted both to support and to oppose slavery and imperialism, the former on the grounds of rights to property, ascriptive understandings of agency and capacity, and (local/state) self-government, and the latter on the grounds that freedom from oppression was an indefeasible right of all human beings. Protestant Christian theology has been prominently adduced in support of compact and covenant theories of the origins of legitimate political authority, and to both justify and oppose chattel slavery, women's equality, the expansion of the social welfare state, the rights of organized labor, the civil rights movement, and the Vietnam War. Liberalism, republicanism, ascriptive Americanism, Protestant Christian nationalism, and other recurring frameworks have reappeared in different mixes, from the policy programs of the original Democratic Party forged by Thomas Jefferson and Andrew Jackson to late twentieth- and early twenty-first-century New Democrats like Bill Clinton and Barack Obama, and from Henry Clay's Whigs to Abraham Lincoln and Ronald Reagan. Donald Trump may not know much about American history and American political thought, but he intuitively knows very well that Americans respond to republican themes of corruption and decline (a populist staple), to invocations of natural rights to liberty generally, and religious liberty especially, to Christian providentialism, and to ascriptive, racist, and ethno-centric white Christian nationalism.

As such, while known by its continuities, American political thought has always been both porous and mutable. It is a tradition with defining touchstones and a cognizable heritage. But it is also a tradition that is alive and changing. Traditionalist conservatives and forward-looking partisans of change will hold very different views about both the reality and the desirability of recognizing bedrock foundations and longstanding continuities, about the locus of government power authorized to tell you what to do, and about inviting and pursuing new directions, departures, and transformations. And they will draw creatively from American political thought's well of disparate frameworks and ideas in their electoral and movement campaigns and mobilizations aimed at rallying and recruiting the political support of the American people.

Today, these arguments continue to play out along multiple dimensions. In what follows, I consider a few of the most prominent and politically significant.

Boundaries, Categories, and Intersectionality

The French political theorist Michel Foucault – who, along with other French poststructuralists, deconstructionists, and postmodernists, developed a powerful following on the American academic Left in the 1980s – was perhaps the most influential proponent of the idea that the imposition of categories, both inside formal institutions of government and outside them, played a crucial, and perhaps superintending, role in governing: a process he called "governmentality." Categorization and classification, often in the form of a binary, imposed clear borders, which are wielded as instruments of power. As such, linguistic categories are not "only words." Classifications and definitions are implements of discipline, rule, coercion, and control. Language itself – perhaps especially language, the naturalized, all-but-invisible fabric of the episteme – is a major instrument of the marshaling, institutionalization, and reproduction of the prevailing regime of power. One might say that it is an administrative tool made use of and structurally implemented by the oppressor against the oppressed, the agent against the subject, the ruler against the ruled, except that Foucault and Foucauldians understand the operation of political power not as constructed by such binaries and stable hierarchies, but as constitutively diffuse and pervading: for Foucauldians, the agent does not exist.

While Foucault and other French theorists put wind in the sails of these insights, they arrived less as a revelation than a confirmation to many, bringing a new conceptual vocabulary to underwrite the renewal of a radical critique of an old problem. Beginning in the 1980s, political writing about the coercive and controlling effects of classification and categorization as an instrument of governing power – often originating in the ostensibly private sphere – cohered into an extensive scholarly literature.

The basic idea that "governmentality" or "administration" took place in the spaces that liberal political thought had consigned to the ostensibly a-political private sphere was, of course, not news to feminists. As we have seen, the first-wave feminist Charlotte Perkins Gilman had explored how the (male) understanding – and, hence, imposition and enforcement – of the female role purportedly prescribed by the laws of nature served to coerce and control women in ways that were profoundly damaging to their psyches, potential, and freedom. Second-wave feminists took up the theme with a vengeance, forming "consciousness-raising" groups to explore the ways that these processes had been accepted, operating largely unconsciously and unseen, dictating the course of their lives, and even the contours of their own minds and selves, as a form of internal colonization. (Black Power thinkers were also pushing back against similar forms of internalized forms of erasure and self-hatred imposed by the dominant culture's racism and white supremacy.) At the same time, some were finding themselves coerced into categories, classifications, and binaries even by those whom they might have otherwise considered their comrades and allies. To them, this felt like a violent act that (as the poet Adrienne Rich described it) "split them at the root."

Black women led the way in considering the violence wrought by classificatory categories and imposed binaries of identity. They hardly needed poststructuralist French political theory to have noticed the phenomenon. As far back as the mid-nineteenth century, the ex-slave and evangelical abolitionist/feminist Sojourner Truth had alighted upon the ways in which the women's rights advocates who had issued the landmark Seneca Falls Declaration (1848) did not seem to promise much to her because, while certainly a woman, she was also black. She levied the charge of invisibility, or being unmapped. As second-wave feminism was cresting in the early 1970s, Toni Morrison, harking back to the "classifying signs" posted across the Jim Crow South that "told you who you were, what to do," trenchantly observed the ways that the middle-class white women's liberation movement of her own time, with which she might have otherwise been sympathetic, mistakenly took the assumptions and experiences of its highly circumscribed membership as speaking for all women, notwithstanding the palpable ways in which it ignored black women's problems and lives.[1] The poet Nikki Giovanni expressed similar views during the second wave, as did the political theorizing of Boston's black radical lesbian feminist Combahee River Collective (1974–1980). Audre Lorde and Adrienne Rich reflected upon the intersection of race, sex, and lesbian sexuality. Others, like the painter and philosopher Adrian Piper, considered the problem of the categories imposed by presumed racial binaries through sustained engagement with the phenomenon of "passing" – a topic that had drawn the attention of earlier black thinkers like James Weldon Johnson, Nella Larson, and George Schuyler.[2] In doing so, Piper interrogated the relationship between chosen and imposed identities – the nature of the self that, in a liberal society, is presumed to be legitimate political authority's wellspring and foundation.

The black–white binary/dualism as the alpha and omega of American race relations was problematized and interrogated as well. Moving beyond the emerging problem of perpetual mitosis as a succession of previously neglected identities were added to the list, the Chicana lesbian feminists Cherríe Moraga, Gloria Anzaldúa, and others sought – including through autobiography and art – to arrive at a genuinely revolutionary way of seeing that would be adequate to the task. This new vision would begin with a new language, appropriate (as bell hooks put it) to "a liberatory ideology that can be shared with everyone." Hooks became perhaps the most persistent critic of what she described as the "dogmatic" "absolutist," and hence schismatic splintering on the revolutionary Left. The cascade of divergences and divisions, hooks charged, were being instigated by revolutionary Leftists who were themselves drunk on "exercising authority and power," and sought their own form of "hegemonic control." This sort of identity politics, she argued, was ugly and counterproductive. It was a dead end.

Anzaldúa, born in Texas's Rio Grande Valley and speaking from and about the position of the mestiza, considered binaries, dualisms, and classifications as a problem of borders and borderlands. In "A Manifesto for Cyborgs" (1985), invoking the science fiction of Samuel Delany, Octavia Butler, and others, the biologist Donna Haraway issued a visionary "posthumanist" statement that problematized the purported – and, increasingly, she observed, unsustainable – boundaries between human and animal, human/animal and machine, and, finally, biological and mechanical (as embodied, for instance, in the idea of the "monster"). "This essay," Haraway, announced, cutting radically against the taxonomic foundations of the biological sciences in which she had been trained, "is an argument for *pleasure* in the confusion of boundaries and for *irresponsibility* in their construction." In its own way, Haraway's anti-taxonomic vision, like that of bell hooks, was a plea for the transcendence of Left "identity politics," and for a new politics of perpetually unfolding affinity.

In time, a more systematic academic literature on "intersectionality" led by the legal scholar Kimberlé Williams Crenshaw and the sociologist Patricia Hill Collins began to consider the legal and sociological implications of societal and governmental classifications and categories. This work was infused by a deeper philosophical grounding in the influential treatise on gender by the UC-Berkeley philosopher Judith Butler. Butler's *Gender Trouble* (1990) unleashed a major movement for political and social reform that aggressively challenged the gender–identity binary. This, in turn, ignited sometimes intense political controversy and contestation about the prevailing classifications used by governments and private actors that defined people by their bodily (genital/reproductive) attributes for purposes of the census, sports teams, access to restrooms and locker rooms, and other matters and spaces. During President Barack Obama's administration, the Justice Department and the US Department of Education's Civil Rights Division newly reinterpreted Title IX of the Education Amendments of 1972 (which had proscribed discrimination on the basis of "sex") to require educational institutions receiving federal funding to allow individuals to use whichever restroom conformed to their own self-understanding of their gender, regardless of the "sex" assigned to them at birth on the basis of their bodily/genital characteristics. After Donald Trump's election as President, with strong Religious Right support, these new rules were repealed in one of her first acts upon taking office by Trump's Education Secretary, the conservative evangelical Christian activist Betsy DeVos. It was not long, however, before the the US Supreme Court issued a stunning rejoinder in *Bostock v. Clayton Country* (2020) by interpreting the bar on sex discrimination in the Civil Rights Act of 1964 as prohibiting employment discrimination based on either sexual orientation or gender identity.

> Does being female constitute a 'natural fact' or a cultural performance, or is 'naturalness' constituted through discursively constrained performative acts that produce the body through and within the categories of sex?
> Judith Butler (1990)

The Persisting Problem of the Color Line

While much of the new thinking about classifications, boundaries, and categories took up the question of conceptual structures – including the category of "white" or "whiteness" – the politics of race continued to be significantly defined by the liberal paradigm that still accepted the categories of black and white, and sought to vindicate the longstanding promise of equal rights under the law. It was not as if, even under the traditional categories and frameworks, the possibilities had been realized and exhausted. The problem of race and racism in American society is, if anything, as salient in the early decades of the twenty-first century as it was when W.E.B. Du Bois pronounced its centrality in *The Souls of Black Folk* (1903).

When Ronald Reagan launched his ultimately victorious candidacy as the Republican Party nominee for the presidency from the Neshoba County Fairgrounds, outside of Philadelphia, Mississippi (1980) – the infamous site of the brutal Ku Klux Klan murders of the young Freedom Summer (1964) civil rights activists James Chaney, Andrew Goodman, and Michael Schwerner – it probably surprised very few African-Americans, who had sensed since at least 1964 that the modern conservative movement, which had at long last ascended to power, was fueled in significant part by a sense of racial, and perhaps racist, backlash and retrenchment. Reagan had championed the causes of "states rights," and won the enthusiastic support of groups like white southern evangelical and fundamentalist Christians (including the rising "Moral Majority," founded by the erstwhile segregationist Southern Baptist minister the Reverend Jerry Falwell) and law enforcement, with whom American blacks had a profoundly troubled history. It is hardly surprising that many African-Americans apprehended the modern conservative movement as aggressively hostile, if not white supremacist. While the Reagan coalition extended beyond this – and there were prominent black conservatives like Thomas Sowell, Walter E. Williams, Shelby Steele, and Clarence Thomas – many black Americans came to believe that they were once again under siege, both directly, and by the accumulated effects, across an array of fronts, of the ensuing Reagan administration's policies.

Although the old-line civil rights groups tried to fight back, newer initiatives, like the Reverend Jesse Jackson's multicultural National Rainbow Coalition (1984), challenged Reagan's policies while campaigning for, among other things, jobs, a living wage, ballot access and voting rights, civil rights, criminal justice reform, and environmental justice. Notable, too, was a relatively new form of black musical – and, often, political – expression: rap and hip-hop. Political rap and hip-hop had clear antecedents in the spoken-word musical statements of the late 1960s Black Arts movement, from artists like the Harlem-based the Last Poets (Jalal Mansur Nuriddin, Abiodun Oyewole, Umar Bin Hassan – though the group had several iterations) and Gil Scott-Heron. These musicians had deep roots in their era's black nationalist and black Muslim movements. They deftly expressed the pent-up anger at the oppression of peoples of African origin in the United States, as well as the pride, joy, and deep cultural resources of dark-skinned peoples through the magnetism of the music and its transformative beats, which, as fused with jazz, funk, soul, and spiraling, rhythmic and rhyming lyrics, would revolutionize popular music in America – and, indeed, the world. The styles of the seminal self-titled first album by the Last Poets (1970) in songs like "When the Revolution Comes," and of Gil Scott-Heron ("The Revolution Will Not Be Televised" and "Whitey on the Moon" – also both 1970), joined with Afro-Caribbean currents to create rap and hip-hop. (Most credit the DJ Kool Herc for introducing the turntables and their distinctive breaks at a legendary South Bronx block party in 1973.) A rising generation of artists, including Grandmaster Flash and the Furious Five

("The Message," 1982), NWA ("Fuck tha Police," 1988), and Public Enemy ("Fight the Power," 1989), took these stylings to new heights, both musically and in cultural and political prominence, as they chronicled the ravages that drugs, guns, violence, poverty, discrimination, police abuse, and mass incarceration had wrought on black America. As they expressed their rage and demanded political action, they were met by indifference and retrenchment across the Reagan–George H.W. Bush years. But they had nevertheless drawn the nation's attention – and incurred its backlash, including from New Democrats like Bill Clinton and Tipper Gore. Hip-hop continued to develop its political voice into the 1990s and beyond with artists like Tupac Shakur ("Brenda's Got a Baby," 1991), Nas (*Illmatic*, 1994), Lauryn Hill ("Lost Ones," 1998), Frank Ocean ("Bad Religion," 2012), Beyoncé ("Freedom," 2016; "Formation," 2016), Kanye West ("We Don't Care," 2004), and Kendrick Lamar (*To Pimp a Butterfly*, 2015; *DAMN.*, 2017), as its styles, motifs, and beats moved to the center of American music and culture.

In the early 2000s, a succession of police killings of unarmed black men and women, and unpunished civilian killings of black people – an old phenomenon, newly captured on camera in a video age – inspired mass action and resistance in places like Ferguson, Missouri. A Movement for Black Lives (Black Lives Matter/BLM) was launched. Decrying "the sustained and increasingly visible violence against Black communities in the US and globally," the movement's Platform (2016) began by emphasizing its roots in the community, its inclusivity, and its broad remit to fight "the ravages of global capitalism and anti-Black racism, human-made climate change, war, and exploitation." Declaring that it stood "with the descendants of African people all over the world," and its support for "reparations for the historic and continuing harms of colonialism and slavery," the movement announced both long- and short-term demands. In the broadest sense, BLM demanded an end to "the war on black people." More concretely, the movement demanded community control, political power, reparations, economic justice, and a broad public commitment to appropriate investment and divestment consistent with that program. At the same time, there was a renaissance of black political thought on race in America by writers like Ta-Nahisi Coates, Charles Mills, Claudia Rankine, Keeanga-Yamahtta Taylor, Ibram X. Kendi, Imani Perry, John McWhorter, Glenn Loury, and Thomas Chatterton Williams, along with studies of specific concerns facing black people in the US, such as structural racism and historical legacies, intersectional and mixed-race identities, police violence, and mass incarceration. The sense of urgency of this work was augmented by the rise of an open and avowedly racist white supremacist "Alt-Right," and the election of the most virulently racist President since Woodrow Wilson, the Republican Donald Trump.

Contemporary Conservatism

One way to look at contemporary American conservatism is as a family of ideas and instincts that rejects nearly all the presuppositions described above concerning borders, boundaries, categories, and classifications. Conservatives consider these to constitute the very foundations of a well-ordered society that is legitimately charged with telling you what you can and cannot do. They believe that many of society's most familiar categories are not artificial but natural – they are rooted in ascertainable transcendent truths, and grounded in what conservatives take to be the empirical reality of actual human nature, and the self's legitimate needs and aspirations. As such, they appropriately structure and order the world.

While man-made, conservatives believe, borders – including national borders – commonly set clear and essential parameters for determining who is in and who is out. Sentimentalists may loosely decry "exclusion." But exclusion is an essential prerequisite to inclusion: it enables a genuine community of shared affinities and interests. Borders make democratic self-rule and civic equality realistic possibilities. Membership implies a club. And membership entails a claim to – yes – privileges. When their parameters are appropriately set, boundaries appropriately distinguish between "this" and "that." They are the lines on the map of all free societies. While radical feminists (especially), socialists, and others on the Left are quick to point out the oppressive effects of the (liberal) public–private distinction, conservatives are profoundly sensitive to the consequences of eliding, if not eliminating, this distinction. Among these, they insist, are the loss of individual freedom and choice about matters of religious faith, the upbringing and education of one's children, and about a thousand daily matters of how one wants to live and work, and of what one thinks, says, and does. If the boundaries demarcating the public and private spheres are eliminated, elided, or blurred, all of these matters are put in the hands of those who happen to win a popular vote. What's worse, they are then put in the hands of those who direct the coercive enforcement apparatus of the state, no matter how insular and removed from the purportedly legitimating authorization of a popular majority.

American conservatives frequently recur to the boundaries set by the country's Constitution as foundational to, and constitutive of, liberty, equality, and the possibility of self-government in service of the common good. The "compound republic" described and defended by James Madison in Federalist #51 had, first, advisedly separated the powers of the national government and then set boundaries between the powers of the national government and those of the states. Conservatives have insisted on the legal enforcement of the boundaries and categories the US Constitution sets on the powers of government, as they were initially designed by the nation's founders, and as reinforced by the "formalist" constitutional thought for which conservatives have long been known (and which has long been criticized by progressive and liberal "realists" and "pragmatists"). Congress (with a few limited exceptions) is empowered to legislate – to make the laws, and only to legislate and make the laws. The executive is empowered to enforce the laws, and not to make them. The judiciary is empowered to apply the laws as part of its highly limited, if important, function of resolving disputes – "cases or controversies" – between opposed parties in individual cases, and not to either make or enforce laws. The national government was allotted certain enumerated powers. As underlined by the Tenth Amendment, all residual powers of government are reserved to the states, or to the people. The Constitution provides, moreover, for the protections of the fundamental rights of individuals against all governments. This framework for liberty under law is premised on boundaries and categories. And liberals and leftists, perhaps inflamed by their particular obsessions with race and gender, who speak facilely of the "tyranny" of boundaries and categories, many conservatives would say, are blithely disregarding no less than the institutional architecture of freedom.

Reckless generalizations about the pernicious effects of the very idea of borders, boundaries, and categories notwithstanding, many conservatives also defend the substantive categories that have been aggressively challenged by reformers, progressives, liberals, and leftists. In the teeth of the tenor of the times, for instance, conservatives have consistently defended a host of traditional moral understandings. These defenses entail unapologetic judgments about right and wrong, true and false, better and worse, to which they frequently understand themselves as making an exclusive claim. Harking back to ancient political thought and longstanding republican themes concerning individual and civic virtue, many conservatives proudly make distinctions between the better sort of people, and their inferiors, and defend the claims of the better sort of a right to rule. Conservatives believe in hierarchies. They believe that those who are virtuous, whether by lights of classical or Christian understandings, have rightful claims to leadership. Only the virtuous, after all, are prepared for statesmanship. Virtuous statesmen – and citizens – will set boundaries, apply categories, and make moral judgments and distinctions.

The classifications, categories, and hierarchies in which conservatives believe, and which they find inherent in, and seek to implement through, American law do not, they insist, originate in the mere political preferences or ideological presumptions of American conservatives. They are intrinsic to the natural order of the world. Most, perhaps, attribute that order to the intent and design of a Creator God. As such, for conservatives, the self at the foundation of legitimate authority in a free society is understood by objective standards, and not by the individual's subjective claims concerning who and what they are or want, or by their (ostensibly) arbitrary "personal preferences."

So, too, each person's rightful status and place. Historically, many people

– including, but hardly limited to, conservatives – have argued that God had decreed racial hierarchies, or at least racial separatism, with "yellow," "black," and "white" dispersed to different continents across the globe. Many, whether following the Bible or interpreting physical and (ostensible) psychological differences and distinctions, have argued as well that God created men and women for different purposes and, as such, they should be understood to inhabit and assume duties in separate spheres. Many conservatives insist today that the binary of man and woman – male and female – has been ordained by nature, and that any effort to collapse these categories is a frontal, ideologically motivated assault on the natural order. Men and women, moreover, were created by God and nature with procreative purposes in mind. As such, marriage is by definition an institution that is properly – and only – a union of one man and one woman.

American conservatism is suffused with such distinctions, definitions, categorizations, and judgments. Murder is proscribed by God and morality. Abortion is murder. Husbands are responsible for supporting their wives and children. To hold the state responsible for the financial support of families is for the state to displace the family and, in the cases of exigent circumstances, churches, where needed assistance can be provided in ways that reinforce, as opposed to undercut, the moral order. The natural order dictates that those who work shall receive, and that those who do not shall not. Those who classify people by race for purposes of public policy are flouting the principle that all of us, by virtue of our shared humanity, are entitled to equal treatment and equal justice under law. And so on. To be sure, as discussed earlier in this book, conservatives vary in their presuppositions, views, and policy positions, including on issues like abortion, same-sex marriage, affirmative action, and the appropriate nature and extent of the social welfare state. But it is fair to say that most conservatives will hold moral arguments to be a touchstone of political thought. They will reject moral relativism. They will argue that the concepts, categories, and moral foundations set by traditional understandings of western civilization are superior to other cultures and thought traditions in making a good and free life possible. And many will go even further to argue, in an exceptionalist vein, that the political system of the United States is the pinnacle achievement in this regard. Some will go so far as to accuse progressives, liberals, and leftists with working to undermine the great American experiment in genuine self-government and liberty under law, which is rooted in objectively discerned transcendent truths. They will arraign them for doing so by recklessly introducing dubious relativist, historicist, nihilist, radically egalitarian, cosmopolitan, and utopian new departures. When they think of "sustainability," conservatives do not think about climate change. They think of the sustainability of a country and a political culture that is moving toward abandoning its core foundations.

Legitimate, and good, governments will order the collective life of the polity in ways that take account of these truths, realms, and orders, and provide the context in which people can best live in harmony with them. Illegitimate, and bad, governments, whether out of ignorance, carelessness, or the perversity of human will – perhaps catastrophically inspired by some unrealistic utopian dream or simple will to power – will either disregard or deliberately flout the imperatives following from real-world facts and human nature, and construct governing institutions and orders that run the gamut from ineffective and dysfunctional, to morally, intellectually, and politically bankrupt and disastrous.

As such, conservatives will insist – against a rising tide of ignorance, resistance, and opposition, to which political modernity is especially prone – upon defending longstanding lines, borders, categories, hierarchies, and institutions as rightly and traditionally constituted (family, religion, the nation, the rightly ordered state) in a way that will anchor the polity in genuine and reliable foundations. Should the anchor drag, conservatives take it as their high responsibility and mission to re-ground and revitalize the polity's constitutive people, and to re-root the institutions of civil society and government in ways that are sustaining and conducive to the individual and collective good.

Contemporary Liberalism

But liberals, too, in their own way, believe in boundaries and categories, resting on foundations. Liberal political theory is also constructed on dualisms and binaries: public and private; government and civil society; the individual and the social (or common); authorized/legitimate and unauthorized/illegitimate. Liberal political theory, which arose in the context of the bloody religious wars of sixteenth-century western Europe, was forged as an alternative to the then prevailing understandings of political authority premised upon convictions of the content of fixed, transcendent truths. These irreconcilable understandings had ignited an endless succession of wars and persecutions. The liberal answer to this political problem was to sharply limit the status of truth claims in the public sphere, while providing a protected space for them in the personal and private realms (liberalism's foundational "public–private distinction"). This re-conceptualization of politics required a re-grounding of our understandings of the legitimate source of political authority away from some supreme conception of Truth and the Good. Proto-liberal and liberal political thought innovated by rooting political authority in decisions made by the sovereign individual (liberalism's foundational "individualism"), and, more precisely, in the individual's decision, theoretically posited as made in a hypothetical "state of nature," to preserve his life and to protect what would otherwise be his uncertain enjoyment of his natural rights to life, liberty, and property (or "the pursuit of happiness") in an ungoverned world.

Ever since the "bracketing" of this notion of fixed, transcendent truths as the cornerstone of good and legitimate government, traditionalist, non-liberal, or anti-liberal conservatives would insist that it amounted to an "abandonment" of essential ties and tethers, an unmooring of the polity that had set human communities tragically adrift without a *telos*, or end. The effects of this unmooring could be quotidian and atmospheric. The liberal unmooring could underwrite an absence of meaning and purpose along the lines described by Nietzsche's "last man." It could spur a perpetual quest by individuals for elusive satisfaction in fleeting pleasures and empty achievements of technique. The effects of a society's abandonment of Truth and the Good could also be dramatic, and existential. It could provide fertile ground for the growth of an amoral positivism holding that there was ultimately no moral grounding for the social order. This could result in a potentially catastrophic secular, positivistic, historicist, and ultimately nihilistic moral relativism, in which anything was possible, and sanctioned. In a blatant betrayal of their promise, some have argued, this makes liberal societies prone to tolerate – if not celebrate and actively promote – great moral evils.

The confluence of these quotidian and existential flaws might well prove fatal. Liberal societies might be uniquely debilitated in defending themselves against existential threats – internal and external, intellectual and practical. Perversely, liberals may be more inclined to defend the freedom of speech of those making truth claims, and the political rights of anti-liberals, than to strenuously defend their own views and positions. The same relativistic and tolerant stance may lead to a demoralized resistance to external foes who seek to conquer and rule free liberal polities, taking advantage of liberal freedoms to ultimately subvert them. Given that the ability to govern itself supplies the very *raison d'être* of modern, liberal social contract theory, many conservatives have insisted that liberal political theory is ultimately self-undermining, contradictory, and incoherent.

As liberals saw it, however, the very categories that liberalism offered in its contractualist theory of the state – evident, for instance, in both the contending late twentieth-century social welfare state liberal theory of John Rawls, on the one hand, and the libertarian liberal political theory of Robert Nozick, on the other[3] – promised all of the good things for which liberal polities, including liberal democracies like the United States, are valued and esteemed: peace, good order (the rule of law), legitimate and limited government, liberty, guarantees for the enjoyment of rights (including religious and economic liberty, due process, and the freedom of speech, press, and thought), (civic and legal) equality, economic prosperity, and collective (national) and individual autonomy and independence. Yes, societies committed to "liberal neutrality" largely avoided propounding or enforcing a substantive vision of human flourishing – of individual virtue and the good. But their theories of constitutional government provided the political and legal architecture for individuals to freely choose their own ends, and to pursue those ends according to their own individual natures, desires, wants, needs, and tastes to the maximum extent possible, consistent with the minimum background conditions necessary to preserve the collective liberal order.

As such, the categories structuring liberal theories of government, the borders, boundaries, binaries, and dualisms of which liberalism was not simply unembarrassed but proud – legitimate versus illegitimate powers of government (constitutional government, the rule of law), the powers of government versus individual rights held to be off-limits to government (the public–private spheres, natural and constitutional rights) – set the foundations for the best possible form of government consistent with the aspirations to human dignity, equality, and liberty. Far from being indifferent to moral ideals and human fulfillment and flourishing, by bracketing those ideals in its underlying theory of the state, a "liberal morality" set the institutional conditions for both individual and collective happiness, human flourishing, and individual and societal accomplishment and achievement.[4] Liberal political orders provided the conditions that offered the possibility of the freest, richest, and happiest societies that human history had ever known.

Liberals have sought to defend their political understandings against what, in recent years, has become a relentless assault from the Left and Right alike. To perpetually attack the very idea of categories, binaries, dualisms, and spheres as "hegemonic" ideological fictions imposed upon civil society and the polity as instruments of illegitimately hierarchical ruling systems of domination and subordination, as liberals have accused the Left of doing, is a dangerous game. It threatens to undermine and eviscerate the conditions that have underwritten free societies under the rule of law, the pillars, as liberals had come to understand it, by the lights of a progressive, evolutionary, developmental frame, of western civilization itself. If the prevailing western liberal order, despite its presumptions to be committed both in principle and in practice to advancing freedom, equality, democracy, and the rule of law, is pervasively constituted by oppressive systems of domination and subordination, and if its appeals to limited government, the rule of law, and individual rights are subterfuges, then politics is about power, pure and simple. You either have it or you do not. The superintending political goal becomes to seize it, and rule – theoretically, without limit – in the interest of . . . one is tempted to say "the powerless." But, of course, once the powerless seize power, they are no longer powerless. The positions are simply reversed.

The conviction that politics is at its core about power, liberals contend, and that worthwhile political thought and engagement are directed toward the revolutionary overthrow of the prevailing system of power which liberals have distractingly defended through appeals to an ideological false consciousness concerning "fairness," "limited government," "freedom," and "individual rights" (all, at base, simply masks for power), is a recipe for authoritarianism and totalitarianism (though others would point out that, in its origins, liberalism itself, which was aimed at the revolutionary overthrow of the prevailing systems of power, was doing exactly the same thing).

In the late twentieth and early twenty-first centuries, "liberal" conservatives and "liberal" liberals like Mark Lilla[5] have argued that these tendencies are ascendant on the Left in the thought, and conduct, of the (mostly) academic proponents of poststructuralism, postmodernism, critical theory, critical race theory, and radical (as opposed to liberal) feminism, as they have come to predominate in the one institution of civil society in which the Left has been able to put its ideology into effect, by stepping into positions of power and authority, and ruling: the American college and university. There, diverse strands of the academic Left have imposed aggressive codes concerning right-thinking speech and conduct and ruthlessly enforced them, with little regard for bourgeois ideas like limited government, fairness, liberal neutrality, and individual rights, and due process rule of law protections. Along the way, these anti-liberals in the academy have tutored their eager students to understand and position themselves as either victims of oppression or righteous fellow-travelers, duty-bound to renounce their "privilege" and stand in solidarity with the oppressed. Wielding allegations of racism, sexism, heteronormativity, colonialism, neo-colonialism, and cultural appropriation, these leftist scholars and students – and the university administrators and bureaucratic cadres drilled in their understandings, and empowered to propagate and enforce them – have set themselves against the racist and sexist "violence" allegedly perpetrated by American colleges and universities. By "violence," these engaged critics mean not physical assault – which is rare – but rather the use of language or social behavior by members of "privileged" groups in ways that ostensibly serve to reinforce systems of domination and oppression ("structural racism") operating, in part, through the quotidian use of language and other forms of expression ("micro-aggressions", "cultural appropriation"). The use of pronouns that inscribe a traditional gender binary ("he/she"), for instance, is held to be a "violent" political act, if not an assault, upon a student who does not self-identify along a traditional gender binary. Students are assigned literature and political theory either testifying to the harm done by what early critical race theory characterized as "words that wound,"[6] or, in the case of many of the classics of western literature (often by power-wielding "straight white males"), taken as symptomatic of, and malignantly re-inscribing, the systems of domination and oppression at the heart of the western political project. Health statistics, including statistics concerning rates of suicide, anxiety, and depression, are adduced to demonstrate the concrete effects of living under such conditions. Linguistic regimes are analogized to physical assaults: they have wrought real physical damage on "black bodies." (The trope of the subaltern "body" has become pervasive in the literature.)

Under such conditions, to speak of "the freedom of speech" is an abomination. And the provision of "safe spaces" in which the besieged and assaulted can find shelter, and at least a moment's respite – a dollop of freedom – among similarly situated others, has become a non-negotiable demand, along with compulsory workshops in the language and behavior appropriate to a diverse academic community. In moving forward on these fronts, as informed by these ideas, students and (sometimes) university administrators have spurned the binary/dualism so central to liberalism, including the understandings of the distinctions essential to the rule of law, such as those between speech and conduct, thought and action, and physical injury and verbal offense or affront.

Capitalism, Socialism, and Neoliberalism

The collapse of the Soviet Union and the dismantling of the Berlin Wall (1989) rung down the curtain on what Whittaker Chambers described as the "great alternative faith" of mankind, on offer to those spurning the promise of free, western, liberal capitalist societies like the United States, whose pillars were belief in and submission to God, and, consequently, a foundational commitment to liberty under law. To Chambers and other conservatives, the exceptionalist United States stood – barring nefarious subversion – as a beacon to the world both in its rootedness and in the power it brought to bear – hard and soft – in the global fight against communism. The Whittaker Chambers devotee, sponsor, and friend, William F. Buckley Jr., the impresario of the modern American conservative movement, insisted that the United States' commitment to "free enterprise and limited government" was inextricably tied to its bedrock Judeo-Christian faith. Christian individualism and atheistic socialism were antonyms. As he put it at the height of the Cold War in *God and Man at Yale* (1951), "I . . . believe that the duel between Christianity and atheism is the most important in the world. I further believe that the struggle between individualism and collectivism is the same struggle reproduced on another level."

Soon after the fall of the Berlin Wall, the neoconservative political theorist Francis Fukuyama's "End of History" thesis (1992) posited that, after a prolonged period of existential, civilizational struggle between market-oriented bourgeois liberalism and its challengers, whether communism or religious orthodoxy, there was only one contender left standing: bourgeois liberal democracy. The West, and its exemplar and leader, the United States of America, stood astride the globe like a colossus, triumphant – the winner in the battle of ideas. As indicated by the full title of his book – *The End of History and the Last Man* – Fukuyama, drawing from Nietzsche, was hardly unconflicted about the triumph of the liberal world-view. (Nietzsche's "last man" is shallow, empty, and lazy; his life is self-centered and self-indulgent, if only half-heartedly, because, after all, why bother? It was an aspiration-free life of listless, bovine wallow.) Nevertheless, at the end of the twentieth century, moving forward, American-style liberalism was, Fukuyama insisted, the only credible game in town.

But how should we think about a post-Cold War world in which the United States and its capitalist economic system seemed not only to win the global war of ideas, but also to preside unchallenged as the dominant force – a hegemon – in global politics and economics? Some were troubled. Fukuyama's mentor Samuel Huntington soon published a rejoinder to his student in *The Clash of Civilizations and the Remaking of World Order* (1996). There, Huntington warned that, far from welcoming these developments, many around the world remained defiantly unreconstructed: they would stand and fight against the western, American, secular, liberal capitalist hegemony.

> The combination of economic and political freedom produced a golden age in both Great Britain and the United States in the nineteenth century.
>
> Milton and Rose Friedman (1980)

Others argued that, far from being a fixed entity, liberal capitalism was entering an ominous new stage. Market-oriented economic thought had been refined and developed across the second half of the twentieth century in ways that were as stealthy as they were revolutionary. Because this new thought had been retrofitted for enlistment in the day-to-day operations of law and public policy, its subcutaneous influence had become pervasive. The "microeconomic revolution" forged by the Chicago School of Economics (Aaron Director, Gary Becker, George Stigler, Milton Friedman) and the associated Law and Economics (Richard Posner, Frank Easterbrook) and Public Choice (James Buchanan and Gordon Tullock) schools and movements had formulated sophisticated theories of micro- and macroeconomic policy, law, and public policy that were designed to be enlisted by lawyers, judges, and other government officials making real-world legal, social, political, and economic decisions. The models associated with these theories were premised on individual choice foundations that worked to reinforce the economic, moral, and political claims of free markets against those of collective decision-making, or even collectivities ("society"), which, they explained via sophisticated mathematical models, for most purposes, did not actually, functionally, exist. Relatedly, although starting from different foundations, the Austrian Economics advanced by Ludwig von Mises and Friedrich Hayek mounted influential critiques of centralized economic planning, and argued for highly decentralized, and often individualized, decision-making. Thinkers from these diverse schools were brought together under the auspices of the Switzerland-based Mont Pelerin Society, where members from around the world – from Augusto Pinochet's brutal Chilean military dictatorship to Margaret Thatcher's Great Britain and Ronald Reagan's America – could till common intellectual ground that would inform both domestic public policy and the broader global political and economic order.

If strong-form economic liberalism had long had its detractors in the domestic United States who had sought to tame, if not displace, its more brutal social, political, and economic effects, the new heights it seemed to reach globally in the early twenty-first century inspired its own set of harsh critiques of "neoliberalism," critiques which have coalesced into a powerful strain of contemporary American (and global) political thought.

These developments have not been without ironies concerning borders, boundaries, and categories. Most American conservatives committed to the understanding of capitalist markets as knowing no (or few) bounds have pushed back against efforts to block the free flow of capital and labor across national boundaries. They have argued that markets work best – both generally, and for Americans – when there is a free flow of the factors of production, which directs resources to their most productive uses. These dynamics allow for the production of the best and most needed goods most efficiently, at the best price. This, in turn, satisfies consumer demands, generates wealth, and provides jobs. In the long run, it raises the standard of living of Americans, and of people around the world. Because they are convinced both that these dynamics are real, and that they are a good thing, conservatives have generally supported free trade and the free movement of peoples across national borders (immigration). The anti-neoliberal Left, on the other hand, has attacked the abandonment of national borders, arguing that a robust understanding of the bordered nation is indispensable to sovereign democratic control over people's economic lives and destinies. The attitudes on the anti-neoliberal Left toward national borders, to be sure, are complicated by the Left's general support for immigration – even, at times, for "open borders" – which is a product of its ongoing concern over discrimination on the basis of race, ethnicity, and national origin. But when it comes to economics, at least, it seems, borders have a new currency with some strains of the American Left.

These new currents of thought have led to what at first blush seem like strange bedfellows. A host of anti-globalization thinkers like David Harvey, Nancy Fraser, Michael Hardt and Antonio Negri, and Wendy Brown have argued that borderless capitalism is in the process of destroying democracy and popular rule. Some of the most prominent of these thinkers, like Brown and Fraser, have challenged neoliberalism in part through the enlistment of radical "Critical Theory" forged in the interwar years at Germany's Frankfurt School by scholars like Theodor Adorno, Walter Benjamin, and Herbert Marcuse, many of whom came to the United States as political exiles from Nazi Germany.[7] Marking a return, if not purely or exclusively, to the materialist understandings of classical Marxism (Sigmund Freud's and Antonio Gramsci's understandings of desire and consciousness were also in the mix), critical theorists are strongly inclined toward a global perspective emphasizing the foundational relationship between capitalism and exploitative political power, in what some of them have boldly described as a new capitalist/neoliberal "empire." Critical theorists, for instance, have drawn special attention to our own era's satanic mills that – typically forgotten and sight-unseen in a hollowed-out, de-industrialized United States – mass-produced iPhones and sneakers. In this new imperialism, the exploitation, abuse, and cost externalities that fuel the ostensibly successful global capitalist order, critical theorists have explained, are often shifted offshore and out of sight, like the empire's domestically invisible wars and its ravaging of the global environment, though developments like climate change have now come to threaten the very future of human life on earth. Critical theorists underline that the ultimate source of these problems is neoliberal capitalism itself.

These scholars have sometimes recognized shared common ground with anti-liberal traditionalist conservative American political thought advanced today by an ascendant Catholic Right, which includes thinkers like Patrick Deneen, Sohrab Ahmari, Rod Dreher, and Ross Douthat, whose hostility toward materialistic liberalism is consonant not simply with Catholic traditionalism, but also with the organicist conservative thought of figures like Richard Weaver and (in their own idiosyncratic ways) Wendell Berry and Jane Jacobs. Whether coming from the Left or traditionalist Right, all of these thinkers emphasize the ravages wrought by liberal individualism run amok, in the economic as in other spheres of life. They call for a revival of the claims of the community, anchored in a commitment to collective self-determination and the common good.

The Resurgent American Left

In the aftermath of the 2008 financial crisis – and the federal government's business-friendly response – the Left found a growing audience both for its diagnosis of the systematic dysfunctions that had precipitated the meltdown, and for its longstanding critique of the country's economic system and its politics. At the heart of both was an emphasis on the ways that vicious cycles of economic and political inequality were undermining American democracy. Under capitalism as it was currently practiced in the United States – especially since the 1980s – economic and political power were flowing upward to an ever-smaller group of people, and the gap between their power and the power of everyone else was widening at an astonishing rate not seen since the late nineteenth-century Gilded Age.[8]

At the 2011 Occupy Wall Street protests at Zuccotti Park in lower Manhattan, soon joined by similar protests elsewhere, the protesters chanted "We are the 99%." The message was that the small sliver of the top 1% was increasingly in the driver's seat in American politics, and was leveraging its newfound power to further enrich itself, and seize even more. In the process, the civic solidarity presuming a commonality of interests necessary to hold a polity together was disintegrating: the vast majority were being ruled by a tiny minority, imperiling republican government. This was bad enough in itself. It was illegitimate. But it was made worse by the fact that, increasingly, the top 1% seemed to be more focused on consolidating their wealth and power than advancing the broader public good. The 2008 financial collapse had only clarified this reality.

Members of the rising Left argued that the new plutocracy had been long in the making. It was the bitter fruit both of deep structural trends under "late capitalism" and of systematically skewed policy decisions: the decline of the power of organized labor; the rise of a non-unionized and precarious service and gig economy; financial deregulation; the dismantling of the social safety net; the political demobilization of the poor and working classes; the withdrawal of support for public higher education and the student debt crisis; and the green light provided for corporate power and influence by a conservative Republican Supreme Court, including by its campaign finance decision in *Citizens United v. Federal Elections Commission* (2010).

The Occupy Wall Street movement sparked a broadening circle of mobilizations on the American Left. With roots tracing back to Eugene V. Debs, the Democratic Socialists of America (DSA), founded in 1982 by Michael Harrington, saw a surge in new memberships. Although the DSA frequently endorsed Democratic Party nominees – and had enthusiastically endorsed Barack Obama for President in 2008 – it broke with the party establishment to endorse Vermont Senator Bernie Sanders over Hillary Clinton in the 2016 Democratic primaries. (While calling for Donald Trump's defeat, the DSA withheld its endorsement for Clinton in the general election.) As such, part of the challenge now involved an effort by the Left to remake – to reclaim – power within the Democratic Party.

A closely allied environmental movement focused on climate change spoke with renewed prominence and force in the 2011 protests against fracking and the construction of the Keystone XL Pipeline. While discussions about rallying support for a "Green New Deal" (GND) had begun as early as 2006, in 2018 Massachusetts Senator Ed Markey and New York City Representative Alexandria Ocasio-Cortez formally introduced a non-binding GND program in Congress aimed at saving the planet from the looming environmental catastrophe by working toward net-zero carbon emissions. Although some important writers lamented that it was already too late, these activists argued that, while the window was closing fast, there was still time to wean Americans – and, it was hoped, the world – from fossil fuels and aggressively support clean energy.

GND proponents lent their support not only to the broader movement targeting economic inequality but also to the segment of the rising Left focused on racial injustice. The economically disadvantaged and people of color, it was understood, were disproportionately affected by environmental and global health catastrophes like the 2020 Covid-19 pandemic. In yet another uprising against the policies of both the contemporary Republican Right and establishment Third Way New Democrats, African-American Black Lives Matter activists and writers like Michelle Alexander and Bryan Stevenson spearheaded a resurgence of black thought concerning egregious disparities in the country's criminal justice system and, for that matter, the place of African-Americans in America more generally.[9] This thought went well beyond reform of particular policies, not only to questions of systematic bias but also, once again, to the question of whether rectification of the crimes of the past and present was even possible. In the arts, from as far back as the 1950s, with Ralph Ellison's *Invisible Man* (1952) and the formation of the Sun Ra Arkestra, to George Clinton's Parliament-Funkadelic in the 1960s and beyond, the Afro-futurist genre had enlisted science fiction and space-age themes both to convey African-Americans' perpetual sense of being extraterrestrial alien others, and their lost worlds and identities, and to imagine a community in another galaxy free from the relentless accretions of a racist American history. Some, like Randall Robinson and Ta-Nahesi Coates, argued with renewed vigor for reparations for slavery. With notable synergies but in a different key from Afro-futurism, Afro-pessimists like Frank Wilderson III proclaimed that, given slavery and its ongoing post-emancipation legacy, African-Americans would never be afforded full civic membership in the United States in the way that, some argued, other people of color could reasonably hope for and achieve. In the US, blackness was uniquely and hopelessly constituted by slavery. As such, the existential position of African-Americans was that they would never be free, rights-bearing liberal agents, or full members of the republican social and civic spaces and sphere upon which democratic and republican government are premised. African-Americans were consigned instead by slavery to permanent social and civic death, as enemy others, to be violently suppressed. As far as full civic inclusion in the United States was concerned, they might as well focus on life on Mars.

As Afro- and climate pessimism suggest, not all on the Left are sanguine that ordinary politics – or, for that matter, anything – can save American society, considered as a distinct and distinctive polity, or as part of a wider world. Notwithstanding this, although recognizing the gravity of the challenges they face, and the difficulty of the predicament, many – and perhaps especially the young – retain at least some faith and hope that these contemporary movements and mobilizations might augur a resurgent Left politics in the early twenty-first-century United States that offers a sense of genuine political possibility.

Conclusion: The Futures of American Political Thought

To study political thought is to study the ways foundational political ideas are implicated in the formation of political consciousness, and provide normative guidance for the enactment of laws, the formulation of policy, and the design, functioning, and assessment of political institutions. It involves a consideration of the interplay between ideals, ideas, and abstract principles and real-world challenges, predicaments, and problems. To study American political thought is to study the way these dynamics have operated in a single country, the United States of America, over the course of its history. Students of American political thought have made a number of observations about these dynamics. They sometimes agree. Just as often, they spar, and vigorously dissent.

As noted at the outset of this chapter, my own view is that, since the country's inception, American political thought has been characterized if not by agreement on a defining creed, then at least by a tradition of contention that has centered on the core concepts of that creed: freedom, equality, and democracy. Patterns have emerged in the frameworks that Americans have used to think about and apply those concepts. Liberalism, republicanism, and ascriptive Americanism are all frameworks – ideologies, even – that have shaped the ways Americans have integrated these disparate, and sometimes contradictory, creedal principles and applied them to their concrete political realities and problems. Some have celebrated these dynamics. Others have challenged or condemned them as an iron cage that has either rendered other principles and ideals invisible, or taken them off the table politically – if not cast them out as dangerously alien and subversive.

Today, the United States, like other countries around the world, faces both continuing realities and challenges and a concatenation of novel problems. Concentrations of economic power; new technologies that have altered the economy and ecology of information and the nature of work; the reclamation and mobilization of personal and political identities; partisan, factional, and geographic polarization; questions of civic inclusion and exclusion and environmental sustainability – all raise questions concerning the usefulness of extant ideas, frameworks, and paradigms in arriving at defensible and desirable political solutions and settlements.

This book has canvassed more than two centuries' worth of the same dynamics as they played out in different times in the nation's history. This past is not merely prologue: it is actively present. Contemporary political actors – presidents, members of Congress, state and local politicians, party leaders, social movement and protest activists, and politically minded journalists, among others – commonly invoke the ideas of and about the nation's past in vying to shape its future. The conservative Tea Party movement of the early 2000s, for instance, chose its name to invoke the symbolism of the revolutionary era patriots. The Tea Party made arguments that specifically linked contemporary political causes to the claims made long ago by the country's founders. In the face of charges that his occupation of the White House, his manner, and his programs were unprecedented, President

Trump, in symbolic counterargument, placed a portrait of Andrew Jackson prominently in the Oval Office. Social movement actors of a different ilk have identified themselves with the civil rights movement leader Martin Luther King Jr. and proponents of Black Power, the Black Panthers, and Malcolm X. In his Dust Bowl Ballads, the folk singer Woody Guthrie compared the bankers foreclosing on the indebted common people's farms and homes to the men who killed Jesus, as did, in a different way, the populist/Democratic presidential candidate William Jennings Bryan, who proclaimed that, under his leadership, the common man would not be crucified "upon a cross of gold." In calling for the creation of a modern, activist national government newly committed to public-spirited national policy, the progressive Herbert Croly argued that, under current conditions, the nation now needed to enlist Hamiltonian means to achieve Jeffersonian ends. Theodore Roosevelt and, later, Barack Obama, both made major speeches in Ossowatamie, Kansas, to claim the mantle of Abraham Lincoln while launching new initiatives spearheaded by an active and aggressive national government committed to protecting and advancing rights. The Democratic Party had long held annual Jefferson–Jackson Day dinners to rally its supporters by appealing to the spirit of the party's illustrious founders. The Jefferson–Jackson label was recently retired, however, as more and more African-Americans, a core party constituency, persuaded the rest of the party leadership that it mattered to them that Jefferson and Jackson were slaveholders. In campaigning against abortion rights, conservative evangelical Christians had claimed to be following in the footsteps of earlier Christian abolitionists, while downplaying the degree to which many antebellum Christians, especially in the South, had also invoked the Bible and Christian principles to justify, rather than oppose, chattel slavery. Appealing to their own early twentieth-century namesakes, modern-day "progressives" have downplayed the sometimes shocking statism of key elements of the earlier progressive movement, and its occasional spurning of what some of their predecessors described as the United States' obsolete Constitution, while their conservative opponents have played them up. Those conservatives have lately placed considerable emphasis on the scientific racism of many early twentieth-century progressives, an accurate charge that is nevertheless problematic, given that some of that era's greatest champions of racial equality and justice like Jane Addams and W.E.B. Du Bois were also progressives, and that, although they may have started from different premises, the conservatives of the same era were often just as virulently racist as its more problematic progressives.

One thing the study of American political thought can do is to help students critically interrogate claims of lineages and legacies. They are far from self-evident. The past rarely maps neatly onto the present's very different context. Even the most sensible invocations of historical lineages and legacies involve complex decisions about continuity and change, and what is remembered and forgotten. But it is always a good time to remind ourselves that, in critical respects, the past has shaped the present. Because it underwrites contemporary political understandings, and is enlisted as a resource in contemporary political causes and campaigns, the past, and the thought and ideas of Americans who have come before, plays a major role in the process of making the American future.

The study of American political thought helps us to situate our short lives as Americans, and interested students of America, in the stream of time. As such, this study should be an important part of the broader process of arriving at an understanding of the meaning of our lives, individual and collective, in the time in which we live.

Questions

1. Is it possible to model the dynamics of American political thought over the long term as conforming to a developmental pattern – either as consistent, static, or stable, as an upward or downward trajectory (or, put otherwise, a story of progress or decline), or as cyclical (such as between ordinary times and periods of reform or revolution)? How much would you say that political thought is either deeply entrenched or open-ended?
2. In a free society, should we recognize the contours of the self that is commonly considered the wellspring of all legitimate political authority by the lights of individuals' own experiences and understandings of who they are, or by the lights of objective understandings of the human person as created in the image of God?
3. Much has been said in recent years about the rise of "identity politics" in the United States. Is there anything new about this? Is an emphasis on the politics of identity more of the same? Is it a step forward, or a disturbing retrenchment? Does it open up, or foreclose, desirable political possibilities?
4. How appropriate is it to describe contemporary American politics – or, for that matter, the long history of American political thought – as a battle between conservatives and liberals/progressives?
5. Do you think it is appropriate to continue to study American political thought through the lenses of "big-picture" ideological frameworks like liberalism, republicanism, or ascriptive Americanism?
6. What, if anything, does the study of American political thought bring to our study of American politics that the traditional empirical study of American politics through the lenses of parties, elections, political institutions, political behavior, interest groups, and social movement mobilization does not?

7. Is the study of American political thought meaningfully different from the study of political theory more generally? If so, how and in what way?

8. Are you optimistic or pessimistic about the future of the country? How much of that is related to the current state of American political thought?

Notes

CHAPTER 1 THEMES AND FRAMEWORKS IN AMERICAN POLITICAL THOUGHT

1 Locke: "[T]he beginning of politic[al] society depends upon the consent of the individuals to join into, and make one society; who, when they are thus incorporated, might set up what form of government they thought fit." *Second Treatise of Civil Government* (1689), Ch. VIII. In the Declaration of Independence, Thomas Jefferson slightly altered Locke's formulation of the animating rights to "life, liberty, and the pursuit of happiness."

2 Locke: "[F]reedom of men under government is to have a standing rule to live by, common to every one of that society, and made by the legislative power erected in it; a liberty to follow my own will in all things, where that rule prescribes not; and not to be subject to the inconstant, uncertain, unknown, arbitrary will of another man." Ibid., Ch. IV.

3 Isaiah Berlin, "Two Concepts of Liberty" (1958); Benjamin Constant, "The Liberty of the Moderns and The Liberty of the Ancients" (1819).

4 Jean-Jacques Rousseau, *The Social Contract and Discourses* (1761), Book IV, Ch. 8.

5 Believing this to have been a mistake, the framers of the pro-slavery Constitution of the Confederate States of America (1861) remedied the omission by announcing its promulgation by "We, the people of the Confederate States ... invoking the favor and guidance of Almighty God ...."

6 Isaac Kramnick, "'The Great National Discussion': The Discourse of Politics in 1787" (1988).

7 Rogers M. Smith, "Beyond Tocqueville, Myrdal, and Hartz: The Multiple Traditions in America" (1993); Rogers M. Smith, *Civic Ideals: Conflicting Visions of Citizenship in US History* (1999).

CHAPTER 2 SETTLEMENT, THE ROAD TO REVOLUTION, THE FOUNDING, AND THE EARLY REPUBLIC

1 Early in the nation's history, a number of states in the federal system did, increasingly controversially, require religious tests for public office. These were gradually eliminated in the first half of the nineteenth century.

2 Thomas Jefferson's University of Virginia (1819) was a deliberate exception.

In designing UVA, Jefferson omitted the usual campus chapel, and replaced it with the Rotunda, a classical structure modeled on the Roman Parthenon, which served as the library, and was meant to reflect the "authority of nature and power of reason."

3 See, e.g., *Somerset v. Stewart* (1772), a decision by Great Britain's Kings Bench, written by Lord Mansfield, which declared chattel slavery a practice contrary to common law and right, "so odious, that nothing can be suffered to support it, but positive law."

4 Jon Elster, *Ulysses Unbound: Studies in Rationality, Precommitments, and Constraints* (2000); Federalist #1 (Hamilton).

5 *McCulloch v. Maryland*, 17 US 316 (1819).

6 Federalist #78. This was another Hamilton argument reprised by John Marshall, in this case in *Marbury v. Madison* (1803).

7 See Hanna Pitkin, *The Concept of Representation* (1967).

8 See Herbert Storing, *What the Antifederalists Were For* (1981); Saul Cornell, *The Other Founders: Anti-Federalists and the Dissenting Tradition in America, 1788–1828* (2012).

9 David Siemers, *Ratifying the Republic: Antifederalists and Federalists in Constitutional Time* (2002); Jeffrey Tulis and Nicole Mellow, *Legacies of Losing in American Politics* (2018).

CHAPTER 3 ANTEBELLUM POLITICAL THOUGHT

1 See Russell Muirhead, *The Promise of Party in a Polarized Age* (2014); Nancy Rosenblum, *On the Side of the Angels: An Appreciation of Parties and Partisanship* (2010); Russell Muirhead and Nancy Rosenblum, "The Uneasy Place of Parties in the Constitutional Order," in Mark Graber, Sanford Levinson, and Mark Tushnet (eds.), *The Oxford Handbook on the US Constitution* (2015).

2 Christian Fritz, *American Sovereigns: The People and Americans' Constitutional Traditions Before the Civil War* (2008).

3 A.G. Hopkins, *American Empire: A Global History* (2018).

4 Avishai Margalit, *On Compromise and Rotten Compromises* (2009); Amy Gutmann and Dennis Thompson, *The Spirit of Compromise: Why Governing Demands It and Campaigning Undermines It* (2014).

5 Paul Frymer, *Building an American Empire: The Era of Territorial and Political Expansion* (2017).

6 See Sean Wilentz, *Chants Democratic: New York City and the Rise of the American Working Class, 1788–1850* (1984).

CHAPTER 4 SECESSION/CIVIL WAR/RECONSTRUCTION

1 Eric Foner, *Free Soil, Free Labor, Free Men: The Ideology of the Republican Party before the Civil War* (1970).

2 *Bradwell v. Illinois* (1873).

3 Richard M. Valelly, *The Two Reconstructions: The Struggle for Black Enfranchisement* (2004).

CHAPTER 5 INDUSTRIAL CAPITALISM, REFORMISM, AND THE NEW AMERICAN STATE

1 John Kenneth Galbraith, *American Capitalism: The Concept of Countervailing Power* (1952).
2 Tim Wu, *The Curse of Bigness: Antitrust in the New Gilded Age* (2018).
3 Mark Twain and Charles Dudley Warner, *A Gilded Age: A Tale of Today* (1873).
4 Andrew Carnegie, *Wealth* (1889).
5 Sidney Tarrow, *Power in Movement: Social Movements and Contentious Politics* (1998).
6 These dispatches were subsequently published by Tarbell as *The History of the Standard Oil Company* (1904).
7 Dorothy Ross, *The Origins of American Social Science* (1991); Thomas Haskell, *The Emergence of Professional Social Science: The American Social Science Association and the Nineteenth-Century Crisis of Authority* (1977).
8 Modern liberals like Franklin Roosevelt (or, for that matter, Barack Obama, Joe Biden, and Nancy Pelosi), to the consternation of those who now came to be called "classical liberals," insisted that their efforts to augment and leverage the powers of government under conditions of an unprecedented consolidation of private wealth and power served to rescue and vindicate the fundamental liberal principles of liberty and equality and, via a renewed commitment to the protection of civil liberties and civil rights, the protection of public and private rights.
9 Bruce Ackerman, *We the People: Foundations* (1993).

CHAPTER 6 THE NEW DEAL LIBERAL ORDER: COLLAPSE, CULMINATION, OR "GREAT EXCEPTION"?

1 When the Supreme Court struck down the first incarnation of these codes, which were written by private businesses under federal government auspices, for, among other constitutional transgressions, amounting to "delegation [of legislative power] running riot" (*Schechter Poultry v. US*, 1935), they were revised to provide for greater direct government involvement and control.
2 See John Stuart Mill, *On Liberty* (1859).
3 Will Herberg, *Protestant, Catholic, Jew: An Essay in American Religious Sociology* (1955). See Kevin M. Schultz, *Tri-Faith America: How Catholics and Jews Held Postwar America to Its Protestant Promise* (2011); Wendy Wall, *Inventing the American Way: The Politics of Consensus from the New Deal to the Civil Rights Movement* (2008).
4 Jefferson Cowie, *The Great Exception: The New Deal and the Limits of American Politics* (2016).

CHAPTER 7 RADICAL STIRRINGS, CIVIL RIGHTS, THE CONTENTIOUS 1960S, AND THE RISE OF MODERN CONSERVATISM

1 Jefferson Cowie, *The Great Exception: The New Deal and the Limits of American Politics* (2017).
2 E.E. Cummings, "since feeling is first" (1926).
3 Walter Lippmann, *Public Opinion* (1922).
4 See also Sloan Wilson, *The Man in the Gray Flannel Suit* (1955).
5 Michael Harrington, *The Other America: Poverty in the United States* (1962).
6 "Toward a More Responsible Two-Party System" (1950).
7 Ronald Inglehart, *The Silent Revolution: Changing Values and Political Styles among Western Publics* (1977).
8 Theodore Roszak, *The Making of a Counter Culture: Reflections on the Technocratic Society and Its Youthful Opposition* (1969).
9 Alluding to the English political philosopher Jeremy Bentham's Panopticon, Michel Foucault's *Discipline and Punish* (1975) had explicated a new form of social control through a perpetual, all-seeing, and pervading surveillance that was ultimately internalized.
10 Hannah Arendt, *Eichmann in Jerusalem: A Report on the Banality of Evil* (1963). See also Richard L. Rubenstein, *The Cunning of History: The Holocaust and the American Future* (1975).
11 At the war crimes trials at Nuremberg after the end of World War II, Adolf Eichmann, the Nazi official in charge of Hilter's Final Solution, defended himself on the grounds that he was simply following the law and doing his job. He was subsequently convicted and hanged.
12 See Leroi Jones [Amiri Baraka], *Blues People: Negro Music in White America* (1963).
13 For a more jaundiced take on this peculiarity, see Woody Guthrie's "Do-Re-Mi" (1940) or Phil Ochs's "The World Began in Eden and Ended in Los Angeles" (1969).

CHAPTER 8 THE IDENTITY AND POST-MATERIALIST LEFT, THE NEW RIGHT, AND THIRD WAY LIBERALISM

1 Those adopting this schema argue that there was subsequently a third wave across the 1990s into the early 2000s, and that we are currently seeing a fourth wave.
2 Common parlance at the time, for instance, required that a woman be formally designated as either "Miss" or "Mrs." – in other words, as either not yet married or married. It meant something when, in 1972, the feminist activists Gloria Steinem and Dorothy Pitman Hughes founded *Ms.* Magazine, flying under the banner of a self-chosen honorific, independent of the woman's marital status.
3 By contrast, among 1930s feminists, it had been the radicals who had sub-

scribed to difference feminism, while more moderate liberal middle-class women had argued from an anti-essentialist position.

4 Both Lorde and Giovanni's writings were included in the pioneering compendium of black feminist thought, Toni Cade Bambara's *The Black Woman: An Anthology* (1970).

5 As such, Ginsberg anticipated the outlook and understandings of the later academic framework and research agenda known as "Queer Theory," which mounted a sustained challenge to "heteronormativity."

6 Holly Near, "Singing for Our Lives" (1990).

7 The 1924 law did not apply to immigrants from the western hemisphere, which meant that it did not include Latino immigrants. The quota for Asians was zero: the 1924 law barred *all* Asian immigration.

8 *Johnson v. M'Intosh* (1823); *Cherokee Nation v. Georgia* (1831); *Worcester v. Georgia* (1832).

9 Helen and Scott Nearing, *Living the Good Life: How to Live Sanely and Simply in a Troubled World* (1954).

10 For subsequent reflections and extensions, see J. Baird Callicott, *In Defense of the Land Ethic: Essays in Environmental Philosophy* (1989) and *Beyond the Land Ethic: More Essays in Environmental Philosophy* (1999), and Paul W. Taylor, *Respect for Nature: A Theory of Environmental Ethics* (1986).

11 The Clean Air Act (1963); the Clean Water Act (1972); mandatory seatbelt laws (1966); and the creation of a new Department of Transportation (1966), and, within it, of the National Traffic Safety Agency (1966), the National Highway Safety Agency (1966), and the National Highway Safety Bureau (1966) – regulatory agencies that soon issued the Federal Motor Vehicle Safety Standards. Other influential contemporaneous works in the new environmental philosophy and ethics were Lynn White Jr.'s "The Historical Roots of Our Ecological Crisis," *Science* (1967) and Garrett Hardin's "The Tragedy of the Commons," *Science* (1968).

12 See Edward Banfield, *The Unheavenly City* (1970); James Q. Wilson, *Thinking About Crime* (1975); and George Kelling and James Q. Wilson, "Broken Windows" *The Atlantic* (1982), which argued that allowing a creeping sense of disorder by not punishing purportedly minor crimes like vandalism and turnstile-hopping will have cascading effects that lead to increased rates of both minor and more serious, violent crime.

13 "Congress shall make no law respecting an establishment of religion . . . ." US Constitution, First Amendment. This provision had recently been held by the Supreme Court to limit the conduct of the states as well, through its "incorporation" via the Fourteenth Amendment's due process clause (*Everson v. Board of Education*, 1947).

14 For (allegedly unpatriotic, if not treasonous) Vietnam War draft resisters who had fled to Canada.

CHAPTER 9 CONCLUSION

1 Toni Morrison, "What the Black Woman Thinks About Women's Lib," *The New York Times Magazine* (August 22, 1971).

2 James Weldon Johnson, *The Autobiography of an Ex-Colored Man* (1912); Nella Larson, *Passing* (1929); George Schuyler, *Black No More: Being an Account of the Strange and Wonderful Workings of Science in the Land of the Free, AD 1933–1940* (1931).

3 John Rawls, *A Theory of Justice* (1971); Robert Nozick, *Anarchy, State, and Utopia* (1974).

4 Stephen Macedo, *Liberal Virtues: Citizenship, Virtue, and Community in Liberal Constitutionalism* (1990); William Galston, *Liberal Purposes: Goods, Virtues, and Diversity in the Liberal State* (1991).

5 Mark Lilla, *The Once and Future Liberal: After Identity Politics* (2017).

6 Mari Matsuda, *Words That Wound: Critical Race Theory, Assaultive Speech, and The First Amendment* (1993); Catharine MacKinnon, *Only Words* (1993).

7 Stuart Jeffries, *Grand Hotel Abyss: The Lives of the Frankfurt School* (2016). Brown, however, was also a student of the American democratic theorist Sheldon Wolin. See Wolin, *Politics and Vision: Continuity and Innovation in Western Political Thought* (1960); Wolin, *Democracy Incorporated: Managed Democracy and the Spector of Inverted Totalitarianism* (2008).

8 See Thomas Piketty, *Capital in the 21st Century* (2014).

9 Michelle Alexander, *The New Jim Crow: Mass Incarceration in the Age of Colorblindness* (2010); Bryan Stevenson, *Just Mercy: A Story of Justice and Redemption* (2014).

Index